Communication in IT

Strategies for Managing Teams,
Stakeholders and
Successful Projects

Communication in IT - Strategies for Managing Teams,
Stakeholders and Successful Projects
Copyright © 2024 by Angel Marqués
All rights reserved.

No part of this book may be reproduced, stored in a retrieval system, or transmitted in any form or by any means—electronic, mechanical, photocopying, recording, or otherwise—without prior written permission from the author, except in the case of brief quotations for book reviews or similar purposes permitted by copyright law.

This is a work of non-fiction. All content and interpretations herein are based on research and analysis by the author. Any resemblance to real persons, living or dead, is purely coincidental.

Published by Angel Marqués Sánchez
ISBN: **9798301285875**

Hello! I would greatly appreciate it if you could share your opinion by leaving a review on Amazon. Reviews not only help other readers discover the book, but they're also essential for supporting future projects.

If you have a few minutes, please visit the review page by scanning the QR code below.

INTRODUCTION: COMMUNICATION AS THE BACKBONE OF IT PROJECTS...... 6
    Highlight the unique challenges faced by IT professionals in coordinating across diverse teams and stakeholders. 10
    Equipping readers with practical strategies to enhance communication, manage deliverables, and achieve project success. 14

CHAPTER 1: UNDERSTANDING THE FOUNDATIONS OF COMMUNICATION IN IT 19
    Common challenges in IT communication 25
    Overview of IT methodologies and how communication fits into these frameworks. 29

CHAPTER 2: TEAM COMMUNICATION: BUILDING COHESION WITHIN YOUR GROUP 39
    Understanding team dynamics: balancing technical expertise and interpersonal skills. 48
    Tools for effective team communication 59

CHAPTER 3: COMMUNICATING WITH STAKEHOLDERS: MANAGING EXPECTATIONS 70
    Techniques for presenting technical information in a clear and actionable way. 77
    Building trust through regular updates, transparent reporting, and responsive communication. 85

CHAPTER 4: BRIDGING THE GAP WITH THIRD-PARTY TEAMS 92
    Managing dependencies, contracts, and deliverables through structured communication. 97
    Resolving conflicts and ensuring alignment between third-party teams and internal goals. 105

CHAPTER 5: NAVIGATING COMPANY POLICIES AND INTERNAL COMMUNICATION STANDARDS 113
    Strategies for aligning team practices with organizational standards. 122
    Leveraging tools and platforms to streamline communication and documentation. 131

CHAPTER 6: CONNECTING WITH THE END CUSTOMER 142
    Managing customer expectations and ensuring satisfaction through clear communication. 152

Building long-term relationships with clients by delivering consistent and transparent updates. 163

CHAPTER 7: MANAGING DELIVERABLES: COMMUNICATION AS A CONTROL MECHANISM 181

Handling revisions, delays, and scope changes through proactive communication. 193

Practical tools for tracking progress and maintaining alignment across teams. 201

DISCOVER MORE 218

Introduction: Communication as the Backbone of IT Projects

In the dynamic world of IT consultancy and large-scale projects, success hinges on more than just technical expertise or resource availability. The pivotal factor is often something less tangible yet deeply influential: communication. Imagine a scenario where a multi-million-dollar IT infrastructure upgrade stalls—not because of coding errors or hardware failures, but due to a simple miscommunication during a routine meeting. Stakeholders believed one set of deliverables was prioritized, while the development team worked on something entirely different. The result? Missed deadlines, budget overruns, and frustrated clients. This all-too-common story underscores a hard truth: even the most sophisticated projects are vulnerable to breakdowns when communication falters.

This example might feel familiar to many professionals in IT, as projects today demand the collaboration of diverse teams, stakeholders, and external vendors. Each group comes with its own objectives, technical language, and workflows, making the risk of misunderstandings almost inevitable. What seems like a minor gap in communication—a vague email, an ambiguous requirement—can cascade into significant disruptions. The impact is often felt in ways that resonate far beyond the immediate team, rippling out to affect timelines, customer satisfaction, and, ultimately, the organization's reputation.

Yet, communication is frequently undervalued in the technical realm, where the focus often tilts toward hard skills like coding, system architecture, or project methodologies. While these skills are undeniably vital, they cannot operate in isolation. Projects are not merely a series of technical tasks; they are intricate ecosystems where ideas, feedback, and instructions flow between people. Without a clear and effective conduit for this flow, even the most well-designed systems can collapse under the weight of misaligned expectations.

Strategic communication, therefore, isn't just a soft skill—it's the backbone of IT projects. It's what ensures everyone involved speaks the same language, aligns on goals, and adapts to challenges as they arise. This book begins with a simple assertion: communication is not an optional competency for IT professionals but a critical driver of project success. By mastering it, teams can transform potential pitfalls into opportunities for collaboration and innovation.

Framing Communication as a Strategic Tool

Communication in IT consultancy and large-scale projects is often dismissed as a peripheral concern, something that happens naturally alongside the "real work." However, this misconception overlooks its profound strategic importance. In these high-stakes environments, communication is not merely about exchanging information—it is the framework that shapes decision-making, fosters collaboration, and aligns diverse interests toward a unified goal. It operates as a strategic tool that, when wielded effectively, determines whether a project progresses seamlessly or spirals into chaos.

Unlike casual exchanges, strategic communication in IT projects is deliberate and goal-oriented. It bridges the gap between technical specialists and non-technical stakeholders, translating complex jargon into actionable insights. This is particularly crucial in environments where deliverables must align with organizational priorities, customer needs, and budget constraints. A well-crafted project update or a clear roadmap can mean the difference between proactive problem-solving and costly misunderstandings. Effective communication becomes the bedrock upon which trust is built among team members, stakeholders, and clients, enabling smoother collaboration and quicker resolution of conflicts.

In addition, communication plays a vital role in navigating the inherent unpredictability of IT projects. Projects rarely proceed exactly as planned—requirements evolve, timelines shift, and unforeseen technical challenges arise. Strategic communication ensures that these inevitable changes are managed with transparency and accountability. By fostering a culture of open dialogue and regular feedback, teams can adapt to shifting circumstances without losing sight of the project's objectives. It transforms potential disruptions into opportunities for recalibration, keeping projects on track even in the face of uncertainty.

Moreover, communication serves as the connective tissue in complex, multi-layered project ecosystems. IT consultants and project managers frequently juggle interactions with cross-functional teams, external vendors, and global stakeholders, each with unique expectations and communication styles. Without a strategic approach, these interactions can quickly become fragmented, leading to inefficiencies and fractured relationships. By prioritizing strategic communication, professionals can harmonize these disparate elements into a cohesive effort, driving not only project success but also long-term collaboration and organizational growth.

HIGHLIGHT THE COMPLEXITY OF LARGE-SCALE IT PROJECTS

Large-scale IT projects are inherently complex, involving a labyrinth of moving parts, cross-functional teams, and competing priorities. From integrating legacy systems to deploying cutting-edge solutions, these initiatives demand more than technical expertise—they require meticulous coordination across diverse stakeholders, each with distinct roles, expectations, and levels of understanding. Communication, in this context, becomes the linchpin that holds everything together, ensuring that every component operates in harmony toward the project's objectives.

One of the primary challenges in these projects lies in managing the sheer volume of information that must flow seamlessly across teams. Developers, analysts, project managers, and clients each have unique needs and terminologies, creating a potential breeding ground for misunderstandings. A developer might view a feature from a technical feasibility standpoint, while a client focuses on user experience. Bridging these perspectives requires precise communication that respects each party's priorities while fostering mutual understanding.

The geographical dispersion of modern IT teams further amplifies the complexity. It is now commonplace for projects to involve collaborators spread across continents, working in different time zones and cultural contexts. This diversity, while a strength, also introduces barriers such as language nuances, varying work habits, and distinct corporate norms. In such scenarios, clear and inclusive communication strategies are essential to mitigate misalignment and maintain the momentum of the project.

Furthermore, large-scale IT projects often operate under strict timelines and budgets, with little room for error. A minor miscommunication—whether in requirements gathering, task allocation, or deliverable updates—can cascade into significant delays, cost overruns, or even project failure. The complexity is compounded when multiple methodologies, such as Agile and ITIL, are employed simultaneously, requiring teams to navigate different workflows and priorities. Strategic communication serves as the glue that unites these disparate elements, creating a shared language and vision that enables the project to move forward effectively, even in the face of inevitable challenges.

CONNECT COMMUNICATION TO PROJECT OUTCOMES

The success or failure of an IT project often hinges not on technical expertise but on the strength of communication. While a project's architecture, development tools, and methodologies are critical, their effectiveness depends on how well teams communicate about goals, progress, and potential roadblocks. Clear, consistent communication transforms a well-conceived plan into a deliverable that meets or exceeds expectations; conversely, its absence can unravel even the most robust technical efforts.

Consider the impact of misaligned expectations between stakeholders and project teams. When communication breaks down, stakeholders may receive deliverables that don't align with their vision, leading to frustration, rework, and delays. On the other hand, effective communication ensures that all parties share a common understanding of the project's objectives, timelines, and deliverables. This alignment fosters confidence, minimizes ambiguities, and accelerates decision-making, directly influencing the project's trajectory.

Timely updates and transparent reporting play a pivotal role in risk management. IT projects are rarely linear; unexpected challenges such as resource constraints, technical failures, or scope changes are common. Strong communication channels enable teams to identify and address these issues early, limiting their impact on project outcomes. Regular check-ins, clear escalation processes, and proactive problem-solving keep projects on track, preserving both time and resources.

Moreover, effective communication drives team cohesion and collaboration, which are critical to achieving successful outcomes. In large-scale IT environments, team members often come from diverse disciplines and may have varying levels of familiarity with the project's domain. A robust communication strategy fosters a sense of shared purpose, ensuring that everyone—from developers to stakeholders—is working toward the same goals. When teams feel informed and valued, their engagement improves, resulting in higher productivity, better quality outputs, and a smoother project lifecycle.

EMPOWERING READERS TO TAKE THE LEAD

The ability to communicate effectively is not merely a complementary skill for IT professionals—it is a decisive factor in shaping project outcomes and professional growth. As you delve into this book, you are invited to rethink the way you approach communication in your projects, teams, and collaborations. Strategic communication isn't a passive process; it's a proactive endeavor that demands awareness, intention, and consistent effort.

Every interaction, whether a stakeholder presentation, a team meeting, or an impromptu email, carries the potential to influence the trajectory of a project. With this in mind, the insights and strategies in this book are designed to help you harness that potential. By improving how you convey ideas, manage expectations, and foster collaboration, you can transform not only your own contributions but also the dynamics of the teams and organizations you serve.

This is your opportunity to take the lead, to bridge gaps that often cause frustration and inefficiency, and to elevate your role from task executor to strategic contributor. As you explore the frameworks, tools, and real-world examples provided, consider how they align with your current challenges and aspirations. Reflect on how these approaches can resolve persistent issues in your projects, strengthen relationships with stakeholders, and set new standards for success.

This book is a resource, but its value depends on your willingness to act. Effective communication is a skill that grows with practice and deliberate application. Let this journey be your guide to becoming not just a better communicator, but a true driver of success in the ever-evolving and complex world of IT projects. The time to start is now, and the results will speak for themselves.

Highlight the unique challenges faced by IT professionals in coordinating across diverse teams and stakeholders.

The IT industry operates in a realm of constant flux, where innovation and adaptation are not just ideals but necessities. From the integration of emerging technologies like AI and blockchain to the iterative nature of software development, IT professionals navigate a field defined by perpetual evolution. This dynamic landscape often transforms communication into a high-stakes endeavor, where clarity and precision are vital to ensure alignment across teams, technologies, and objectives. Projects often proceed at breakneck speed, requiring rapid decision-making and the seamless transfer of complex information to prevent derailments.

Compounding these challenges is the sheer scope of IT projects, which frequently span multiple domains, involve diverse stakeholders, and demand integration across various systems. Unlike static or predictable industries, IT thrives on innovation but suffers from its accompanying uncertainty. A single misstep in communication—a vague requirement, an overlooked assumption, or an unclear directive—can cascade into systemic issues, resulting in costly delays or flawed deliverables. IT professionals are acutely aware that their ability to translate intricate technical details into actionable plans often determines a project's success or failure.

Moreover, the collaborative nature of IT work requires individuals with varied expertise to work together seamlessly, despite having distinct terminologies, tools, and priorities. For example, a developer might focus on coding logic, while a project manager emphasizes timelines and deliverables, and a designer prioritizes user experience. Aligning these perspectives demands not only technical proficiency but also exceptional communication skills. Misunderstandings in this environment are not just inconvenient—they can be catastrophic, undermining trust, efficiency, and morale.

In such a fast-paced and interconnected field, communication must go beyond superficial exchanges. It becomes a strategic tool, enabling IT professionals to navigate uncertainty, build consensus, and foster collaboration. Understanding the complexities of this dynamic environment is the first step toward appreciating the transformative power of effective communication—a skill that holds the potential to elevate projects from mere technical exercises to cohesive and impactful successes.

MULTI-DISCIPLINARY TEAMS AND COMMUNICATION BARRIERS

IT projects often bring together a mosaic of professionals, each contributing expertise from their specific domain. Developers, project managers, business analysts, UX designers, quality assurance specialists, and external vendors collaborate to achieve shared objectives. While this diversity drives innovation and ensures comprehensive project development, it also introduces significant communication challenges. Each discipline speaks its own "language," shaped by unique priorities, terminologies, and workflows, making mutual understanding a frequent stumbling block.

For instance, a developer might discuss "code refactoring" with technical precision, while a business analyst focuses on aligning the same task with client requirements. A project manager, meanwhile, may be concerned with timelines and resource allocation, and an external stakeholder might expect a clear outline of the business impact. Without effective channels and strategies for bridging these perspectives, conversations risk devolving into silos of misaligned objectives, leading to inefficiencies or conflicts.

Communication barriers become even more pronounced when stakeholders operate at varying levels of technical fluency. Business executives may require simplified summaries of progress and risks, while technical teams delve into granular details. The disconnect between these layers can result in unrealistic expectations, missed opportunities for innovation, or delayed decision-making. Even when everyone is striving toward a common goal, gaps in understanding can compromise collaboration, leaving teams out of sync and creating frustration.

Overcoming these barriers requires an intentional approach to fostering mutual comprehension and respect for different expertise. IT professionals must master the art of translating complex ideas into accessible language while maintaining technical accuracy. This involves not only choosing the right words but also creating a culture where open dialogue and questions are encouraged. By addressing the communication divides inherent in multi-disciplinary teams, IT leaders can transform diversity into a powerful asset that drives cohesive and high-impact project outcomes.

STAKEHOLDER DYNAMICS AND MISALIGNED EXPECTATIONS

One of the most persistent challenges in IT projects is managing the intricate web of stakeholder relationships. Stakeholders—ranging from internal executives to external clients and third-party vendors—often bring differing priorities, goals, and levels of technical understanding to the table. Balancing these dynamics requires exceptional communication skills, as each group interprets project progress and success through its unique lens. Misaligned expectations, if not addressed proactively, can derail even the most meticulously planned initiatives.

For example, clients may expect rapid delivery of features without fully understanding the time required for proper testing and integration. Meanwhile, internal stakeholders might focus on budget constraints or compliance requirements that clash with project timelines. Third-party vendors, operating under their own agendas, can further complicate matters by introducing dependencies that the core team must navigate. These competing pressures often create tension, with each group unintentionally pulling the project in a different direction.

The challenge intensifies when assumptions are left unspoken or when stakeholders fail to articulate their expectations clearly. A project team might believe they are delivering value through technical innovation, only to discover that stakeholders were prioritizing usability over cutting-edge features. This disconnect, stemming from a lack of alignment in the project's early stages, can lead to scope creep, rework, or strained relationships, adding unnecessary complexity to the project lifecycle.

Effective communication becomes the linchpin for harmonizing these diverse perspectives. IT professionals must engage stakeholders early and often, leveraging structured methods like stakeholder analysis and expectation mapping to clarify priorities. Transparent reporting and consistent feedback loops ensure that all parties stay informed and aligned, minimizing the risk of unwelcome surprises. By addressing stakeholder dynamics head-on, IT teams can build trust, foster collaboration, and create a shared vision that underpins successful project execution.

The Challenges of Globalization and Remote Collaboration

As the IT industry embraces globalization, the landscape of project execution has shifted significantly. Teams are increasingly composed of professionals dispersed across continents, time zones, and cultural contexts. While this global talent pool allows organizations to leverage specialized expertise, it introduces a host of communication challenges that can hinder project cohesion and progress. Navigating these complexities requires IT professionals to adopt innovative strategies for fostering collaboration in virtual environments.

Time zone differences are among the most glaring obstacles in global collaboration. Coordinating meetings, resolving urgent issues, or simply maintaining a steady flow of updates can become arduous when team members operate on opposite ends of the clock. Without deliberate planning, asynchronous communication can lead to delays, misunderstandings, or overlooked messages, particularly in time-sensitive projects. Moreover, the absence of immediate feedback often exacerbates ambiguities, leaving tasks stalled until clarifications are received.

Cultural differences add another layer of complexity, influencing how team members interpret messages, respond to feedback, and interact with authority figures. For example, some cultures may prioritize directness in communication, while others might value diplomacy and subtlety. These differences, if unacknowledged, can lead to misinterpretations or friction among team members. Additionally, variations in work ethics, holidays, and local business practices can create logistical and interpersonal hurdles that demand sensitivity and adaptability.

Remote collaboration technologies, while indispensable, also present challenges. Over-reliance on tools like email, video conferencing, or project management software can lead to communication fatigue and disconnection. The absence of face-to-face interactions often results in weaker team bonds and a diminished sense of accountability. Teams may struggle to foster trust and camaraderie, critical elements for effective collaboration, when their interactions are confined to screens.

Addressing these challenges requires IT professionals to adopt a multi-faceted approach. Scheduling flexibility, cross-cultural training, and proactive use of synchronous and asynchronous tools can help bridge gaps in global teams. By cultivating an inclusive and empathetic communication culture, IT leaders can ensure that diverse, geographically dispersed teams work harmoniously toward shared project goals.

Equipping readers with practical strategies to enhance communication, manage deliverables, and achieve project success.

In the fast-paced world of IT consultancy and large-scale projects, communication often emerges as both the lifeblood and the bottleneck of success. Despite the growing sophistication of project management tools and methodologies, communication breakdowns remain one of the most cited reasons for project failures. Missed deadlines, unclear deliverables, and misaligned expectations often trace back to a failure to communicate effectively. IT professionals find themselves caught in a web of competing priorities—technical innovation, stakeholder management, and team alignment—all of which demand clear, precise, and timely communication. Without strategic approaches, even the most technically sound project can falter.

The sheer complexity of IT projects amplifies the need for practical communication strategies. These projects frequently involve diverse teams, each with its own jargon, priorities, and expertise, and stakeholders who may lack the technical background to fully grasp project intricacies. Bridging this gap requires more than ad-hoc meetings or hastily written emails; it demands intentionality, structure, and clarity. For example, an IT team implementing an enterprise-level system must coordinate with departments ranging from HR to finance, each with its own set of needs and concerns. The failure to establish a cohesive communication plan early on can lead to costly revisions, delays, and strained relationships.

Beyond the internal challenges, external pressures exacerbate the need for effective communication. In a field driven by rapid technological advancement, projects are expected to deliver faster, better, and with greater transparency. Stakeholders demand frequent updates, while customers expect solutions that meet their evolving needs. Navigating this landscape without a strategic communication framework is akin to steering a ship without a compass—there is little room for missteps, yet the path forward is often unclear. By emphasizing the critical role of communication, this book positions itself as an indispensable resource for professionals looking to excel in this demanding environment.

Practical strategies offer a way to move from reactive to proactive communication. This book focuses on equipping readers with tools and techniques that can be immediately applied to real-world scenarios. Whether managing complex stakeholder dynamics, aligning multi-disciplinary teams, or resolving conflicts with third-party vendors, readers will find actionable insights tailored to their unique challenges. By framing the need for these strategies as a response to the pressing demands of the IT industry, the introduction sets the stage for a solutions-driven narrative that empowers professionals to transform their approach to communication.

A ROADMAP TO MASTERING COMMUNICATION IN IT PROJECTS

This book is designed to be more than just a resource; it is a practical guide for IT professionals aiming to navigate the intricacies of communication within complex project environments. The challenges faced in IT consultancy and large-scale endeavors often stem not from technical inadequacy but from the absence of a clear, consistent communication strategy. Miscommunication can erode trust, delay deliverables, and disrupt even the most well-planned projects. Recognizing these pain points, this book offers a structured approach to overcoming them, transforming how professionals engage with teams, stakeholders, and clients.

What sets this guide apart is its solutions-oriented approach. Rather than focusing solely on the theoretical aspects of communication, the content bridges the gap between concept and application. The book acknowledges that IT professionals, whether managing Agile sprints, ITIL processes, or PMP frameworks, need tangible tools to navigate their day-to-day interactions. For instance, how can a project manager effectively communicate scope changes to a resistant client? How can a consultant align a technical team's objectives with the priorities of non-technical stakeholders? These are not abstract questions—they are daily realities for IT professionals, and this book provides actionable answers.

At its core, this guide serves as a roadmap for mastering the multifaceted nature of communication in IT projects. Each chapter is built around practical scenarios and real-world challenges, offering templates, strategies, and case studies that empower readers to take control of their communication practices. Whether it's managing deliverables with global teams, resolving cross-departmental conflicts, or presenting technical insights to executive boards, the book delivers insights that resonate with professionals across the IT spectrum.

By presenting a clear, step-by-step framework for enhancing communication, this book equips readers to not only meet the demands of their current roles but also excel as leaders and collaborators. The goal is not just to solve immediate challenges but to instill a mindset that values and prioritizes effective communication as a cornerstone of professional success. With this roadmap, readers are empowered to turn communication from a persistent obstacle into their greatest asset.

CONNECTING THE STRATEGIES TO TANGIBLE OUTCOMES

Effective communication is not an abstract ideal; it is a measurable driver of tangible success in IT consultancy and large-scale projects. This book emphasizes how mastering communication strategies leads directly to improved project outcomes, enhanced team cohesion, and elevated professional credibility. Every tool, template, and tactic shared within these pages is designed to help readers close the gap between theory and action, transforming communication challenges into opportunities for impact and growth.

For instance, a well-structured stakeholder update is not just a routine task—it can build trust, secure alignment on deliverables, and mitigate risks associated with misaligned priorities. Similarly, resolving a communication breakdown between technical teams and external vendors doesn't just smooth immediate conflicts; it lays the groundwork for long-term partnerships and consistent project performance. By linking these strategies to real-world scenarios, the book ensures readers can immediately see the value of applying these principles to their daily responsibilities.

The practical outcomes of the strategies in this book are rooted in addressing everyday challenges faced by IT professionals. Consider the complexities of managing deliverables across globally distributed teams. Poor communication can lead to missed deadlines and frustrated stakeholders, while a structured approach—tailored updates, clear expectations, and consistent follow-through—ensures projects stay on track. These are not theoretical benefits; they are measurable improvements that affect timelines, budgets, and overall project success.

Ultimately, this book is about empowering readers to achieve results. Improved communication doesn't just solve immediate problems; it enhances professional reputations and builds stronger, more resilient project environments. By connecting the dots between strategies and outcomes, the book positions communication as not just a tool but a transformative element of success, enabling readers to thrive in the dynamic, high-stakes world of IT projects.

Empowering Action for Lasting Impact

This book is more than a collection of strategies; it's an invitation to transform how you approach communication in IT projects. It challenges readers to look beyond the immediate demands of deadlines and deliverables and consider how communication shapes long-term success—for teams, stakeholders, and individual careers. By embracing the tools and practices outlined here, you position yourself as a leader, someone capable of navigating complexity with clarity and foresight.

The strategies offered are not one-size-fits-all solutions. Instead, they are adaptable frameworks designed to address the nuanced challenges you face in your unique professional context. Whether it's aligning multi-disciplinary teams, managing difficult stakeholder conversations, or ensuring seamless coordination in global projects, this book equips you with the confidence to tackle these situations with precision and purpose. The emphasis is not only on knowing what to do but on understanding why and how these approaches drive success.

Taking the next step begins with adopting a mindset of growth and adaptability. Effective communication is not a static skill but a dynamic process that evolves with every project, team, and technology you encounter. This book empowers you to see communication not as a hurdle but as an opportunity to lead, inspire, and innovate within your organization. By committing to this perspective, you amplify your impact and set the stage for sustainable success.

As you turn the pages, you are not just learning techniques—you are building a legacy of excellence in communication. The journey begins with small, intentional changes that create ripple effects throughout your projects and professional relationships. Let this book be your guide to not only mastering the art of communication but also transforming it into the cornerstone of your career in IT consultancy and beyond.

Chapter 1: Understanding the Foundations of Communication in IT

In the fast-paced and highly technical world of IT project management, communication is often seen as secondary to technical expertise. Yet, it is precisely this oversight that frequently undermines the success of even the most well-designed projects. Imagine a scenario where a development team has built a system to precise specifications, only to discover during deployment that the client's needs were misunderstood from the outset. Such outcomes are not rare but emblematic of a widespread issue: the failure to establish clear and continuous channels of communication. This chapter seeks to illuminate why communication is not merely an operational detail but the backbone of IT project success.

At its core, communication in IT projects serves as the glue that binds diverse stakeholders, including technical teams, management, clients, and third-party collaborators. Without effective communication, even the most skilled teams can falter. Misunderstandings about project goals, unclear timelines, or ambiguous expectations ripple through an organization, causing delays, rework, and in some cases, outright failure. Conversely, clear, structured, and transparent communication aligns teams, ensures accountability, and keeps projects on track. It transforms chaos into coordination, bridging the gap between technical precision and strategic objectives.

To appreciate the significance of communication, one must first understand its multifaceted nature in the IT environment. It involves much more than emails and status updates; it requires the careful articulation of technical ideas to non-technical stakeholders, the ability to synthesize complex feedback into actionable plans, and the emotional intelligence to navigate conflicts within teams. In this sense, communication is not merely a skill but a strategic tool that drives decision-making and fosters collaboration. It is through this lens that IT professionals must view their interactions, recognizing that every conversation, report, or presentation is a step toward achieving the broader goals of the project.

This book begins its journey here because communication is the foundation upon which all other methodologies, tools, and strategies rest. IT projects are inherently collaborative, requiring contributions from individuals with diverse expertise, working across geographies and time zones. The success of these endeavors depends as much on how teams interact as on the technology they deploy. By setting the stage with a strong emphasis on communication, we lay the groundwork for understanding how to overcome its challenges and harness its potential to ensure project success.

The Ripple Effect of Effective Communication

Effective communication in IT projects is not just a component of the process—it is the force that drives every aspect of success, creating a cascading impact that touches all elements of a project. When communication flows seamlessly, teams are aligned, stakeholders are informed, and goals are met with efficiency and precision. The benefits extend far beyond the immediate project outcomes, influencing the dynamics of collaboration, the perception of professionalism, and the potential for long-term partnerships.

One of the most noticeable effects of strong communication is the alignment it creates among all project participants. When expectations, goals, and responsibilities are clearly articulated, every team member understands their role and how their contributions fit into the bigger picture. This clarity prevents duplication of effort, minimizes misunderstandings, and fosters a sense of shared purpose. For example, a project manager who provides detailed updates not only keeps the team on track but also ensures that clients and leadership are aligned with the project's trajectory, reducing the risk of surprises or last-minute changes.

The benefits of effective communication extend into the realm of problem-solving. IT projects are rarely free of challenges, but proactive communication can turn potential setbacks into opportunities for innovation. When issues arise, a well-established communication framework ensures they are identified early and addressed collaboratively. This approach not only saves time but also reinforces a culture of accountability and resilience. A development team, for instance, that regularly shares progress and openly discusses obstacles is better equipped to troubleshoot issues before they escalate, keeping the project timeline intact.

Beyond the immediate scope of project execution, effective communication builds trust and strengthens relationships. For stakeholders and clients, regular and transparent updates inspire confidence in the team's capabilities and the project's direction. For team members, open lines of communication create an environment where ideas are valued, and concerns are addressed, boosting morale and fostering collaboration. This ripple effect goes on to enhance the reputation of the organization or individual, opening doors for future opportunities. Simply put, the impact of effective communication extends far beyond the conclusion of a single project—it shapes the foundation of sustained success.

What Happens When Communication Fails

The consequences of poor communication in IT projects can be devastating, unraveling even the most carefully planned endeavors. Unlike technical missteps, communication failures often go unnoticed until they have caused irreversible damage. They manifest as missed deadlines, misaligned deliverables, dissatisfied stakeholders, and frustrated teams, creating a chain reaction that can derail an entire project. These failures reveal a sobering truth: the absence of clear, effective communication is not just an inconvenience—it is a direct threat to project success.

One of the most common outcomes of communication breakdowns is the mismanagement of deliverables. When expectations are unclear or misunderstood, teams often end up working toward goals that do not align with stakeholder needs. A software development team, for instance, may invest weeks building a feature that, unbeknownst to them, has been deprioritized by the client. The result is wasted effort, delayed timelines, and strained relationships. Such scenarios are not rare but are instead emblematic of a systemic issue in IT projects: the failure to establish a shared understanding among all participants.

The impact of poor communication is not limited to the deliverables themselves—it extends to the morale and cohesion of the team. Ambiguity, conflicting instructions, or the lack of timely feedback can create an environment of frustration and mistrust. Team members may begin to disengage, feeling undervalued or unsupported. Collaboration suffers, innovation stalls, and productivity declines. Over time, these issues compound, leading to burnout and turnover, further destabilizing the project and the organization.

Perhaps the most damaging effect of communication failures is the erosion of stakeholder trust. Clients and sponsors rely on consistent updates and transparent reporting to gauge the progress of a project. When these elements are missing or inconsistent, confidence in the team's capabilities dwindles. A single misstep, such as delivering a product that does not meet the client's expectations, can have long-lasting repercussions, including the loss of future business. In the high-stakes world of IT consultancy, where reputation is everything, the cost of poor communication cannot be overstated.

Communication failures reveal themselves in cascading problems that touch every aspect of an IT project. They blur the vision, disrupt the workflow, and damage relationships, making recovery an uphill battle. By understanding these consequences, IT professionals can begin to recognize the critical need for proactive, deliberate communication strategies—a subject that will be explored further in the chapters ahead.

COMMUNICATION AS A STRATEGIC ADVANTAGE

In the complex and competitive environment of IT projects, communication is not merely a functional necessity—it is a strategic advantage. Teams and organizations that prioritize communication as a core competency gain a significant edge in delivering successful outcomes, building trust with stakeholders, and fostering innovation. Far from being a soft skill relegated to secondary importance, communication becomes a driver of efficiency, creativity, and long-term success when integrated purposefully into project strategies.

One of the clearest ways communication serves as a strategic advantage is by ensuring alignment across all levels of a project. From project managers and developers to external stakeholders and clients, consistent and clear communication creates a shared understanding of goals, timelines, and deliverables. This alignment reduces the risk of costly missteps and enables teams to focus their efforts on what truly matters. For instance, a well-structured kickoff meeting that lays out expectations and roles sets the tone for collaboration, giving the project a strong foundation.

Moreover, communication facilitates adaptability, a crucial factor in the ever-changing landscape of IT. Projects rarely proceed without encountering challenges, whether they are technical glitches, shifting client requirements, or unforeseen external pressures. Teams that communicate effectively can respond to these disruptions with agility, using feedback loops to quickly assess the situation, devise solutions, and implement changes. This ability to pivot, supported by open dialogue and shared knowledge, often determines the difference between a project that falters and one that thrives.

Effective communication also enhances stakeholder relationships, which are central to long-term success in IT consultancy. Transparent updates and collaborative discussions demonstrate accountability and build confidence in the team's capabilities. When stakeholders feel informed and involved, they are more likely to advocate for the project and the organization managing it. This goodwill often translates into repeat business, referrals, and a reputation for reliability. In an industry where trust is a key currency, the value of strong communication cannot be overstated.

Treating communication as a strategic advantage transforms it from a routine task into a powerful tool for achieving competitive differentiation. It fosters alignment, adaptability, and trust—qualities that not only enhance project outcomes but also strengthen the foundation of an organization's success. By embedding communication deeply into their project methodologies, IT professionals can turn this often-overlooked element into a defining strength.

Practical Takeaways

Understanding the critical role of communication in IT projects lays the foundation for improvement, but translating that understanding into actionable strategies is what drives change. Practical takeaways empower professionals to close the gap between theory and practice, equipping them with tools to address real-world challenges. In IT, where complexities abound and stakes are high, these strategies are not merely helpful—they are essential for fostering clarity, collaboration, and success.

The first takeaway is the importance of creating structured communication frameworks. Whether it is a recurring team meeting, a shared project dashboard, or standardized progress updates, having predefined channels and formats ensures consistency and prevents critical information from slipping through the cracks. A project manager might implement a weekly status update using a collaborative tool like Jira or Trello, enabling everyone—team members and stakeholders alike—to access real-time information without confusion.

Equally important is the art of tailoring communication to the audience. In IT projects, the diversity of participants—from technical experts to non-technical stakeholders—necessitates a flexible approach. For example, a detailed technical explanation might resonate with a development team but overwhelm a client unfamiliar with the nuances of coding. Translating technical jargon into relatable terms without losing essential details helps bridge this gap, ensuring every party feels informed and valued.

Proactive communication is another critical strategy that cannot be overlooked. Waiting for issues to escalate before addressing them can lead to unnecessary delays and stress. Instead, fostering a culture of openness and early reporting can prevent small problems from snowballing. Teams can adopt a proactive mindset by setting up regular retrospectives or feedback sessions, ensuring a continuous dialogue about what is working and what needs adjustment.

Lastly, leveraging technology effectively can amplify the benefits of good communication practices. Tools like Slack for instant messaging, Zoom for virtual meetings, and Confluence for centralized documentation streamline the flow of information, especially in distributed teams. However, it is essential to avoid overloading team members with too many tools, which can create fatigue and inefficiency. Selecting the right tools and establishing guidelines for their use can strike the perfect balance between accessibility and effectiveness.

These practical takeaways underscore that communication in IT is not a one-size-fits-all endeavor. By embracing structure, audience awareness, proactivity, and appropriate technology, IT professionals can navigate the challenges of complex projects with confidence. These strategies transform communication from a potential liability into a powerful enabler of project success and professional growth.

BRIDGING CHALLENGES WITH FRAMEWORKS

Having explored the profound impact of communication on IT project success—both as a strategic advantage and a potential pitfall—the next step is understanding how to embed communication within established project frameworks. IT professionals often operate within structured methodologies like Agile, ITIL, PMP, or Kanban, each with its unique demands and workflows. Integrating effective communication into these systems is crucial for navigating their complexities and enhancing their outcomes.

By examining the relationship between communication practices and these frameworks, we uncover not only the theoretical alignment but also the practical applications that empower teams to operate seamlessly. The next discussion will delve into how these methodologies inherently support communication, where gaps might exist, and how professionals can bridge those gaps to ensure clarity, collaboration, and alignment throughout a project's lifecycle.

Common challenges in IT communication

Communication in IT projects is both an enabler of success and a frequent source of frustration. In environments where precision, adaptability, and innovation are essential, the ability to exchange information effectively should be a given. Yet, IT professionals often find themselves navigating a web of misunderstandings, misaligned priorities, and linguistic barriers that hinder collaboration. These challenges are not incidental but deeply rooted in the complexity of IT projects, making it crucial to examine why they occur and how they can be mitigated.

At the core of these communication challenges lies the diversity of roles and expertise involved in IT projects. Developers, project managers, designers, and external consultants all bring unique skill sets to the table, each with its own language, priorities, and methodologies. This diversity, while essential for delivering complex solutions, also creates a fertile ground for miscommunication. A single missed connection between these roles can cascade into larger issues, affecting the entire project lifecycle.

The rapid pace of technological change further compounds communication difficulties. IT professionals must frequently adapt to new tools, frameworks, and client demands, all while ensuring that their knowledge is shared effectively within the team. This dynamic environment leaves little room for error, as delays in understanding or implementing a critical update can disrupt timelines and jeopardize deliverables. Communication, in this context, becomes not just a skill but a survival mechanism, essential for keeping pace with evolving requirements.

Moreover, the global nature of many IT projects introduces additional layers of complexity. Teams often span multiple time zones, cultures, and organizational structures, requiring a level of coordination that can feel daunting. Language barriers, differing communication styles, and hierarchical misunderstandings create friction that slows progress and fosters frustration. Understanding these challenges is the first step toward addressing them, laying the foundation for strategies that enable IT teams to thrive amidst complexity.

DIVING INTO SPECIFIC CHALLENGES

The communication challenges in IT projects are as varied as the projects themselves, arising from a mix of technical, organizational, and interpersonal factors. These issues are not isolated incidents but recurring patterns that, if unaddressed, can disrupt even the most meticulously planned initiatives. Exploring these challenges in detail reveals the root causes that hinder collaboration and offers insight into the mechanisms driving these obstacles.

One of the most pervasive challenges is the overuse of technical jargon. IT professionals rely on precise language to describe complex systems, processes, and solutions, but this language often alienates non-technical stakeholders. For example, a software developer explaining an API integration might inadvertently confuse a client unfamiliar with backend terminology. This disconnect can lead to critical misunderstandings, with stakeholders feeling excluded from decision-making and technical teams frustrated by the need to constantly re-explain their work.

Another significant hurdle is the misalignment of priorities. In IT projects, different groups—clients, developers, project managers, and executives—often have competing goals. A client might prioritize rapid delivery to gain a market edge, while developers focus on building a robust and scalable solution, and project managers strive to stay within budget. Without clear communication to reconcile these differences, projects can become bogged down in conflicts or veer off course, with resources wasted on tasks that fail to align with the overall vision.

The issue of information silos is another challenge that frequently plagues IT projects. Teams or departments may withhold information, whether unintentionally or as a result of organizational culture. A development team working on a feature might not communicate updates to the quality assurance team, leading to delays when errors are discovered late in the process. Similarly, management decisions made in isolation from on-the-ground teams can result in unrealistic timelines or requirements that overlook key technical constraints. These silos fragment the project and hinder the free flow of information necessary for cohesive progress.

Finally, the rise of remote and distributed teams introduces logistical and cultural barriers. Time zone differences, reliance on digital communication, and a lack of face-to-face interaction can create misunderstandings that would have been resolved instantly in an in-person setting. Additionally, cultural differences in communication styles—direct versus indirect, formal versus informal—can lead to misinterpretations, especially in high-stress scenarios. These challenges highlight the complexity of modern IT environments and underscore the need for tailored communication strategies that address specific project dynamics.

CONSEQUENCES OF UNADDRESSED ISSUES

When communication challenges in IT projects are left unresolved, the consequences can cascade across every facet of the initiative, undermining both short-term objectives and long-term organizational goals. These repercussions are not confined to operational inefficiencies but extend into financial, relational, and reputational domains, making effective communication a non-negotiable element of success.

One immediate consequence is the erosion of project timelines. Misunderstandings between teams often result in redundant or misdirected work, forcing teams to backtrack and reallocate time to correct errors. For instance, a developer might create a feature based on incomplete requirements, only for the client to reject it during a later review. Such delays ripple through the project, putting additional strain on resources and leading to a domino effect where every subsequent milestone becomes harder to achieve. The cumulative result is not only missed deadlines but also a loss of stakeholder confidence in the team's ability to deliver.

Budget overruns are another inevitable fallout of poor communication. When misaligned priorities or information silos lead to wasted efforts, the cost of rework adds up quickly. Even small missteps, like overlooking a minor compatibility issue, can snowball into larger problems requiring expensive fixes. Additionally, the inefficiencies created by unclear communication—such as repeated meetings to clarify misunderstandings—consume time and money that could have been directed toward innovation or improvement. In an industry where budgets are often tight and highly scrutinized, these overruns can jeopardize not only the current project but also future opportunities.

The relational impact of unresolved communication issues cannot be overstated. Teams facing persistent miscommunication may experience frustration, blame-shifting, and reduced morale. Over time, this toxic environment erodes trust among colleagues, making collaboration increasingly difficult. Stakeholders, too, may lose trust in the organization's ability to execute, leading to strained relationships and, in some cases, the loss of critical business partnerships. For client-facing projects, these issues can tarnish the organization's reputation, as dissatisfied clients share their negative experiences within the industry.

Perhaps most damaging of all is the strategic impact on the organization. Failed or delayed IT projects can hinder a company's ability to innovate, compete, and adapt to changing market demands. A project derailed by communication issues might delay the launch of a critical product, allowing competitors to seize market share. Internally, unresolved communication challenges signal deeper structural problems, such as a lack of cohesive leadership or misaligned corporate values. These broader implications emphasize that communication is not merely an operational concern but a strategic imperative.

The gravity of these consequences highlights the importance of addressing communication challenges proactively. By acknowledging and mitigating these risks, IT professionals can transform potential pitfalls into opportunities for growth and collaboration, setting the stage for sustainable project success.

While the consequences of poor communication in IT projects are substantial, they also present opportunities for growth and transformation. When teams recognize these challenges and address them head-on, they can cultivate stronger collaboration, build resilient systems, and set themselves apart in a competitive industry. Transforming communication issues into opportunities requires a shift in mindset, focusing on the potential for innovation and improvement inherent in every obstacle.

One of the first steps in this transformation is fostering a culture of transparency. When communication barriers such as jargon, silos, or misaligned priorities arise, organizations can use these moments to reflect on their practices and identify gaps in their processes. For example, recognizing that technical terminology alienates non-technical stakeholders can lead to the development of a standardized language or glossary for the project, improving clarity across all levels of the organization. Such proactive measures not only resolve immediate issues but also establish best practices for future initiatives.

Another opportunity lies in leveraging technology to bridge communication gaps. Modern tools such as project management platforms, collaboration software, and real-time communication channels can streamline the flow of information and minimize misunderstandings. For instance, implementing a shared dashboard for all teams to track project milestones can ensure alignment and provide a single source of truth. By embracing these tools and training teams to use them effectively, organizations can transform communication challenges into drivers of efficiency and cohesion.

Interpersonal relationships also stand to benefit when communication challenges are addressed constructively. Misunderstandings and conflicts, if handled openly, can lead to greater empathy and trust among team members. For example, a tense discussion about misaligned priorities can evolve into a productive brainstorming session that clarifies goals and strengthens the team's collective vision. These moments of conflict resolution can create a stronger foundation for collaboration, empowering teams to tackle future challenges with confidence and unity.

Lastly, overcoming communication challenges positions organizations as leaders in their field. Clients and stakeholders notice when a team excels at coordination, clarity, and responsiveness, and this competence becomes a key differentiator in a crowded market. By turning potential pitfalls into opportunities for excellence, IT professionals can enhance not only their project outcomes but also their reputation and influence within the industry. This strategic approach transforms communication from a liability into a cornerstone of competitive advantage, ensuring long-term success for both teams and organizations.

Overview of IT methodologies and how communication fits into these frameworks.

In the intricate world of IT project management, methodologies such as ITIL, Agile, PMP, and Kanban serve as structured blueprints to streamline workflows, manage resources, and achieve objectives. Yet, the success of these frameworks hinges not only on their technical precision but also on the effectiveness of communication that binds every process, task, and decision together. Communication, in this context, acts as the unifying thread, ensuring that the elaborate machinery of methodologies operates cohesively.

Regardless of their distinct approaches, all IT frameworks rely on communication to translate objectives into actions. ITIL's service management processes, Agile's iterative sprints, PMP's phase-driven execution, and Kanban's visual task flows are inherently collaborative. They require teams to share information seamlessly, align on priorities, and adapt to changing circumstances. Without robust communication, even the most sophisticated framework risks becoming a rigid system incapable of addressing real-world complexities.

The value of communication extends beyond task management; it cultivates a shared understanding among stakeholders with diverse roles, expertise, and expectations. In an IT project, developers, business analysts, project managers, and clients must navigate technical jargon, strategic goals, and operational constraints. The ability to bridge these divides through clear and inclusive communication ensures that everyone moves in the same direction, reducing errors and fostering accountability.

Moreover, communication is not merely a tool for execution but a catalyst for innovation and problem-solving. When teams communicate effectively, they create an environment where ideas are exchanged freely, risks are identified early, and solutions are crafted collaboratively. This synergy not only enhances project outcomes but also builds resilience, enabling teams to navigate challenges with agility and confidence. By understanding and prioritizing communication as the foundation of IT methodologies, professionals can unlock the full potential of these frameworks and drive sustainable success.

ITIL: COMMUNICATING IN SERVICE MANAGEMENT

The IT Infrastructure Library (ITIL) is renowned for its structured approach to IT service management, emphasizing processes that ensure services align with business objectives. At its core, ITIL operates through a series of interconnected lifecycles, such as service strategy, design, transition, operation, and continual improvement. While these stages provide a robust framework for delivering consistent and efficient services, their success hinges on a foundational element that often operates behind the scenes—communication.

In ITIL, communication acts as the glue that binds its processes. Consider incident management, where the ability to quickly and accurately communicate issues determines how effectively they are resolved. A service desk team, for instance, must gather precise details from end-users, prioritize incidents based on urgency and impact, and relay critical updates to technical teams. Miscommunication at any stage—whether it's unclear problem descriptions or delays in escalating incidents—can lead to extended downtime, frustrated users, and reputational damage to the organization.

Similarly, in change management, ITIL emphasizes minimizing disruption while implementing updates or modifications. Effective communication ensures that all stakeholders—ranging from IT teams to business users—are aware of impending changes, their potential impacts, and the mitigation plans in place. A breakdown in communication during a major change can result in unexpected outages or resistance from stakeholders who feel uninformed or excluded from the decision-making process.

Another critical aspect is the relationship between IT services and the business they support. ITIL frameworks often stress the importance of Service Level Agreements (SLAs) to align expectations between service providers and their clients. However, SLAs are only as effective as the communication underpinning them. Drafting an SLA requires dialogue to ensure mutual understanding of terms, while regular reporting and feedback loops build trust by demonstrating accountability and responsiveness to evolving needs.

Moreover, the continual improvement lifecycle within ITIL highlights how communication drives progress. Effective feedback mechanisms collect insights from service users and technical teams, transforming challenges and inefficiencies into actionable improvements. This process is inherently collaborative, requiring open channels for reporting issues, brainstorming solutions, and implementing iterative enhancements. Without these communication pathways, opportunities for growth and optimization remain unrealized.

In essence, ITIL's emphasis on process rigor is matched by its reliance on communication as the mechanism that transforms plans into results. For IT professionals working within ITIL frameworks, developing strong communication skills is not optional—it is indispensable. By mastering the art of clear, timely, and strategic communication, service managers can ensure not only the smooth execution of ITIL processes but also the alignment of services with organizational goals and customer satisfaction.

AGILE: COLLABORATION IN ITERATIVE DEVELOPMENT

Agile methodologies revolutionized software development by emphasizing adaptability, rapid feedback, and incremental delivery. Unlike traditional linear approaches, Agile thrives on cycles of iteration where teams produce, test, and refine deliverables in close collaboration with stakeholders. This inherently dynamic environment places collaboration and communication at the center of success, ensuring alignment, transparency, and efficiency at every stage of the process.

In Agile, the hallmark ceremonies—sprint planning, daily stand-ups, sprint reviews, and retrospectives—are all communication-driven. Sprint planning sets the foundation by aligning the team on goals, priorities, and deliverables for the upcoming cycle. Effective collaboration during this phase ensures that everyone, from developers to product owners, has a shared understanding of the work ahead. Miscommunication here can lead to misaligned expectations, incomplete deliverables, or wasted effort on non-priority tasks.

Daily stand-ups serve as microcosms of Agile's collaborative spirit. In these brief yet impactful meetings, team members synchronize efforts, highlight progress, and address blockers. Clear, concise communication during stand-ups helps the team maintain momentum and adaptability. For example, a developer encountering an unexpected challenge might signal it during the stand-up, prompting immediate support or adjustments to priorities. Conversely, poorly managed stand-ups—dominated by vague updates or unresolved discussions—can dilute their purpose and hinder team productivity.

Sprint reviews and retrospectives underscore the iterative and collaborative nature of Agile. Reviews provide a platform to showcase completed work and gather feedback from stakeholders, requiring the team to communicate technical progress in a way that is accessible and actionable for non-technical participants. Meanwhile, retrospectives focus inward, allowing teams to reflect on their processes, celebrate successes, and address areas for improvement. Both ceremonies depend on honest, constructive dialogue to drive continuous enhancement and foster a culture of trust.

Agile's communication extends beyond internal team interactions to include stakeholders, customers, and other external collaborators. Agile prioritizes delivering value, and this requires constant engagement with end-users or business representatives to refine requirements and adjust deliverables. Tools such as user stories and backlog prioritization facilitate this dialogue, ensuring that the team remains focused on outcomes that matter most. A breakdown in communication with stakeholders, however, can result in misaligned deliverables or project delays, undermining Agile's core principle of responsiveness.

In essence, Agile is more than a methodology; it is a communication framework in its own right. Collaboration fuels its cycles of iteration, providing the clarity and connection needed to navigate the uncertainties and complexities of modern development. By fostering open, adaptive, and continuous communication, Agile enables teams to not only deliver better products but also cultivate stronger relationships and a more cohesive working environment.

PMP: STRUCTURING COMMUNICATION IN TRADITIONAL PROJECT MANAGEMENT

The Project Management Professional (PMP) framework is a cornerstone of traditional project management, emphasizing structured processes to guide projects from initiation to closure. Central to PMP's effectiveness is the meticulous management of communication, which ensures that all stakeholders—team members, sponsors, and clients—remain informed and aligned throughout the project lifecycle. Without this structured approach to communication, even the most well-planned projects risk falling into disarray.

PMP identifies communication as one of the ten key knowledge areas, recognizing its critical role in managing stakeholder expectations and maintaining project cohesion. A Communication Management Plan, developed during the planning phase, serves as the blueprint for how information will be shared, who will receive it, and the frequency of updates. For example, a project involving multiple departments and external vendors might specify weekly status reports, daily check-ins for the core team, and monthly executive briefings. By standardizing these practices, the PMP framework minimizes the risk of information gaps or misunderstandings.

Effective communication is also integral to PMP's emphasis on risk management. Anticipating potential risks requires clear and open channels for reporting concerns and discussing mitigation strategies. For instance, during a project's execution phase, a delay in receiving critical supplies might be escalated through a structured communication protocol, enabling swift intervention by the project manager. Conversely, a lack of timely communication could exacerbate delays, leading to a cascade of missed deadlines and additional costs.

In traditional project management, the hierarchical nature of PMP projects necessitates precise and formal communication. Teams often operate within well-defined roles, and clear instructions are essential to prevent misinterpretation. For example, a project plan might dictate exact specifications for deliverables, accompanied by detailed documentation to guide execution. While this structured approach ensures accountability, it also demands that project managers maintain clarity and conciseness in all communications to avoid overwhelming their teams with unnecessary complexity.

Another critical dimension of PMP communication is stakeholder engagement. Sponsors, clients, and end-users often have varying levels of familiarity with the technical aspects of a project. Translating complex project updates into language that resonates with these audiences is a skill that PMP-trained project managers must master. Consider a software implementation project: while developers may focus on technical milestones, executives may only be concerned with cost efficiency and timeline adherence. Effective communication bridges this gap, ensuring that each stakeholder remains invested in the project's success.

PMP's structured approach to communication transforms potential chaos into coordinated effort. It provides a framework for ensuring that the right information reaches the right people at the right time, fostering transparency, accountability, and trust. In the context of large, multifaceted projects, this structured communication is not merely an operational necessity—it is a strategic advantage, enabling project managers to navigate complexity and deliver results with precision.

KANBAN: VISUALIZATION AND FLOW-BASED COMMUNICATION

Kanban, with its roots in lean manufacturing, is renowned for its simplicity and focus on optimizing workflow. Unlike more rigid methodologies, Kanban prioritizes flexibility and continuous delivery, making visualization a cornerstone of its communication strategy. By translating complex workflows into an accessible and transparent format, Kanban empowers teams to communicate effectively about priorities, progress, and challenges without unnecessary meetings or lengthy documentation.

The heart of Kanban communication lies in its board—a visual representation of the work process divided into columns that correspond to different stages of the workflow. Cards, representing tasks or deliverables, move across the board from initiation to completion. This straightforward yet powerful visualization tool provides an at-a-glance understanding of the team's workload, bottlenecks, and task progress. For example, if the "In Progress" column becomes overloaded, it signals a need for immediate attention to prevent delays. This visual clarity reduces the need for verbal explanations, allowing team members to identify and address issues autonomously.

Kanban's emphasis on flow further shapes its communication style. Instead of rigidly scheduled sprints or milestones, Kanban advocates for continuous delivery, where tasks are pulled into the workflow as capacity allows. This approach requires real-time, asynchronous communication to ensure alignment. Teams use the Kanban board as a shared communication platform, updating task statuses, flagging blockers, and prioritizing tasks collaboratively. Tools like comments or tags on digital Kanban boards (e.g., Trello, Jira) enhance this communication, enabling geographically dispersed teams to stay synchronized without constant meetings.

One of Kanban's unique strengths is its ability to highlight bottlenecks and inefficiencies in real time. When tasks pile up in a specific stage, the issue becomes immediately visible, prompting discussions and problem-solving. For instance, if testing tasks accumulate in a QA column, it might indicate resource shortages or unclear requirements. This instant feedback loop fosters proactive communication, enabling teams to address problems before they escalate. In traditional models, such delays might remain hidden until a formal status update, causing unnecessary disruption.

Kanban's flow-based approach also facilitates cross-functional collaboration. Teams working in different domains—such as development, testing, and operations—can converge on a single Kanban board, ensuring transparency across the entire workflow. By visualizing dependencies and task ownership, Kanban minimizes miscommunication between teams. For example, developers can see at a glance whether a feature is ready for testing, while operations can monitor deployment readiness, fostering a smooth handoff between stages.

Kanban's communication ethos revolves around making work visible, maintaining flow, and enabling responsiveness. Its visual and flow-driven nature reduces the friction often associated with more formal communication methods, empowering teams to focus on delivering value. In an era where agility and adaptability are paramount, Kanban's approach to communication ensures that teams can collaborate effectively, resolve issues swiftly, and maintain productivity without sacrificing clarity or cohesion.

BRIDGING METHODOLOGIES: COMMUNICATION ACROSS FRAMEWORKS

In the dynamic landscape of IT project management, it is rare for teams to adhere strictly to a single methodology. Instead, organizations often blend elements of ITIL, Agile, PMP, and Kanban to create a hybrid approach tailored to their unique needs. While this adaptability enhances efficiency and responsiveness, it also introduces complexity—particularly in communication. Bridging these methodologies requires a nuanced understanding of how each framework approaches collaboration and information sharing, ensuring seamless integration across diverse teams and processes.

Each methodology brings its own philosophy to communication. ITIL emphasizes structured workflows and service-level agreements, often relying on formal documentation and escalation channels. Agile champions flexibility and real-time collaboration through ceremonies like stand-ups and retrospectives. PMP focuses on clear hierarchies and comprehensive communication plans, while Kanban streamlines information flow through visualization. These differences can create friction when teams operating within different frameworks attempt to collaborate. For example, an Agile team accustomed to rapid iteration may find itself at odds with a PMP team requiring detailed documentation before advancing.

Bridging these frameworks begins with establishing shared communication norms that respect the strengths and limitations of each approach. For instance, a hybrid team might adopt Agile's daily stand-ups for rapid status updates while utilizing PMP-style milestone reviews for major decision points. Similarly, a Kanban board can serve as a unifying tool, providing visibility into the workflow for both Agile developers and ITIL-driven service managers. By adopting cross-framework tools and practices, teams can harmonize their communication styles without compromising the integrity of their methodologies.

The role of the project manager or team lead becomes particularly critical in this context. These individuals act as translators, ensuring that information flows smoothly between teams operating under different frameworks. For example, they might distill the detailed requirements generated by an ITIL process into actionable user stories for an Agile team. Conversely, they may translate the iterative progress of Agile sprints into structured reports for PMP stakeholders. By tailoring communication to the audience's expectations and needs, project leaders mitigate misunderstandings and foster collaboration.

Technology also plays a pivotal role in bridging methodologies. Modern project management tools such as Jira, ServiceNow, and Microsoft Teams often include customizable features that can accommodate diverse workflows. These tools enable teams to maintain their preferred practices while sharing key information with other groups. For instance, an ITIL team using ServiceNow for incident tracking can integrate their workflow with an Agile team's Jira board, creating a seamless pipeline for escalating and resolving issues. Such integrations ensure that information flows freely across frameworks, reducing the silos that often impede cross-team communication.

Successful communication across methodologies hinges on adaptability and mutual respect. Teams must recognize the value of different approaches and remain open to compromise. By establishing shared goals and leveraging tools that facilitate integration, organizations can overcome the communication challenges inherent in hybrid frameworks. In doing so, they unlock the full potential of their diverse methodologies, achieving outcomes that exceed the capabilities of any single approach.

PRACTICAL IMPLICATIONS FOR IT PROFESSIONALS

For IT professionals navigating environments where multiple methodologies coexist, the ability to communicate effectively across frameworks is not just a soft skill—it's a strategic advantage. Understanding the practical implications of this skill is critical for success, as it directly influences project efficiency, team collaboration, and stakeholder satisfaction. The nuanced requirements of communicating within and across ITIL, Agile, PMP, and Kanban frameworks demand a blend of technical knowledge, adaptability, and interpersonal acumen.

One significant implication lies in task coordination. IT professionals must align their communication style with the expectations of various methodologies to avoid misalignments that can derail progress. For instance, while Agile teams thrive on concise, iterative updates, PMP stakeholders often require in-depth, milestone-focused reports. Professionals who can seamlessly toggle between these styles demonstrate versatility and earn trust across organizational hierarchies. For example, a developer working in a Kanban system might need to provide quick progress updates in a sprint review, then prepare detailed documentation for a PMP-driven project phase.

Another practical implication is the ability to foster collaboration among diverse teams. IT professionals often act as liaisons between departments that operate under distinct frameworks. An infrastructure team adhering to ITIL might need to collaborate with a development team running Agile sprints. In such cases, the professional must translate requirements, expectations, and progress updates into terms that resonate with both groups. This skill not only prevents miscommunication but also helps build bridges between teams, fostering a sense of shared purpose despite differing workflows.

Time management is also deeply affected by cross-methodology communication. Misaligned expectations can lead to wasted time, duplicate efforts, or delays in deliverables. For example, an Agile team might proceed with a user story, only to find later that it doesn't align with the PMP-documented scope. IT professionals can mitigate such risks by proactively identifying potential disconnects and ensuring that all parties are aligned before significant work begins. Regular check-ins and feedback loops become invaluable tools in this context, allowing for continuous alignment and course correction.

Finally, effective communication across methodologies directly impacts career growth for IT professionals. As organizations increasingly adopt hybrid frameworks to balance agility and structure, those who excel in bridging these approaches become indispensable. Whether acting as project managers, technical leads, or individual contributors, professionals who can navigate the intricacies of multi-framework environments are positioned to lead initiatives, gain visibility, and earn credibility in their fields. For example, an IT manager who successfully integrates Agile workflows with ITIL service management demonstrates leadership that transcends technical expertise, showcasing a mastery of both processes and people.

In essence, the practical implications of cross-framework communication are profound. IT professionals who hone this ability not only ensure smoother project execution but also position themselves as vital contributors to their organizations. By embracing the challenges and opportunities of hybrid methodologies, they can drive innovation, foster collaboration, and achieve outcomes that reflect the best of all worlds.

Chapter 2: Team Communication: Building Cohesion Within Your Group

In IT projects, collaboration and clarity are the cornerstones of success, yet they are often overlooked amidst the focus on technical excellence. While the latest technologies and frameworks can streamline processes, the absence of cohesive teamwork and clear communication can cause even the best-laid plans to fail. The complex nature of IT projects, involving diverse roles such as developers, analysts, and testers, makes seamless communication essential. Without it, teams risk working at cross-purposes, leading to inefficiencies and conflicts that derail progress.

Collaboration brings together the diverse skills and expertise necessary for innovation. In IT, where cross-functional teams are the norm, fostering a collaborative culture ensures that each team member's contribution aligns with the project's overarching goals. However, collaboration does not occur in a vacuum; it requires deliberate effort to create an environment where individuals feel valued and supported. This goes beyond assigning tasks—it involves building relationships, encouraging knowledge sharing, and establishing trust among team members.

Equally important is clarity in communication, which acts as the glue holding collaborative efforts together. Clear communication minimizes misunderstandings, ensuring that everyone is on the same page regarding objectives, timelines, and expectations. In IT projects, where ambiguity can lead to costly errors, clarity helps to preempt problems before they arise. When team members understand their roles, responsibilities, and the project's larger context, they can work more efficiently and with greater confidence.

The absence of collaboration and clarity can result in dire consequences, including missed deadlines, bloated budgets, and reduced morale. Teams may fall into silos, limiting the flow of critical information and leading to redundancies or overlooked issues. This chapter introduces strategies to overcome these challenges, laying the foundation for teams to function as cohesive units. By prioritizing collaboration and clarity, IT professionals can unlock their team's full potential and drive successful outcomes in even the most complex projects.

CORE STRATEGIES FOR FOSTERING COLLABORATION

Fostering collaboration within IT teams requires a deliberate approach that balances technical execution with interpersonal connection. Collaboration thrives in an environment where individuals feel a sense of shared purpose, mutual trust, and a commitment to common goals. It is not simply about working together but doing so in a way that leverages the collective strengths of the team. To achieve this, leaders and team members must prioritize psychological safety, clarity in roles, and opportunities for meaningful interaction.

One of the foundational pillars of collaboration is psychological safety. In an IT team, where technical challenges often require innovative solutions, team members need to feel comfortable voicing their ideas without fear of criticism. Psychological safety allows individuals to take risks, admit mistakes, and contribute creative solutions without worrying about negative repercussions. Leaders play a crucial role in fostering this environment by modeling open communication, encouraging diverse perspectives, and ensuring that each member's input is valued. A culture of psychological safety can transform a team's dynamic, making it more adaptable and innovative.

Equally important is defining clear roles and responsibilities. Collaboration becomes strained when team members are unsure about their tasks or when overlapping responsibilities lead to confusion and inefficiency. Clear role definitions ensure that each individual understands their contribution to the project's success and how their work interacts with that of their peers. Tools like the RACI matrix (Responsible, Accountable, Consulted, Informed) can be instrumental in creating this clarity. By outlining responsibilities explicitly and reviewing them regularly, teams can avoid misunderstandings and streamline workflows.

Promoting shared goals is another critical strategy for fostering collaboration. IT projects often involve cross-functional teams with varying priorities, making it essential to unify everyone around a common purpose. Shared goals serve as a north star, guiding the team's efforts and fostering a sense of alignment. Kickoff meetings and regular check-ins can help teams reaffirm these objectives and evaluate progress. By emphasizing collective achievements over individual successes, teams can build a collaborative culture where members feel equally invested in the project's outcomes.

Through these strategies, IT teams can cultivate a collaborative environment that maximizes individual contributions while driving collective success. Psychological safety, role clarity, and shared goals are not standalone initiatives but interconnected elements of a cohesive strategy for effective teamwork. By implementing these practices, teams can overcome challenges, foster innovation, and ensure the seamless execution of complex projects.

STRATEGIES FOR ENSURING CLARITY IN TEAM COMMUNICATION

Clarity in communication is the backbone of efficient teamwork, especially in IT projects where misinterpretations can lead to significant delays, rework, or even project failure. Without a clear exchange of ideas, instructions, and expectations, teams risk falling into confusion, with each member interpreting objectives differently. Establishing clarity requires not only careful planning but also ongoing effort to maintain transparency and alignment as projects evolve.

The first strategy to ensure clarity is standardizing communication channels and practices. In IT projects, teams often rely on multiple platforms for communication—emails, messaging apps, project management tools, and video calls. While each tool serves a purpose, the lack of a consistent communication framework can lead to chaos. Establishing clear guidelines about when and how to use each platform helps eliminate confusion. For instance, project updates might be reserved for a centralized tool like Jira, while Slack is used for informal team discussions. Regularly scheduled meetings, such as daily standups or weekly progress reviews, further reinforce structured communication, ensuring that everyone is aligned on priorities and updates.

Another critical strategy is creating detailed documentation. IT projects often involve intricate processes, complex systems, and technical jargon, making clear documentation essential. Teams should develop comprehensive project charters, requirement specifications, and meeting minutes that leave no room for ambiguity. Documentation should not be static; it needs to evolve as the project progresses, reflecting changes in scope, deliverables, or deadlines. When team members have access to a single source of truth, they can quickly verify information, reducing the risk of miscommunication. Leaders should also emphasize the importance of documentation and ensure it is consistently maintained and readily accessible.

Encouraging active listening and feedback loops is equally important for achieving clarity. Communication is a two-way process, and ensuring clarity requires both the sender and receiver to fully understand the message. Active listening involves focusing on the speaker, asking clarifying questions, and summarizing key points to confirm understanding. Feedback loops further reinforce this practice, allowing team members to validate what they've heard and provide insights or corrections as needed. For example, after a team leader explains a new process, asking team members to restate their understanding can uncover potential misunderstandings early.

By integrating these strategies, IT teams can create a culture where clear communication is a priority, reducing confusion and fostering efficiency. Standardized communication practices, robust documentation, and active listening not only enhance project outcomes but also build stronger, more cohesive teams. These efforts pave the way for better collaboration, fewer mistakes, and a smoother execution of complex IT initiatives.

EXAMPLES AND CASE STUDIES

Real-world examples and case studies highlight the transformative power of effective collaboration and clear communication within IT teams. They provide concrete insights into how theory translates into practice, illustrating the consequences of both strong and weak communication. These examples emphasize the importance of deliberate strategies in fostering team cohesion and alignment.

Case Study 1: Success through Standardized Communication in an Agile Project

An e-commerce company embarked on an ambitious project to integrate artificial intelligence into its product recommendation engine. The team, composed of developers, data scientists, and product managers, initially struggled with scattered communication across email, Slack, and shared drives. Delays and misunderstandings began to snowball, threatening the project timeline. Recognizing the issue, the project manager introduced a centralized communication protocol. All technical updates were logged in Jira, while Slack was reserved for urgent discussions, and Confluence became the repository for project documentation. Daily standups ensured alignment, and a clear channel hierarchy reduced distractions. As a result, the team streamlined workflows, hit milestones on time, and delivered a successful product enhancement.

Example 2: The Cost of Ambiguity in Role Definitions
A global software firm launched a project to develop a cloud-based solution for its clients. Despite having a highly skilled team, the absence of defined roles led to duplication of work and key tasks being overlooked. For instance, two team members began designing overlapping features, while crucial aspects of the system's security remained unaddressed. This misalignment delayed the project by six months and increased costs by 30%. When the team regrouped, they adopted the RACI framework to delineate roles clearly. Accountability and task ownership improved dramatically, and subsequent phases were completed on schedule.

Case Study 3: Building Trust in Cross-Functional Collaboration
In a large healthcare IT project, the team included software developers, medical advisors, and compliance officers. Early in the project, disagreements arose due to conflicting priorities and misunderstandings about technical constraints and regulatory requirements. The project leader implemented a series of trust-building workshops, where team members shared their expertise, discussed challenges, and aligned expectations. Collaborative tools like virtual whiteboards were used during meetings to map out joint solutions. Over time, the team built mutual respect, leading to a seamless integration of compliance needs with technical innovations. The project not only succeeded but became a model for collaboration across the organization.

Example 4: Active Listening to Prevent Scope Creep
A fintech startup developing a mobile banking app experienced scope creep when new features were repeatedly introduced by different stakeholders without proper vetting. The technical team grew frustrated, as timelines became unmanageable. A new project manager addressed this by enforcing active listening and feedback loops. During requirement-gathering sessions, stakeholders were asked to prioritize their requests while developers summarized their understanding of each feature. By instituting feedback loops, the team clarified which features aligned with the core objectives, leading to a more controlled scope and on-time delivery of the product's minimum viable version.

These examples illustrate the importance of fostering collaboration and maintaining clarity within teams. They highlight how structured communication practices, trust-building, and active listening not only resolve challenges but also enhance project efficiency and team morale. By learning from these scenarios,

IT professionals can better understand how to apply effective strategies in their own work environments.

TOOLS AND TEMPLATES

Effective team communication relies not only on strategies but also on the tools and templates that enable streamlined processes, clear documentation, and efficient collaboration. In IT projects, where teams often juggle complex technical requirements and tight deadlines, leveraging the right tools and creating reusable templates can significantly enhance productivity and alignment. These resources ensure that communication is both consistent and accessible, allowing teams to focus on delivering results.

Collaboration Tools for Real-Time and Asynchronous Communication

Collaboration platforms like Microsoft Teams, Slack, and Zoom provide the backbone of real-time communication in IT teams. These tools support instant messaging, video conferencing, and file sharing, enabling quick problem-solving and decision-making. For asynchronous communication, platforms like Confluence or Google Workspace offer a centralized location for storing documents and project updates. For example, a Confluence page dedicated to weekly project updates allows team members across different time zones to stay informed without needing to attend every meeting. By combining real-time and asynchronous tools, teams can create a balance that accommodates diverse working styles and schedules.

Templates for Structured Meetings

Meetings are a critical touchpoint for communication, but they can easily become unproductive without a clear structure. Pre-designed templates for meeting agendas and minutes can help ensure that discussions stay on track and that all key points are documented. For instance, a template for a sprint planning meeting might include sections for reviewing the backlog, assigning tasks, and discussing blockers. Similarly, post-meeting templates that outline decisions made, action items, and deadlines provide a transparent record that team members can reference later. These templates reduce misunderstandings and foster accountability, as everyone knows what is expected.

Project Management Tools for Clarity and Alignment

Project management platforms like Jira, Trello, and Monday.com are indispensable for tracking tasks, deadlines, and dependencies. These tools often come with customizable dashboards that allow team members to see the status of tasks at a glance. By using templates for task descriptions, such as a pre-filled format for defining objectives, required inputs, and acceptance criteria, teams can maintain consistency in how information is conveyed. This clarity minimizes confusion and ensures that all team members, regardless of role, understand what is needed for successful task completion.

Checklists for Communication and Deliverables

Checklists are a simple yet powerful tool for ensuring thorough communication, especially in IT environments where missing a detail can lead to cascading issues. For example, a checklist for code reviews might include items like "confirm adherence to coding standards," "check for potential bugs," and "verify integration with other modules." Similarly, a stakeholder communication checklist could include steps for identifying the audience, tailoring the message, and scheduling updates. These structured approaches help teams avoid oversight and deliver high-quality results consistently.

Templates for Progress Reporting and Feedback

Regular progress updates are essential for maintaining alignment among team members and stakeholders. Standardized reporting templates simplify this process, ensuring that updates are concise and focused. For example, a weekly status report template might include sections for completed tasks, upcoming goals, and identified risks or issues. Feedback templates, on the other hand, encourage constructive conversations by providing prompts for what worked well, what needs improvement, and suggestions for next steps. These tools foster transparency and a culture of continuous improvement, critical for long-term success in IT projects.

By integrating these tools and templates into their workflows, IT teams can significantly enhance both the efficiency and quality of their communication. Whether it's streamlining task tracking, standardizing meetings, or providing structured feedback, these resources ensure that everyone remains aligned and informed. Teams that consistently use these tools not only improve their internal dynamics but also position themselves for better project outcomes and long-term success.

ACTIONABLE TAKEAWAYS

Distilling strategies, tools, and examples into actionable steps ensures that readers can immediately apply the concepts to their own teams. Actionable takeaways bridge the gap between theory and practice, providing clear guidance for IT professionals aiming to enhance team communication and collaboration.

Prioritize Regular and Intentional Communication

Effective communication doesn't happen by chance—it requires deliberate effort. Establish a cadence of structured check-ins, whether through daily standups, weekly team syncs, or biweekly retrospectives. Use these opportunities to share updates, address blockers, and align on priorities. Encourage team members to prepare for meetings by reviewing agendas in advance and bringing specific questions or updates to the discussion. Regular, intentional communication fosters transparency and ensures everyone is aligned on goals and responsibilities.

Create and Enforce Clear Communication Protocols

Clarity in communication starts with well-defined protocols. Standardize the use of communication tools—for example, designate Slack for quick queries, email for formal updates, and Confluence for documentation. Establish guidelines for crafting messages, such as using bullet points for clarity or labeling emails with specific subject lines like "[Action Required]" or "[FYI]." These practices reduce the risk of miscommunication and ensure that team members know where to find information and how to contribute effectively.

Leverage Visual Aids and Summaries

In technical environments, lengthy or overly detailed explanations can lead to confusion. Use visual aids like flowcharts, diagrams, and Kanban boards to represent complex processes or workflows. Summarize key points at the start and end of discussions or reports to provide context and reinforce understanding. For example, a project update might include a high-level Gantt chart summarizing milestones alongside a brief narrative highlighting progress and challenges. Visual and concise communication improves accessibility and understanding for diverse team members.

Encourage a Feedback Culture

Foster an environment where giving and receiving feedback is routine and constructive. Train team members to use structured frameworks like "Start, Stop, Continue" or "Situation-Behavior-Impact" (SBI) to frame feedback positively and effectively. Make feedback part of regular team interactions, whether during retrospectives, one-on-one meetings, or informal check-ins. A strong feedback culture not only improves performance but also strengthens trust and collaboration among team members.

Document and Share Lessons Learned

Every project or task offers an opportunity to refine communication practices. Create a repository for lessons learned, documenting both successes and failures. For instance, after completing a sprint, summarize what communication methods worked well (e.g., using specific templates) and what challenges arose (e.g., delayed responses from stakeholders). Share these insights with the team to build collective knowledge and improve future workflows. Regularly revisiting these lessons reinforces a culture of continuous improvement.

Empower Teams with Autonomy and Accountability

Encourage team members to take ownership of their communication responsibilities. Assign roles such as meeting facilitator, note-taker, or task tracker to distribute accountability. For example, a team member responsible for summarizing weekly updates ensures that everyone stays informed, while another tracking action items ensures follow-through. Empowered teams are more likely to communicate proactively, address challenges early, and maintain high levels of engagement and productivity.

By adopting these actionable takeaways, teams can transform their communication practices into a strategic advantage. These steps promote consistency, reduce misunderstandings, and create an environment where collaboration and clarity drive success. Implementing even a few of these practices can lead to significant improvements in team dynamics, project efficiency, and overall outcomes.

Understanding team dynamics: balancing technical expertise and interpersonal skills.

Team dynamics play a pivotal role in the success of IT projects, influencing everything from collaboration to productivity. In IT environments, projects often involve diverse individuals with specialized skills, working together to achieve complex goals under tight deadlines. This interdependence requires a cohesive team dynamic that fosters both technical excellence and interpersonal synergy. When these dynamics are harmonious, teams achieve greater efficiency, innovation, and adaptability; when dysfunctional, they can derail even the most meticulously planned projects.

IT projects are inherently collaborative, requiring input from developers, project managers, designers, quality analysts, and other stakeholders. Each individual brings a unique perspective and skill set to the table, which can enrich the team's problem-solving capabilities. However, this diversity also introduces challenges. Miscommunication, conflicting priorities, or a lack of alignment between team members can hinder progress. For example, a technically proficient team may struggle to deliver results if interpersonal conflicts or unclear communication channels disrupt their workflow. Team dynamics serve as the framework within which these diverse talents and personalities operate, making their management critical to project success.

A balanced approach to team dynamics acknowledges that both technical and interpersonal skills are essential. Technical expertise ensures that tasks are executed accurately and efficiently, while interpersonal skills create the environment in which technical expertise can thrive. Teams with strong interpersonal dynamics tend to exhibit higher levels of trust, open communication, and mutual respect, which in turn enhances collaboration. For instance, a team that values and practices active listening is more likely to identify and address issues early, avoiding costly delays or misunderstandings.

Leaders play a central role in shaping team dynamics. Effective leaders understand the interplay between technical and interpersonal factors and actively work to cultivate an environment where both are valued. They foster open communication, set clear expectations, and mediate conflicts constructively. Additionally, leaders can act as role models, demonstrating how to balance technical proficiency with interpersonal engagement. By prioritizing team dynamics, IT leaders not only improve individual project outcomes but also contribute to a culture of collaboration and continuous improvement within their organizations.

In sum, team dynamics are not an abstract concept but a tangible factor that directly impacts IT project success. Balancing the technical and interpersonal aspects of team collaboration creates a foundation for achieving shared goals, navigating challenges, and fostering innovation. For IT professionals, understanding and optimizing team dynamics is not just a soft skill but a strategic imperative.

RECOGNIZING THE STRENGTHS AND CHALLENGES OF TECHNICAL EXPERTISE

Technical expertise is the backbone of IT projects, driving innovation and enabling teams to execute complex tasks with precision. Whether it's coding, system architecture, or data analysis, technical skills form the foundation of problem-solving and decision-making in IT environments. Team members with deep technical knowledge often serve as subject matter experts, guiding projects toward optimal solutions and ensuring the technical integrity of deliverables. Their ability to break down intricate problems into manageable components allows teams to meet challenging requirements and navigate unexpected roadblocks.

Despite its strengths, technical expertise can sometimes present challenges that hinder team dynamics. Over-reliance on technical skills may lead to siloed thinking, where team members focus exclusively on their specific tasks without considering the bigger picture. This can result in a lack of alignment between team members, causing delays or inconsistencies in deliverables. For instance, a developer might optimize a feature without fully understanding its impact on the user experience, leading to rework and frustration. Similarly, highly technical individuals may struggle to communicate complex ideas effectively, creating barriers in cross-functional collaboration.

Another challenge lies in the perception of technical expertise within the team. While technical specialists are often seen as indispensable, their influence can inadvertently overshadow contributions from those with complementary but less tangible skills, such as project coordination or client relationship management. This imbalance can lead to team members feeling undervalued, which may diminish morale and collaboration. Moreover, when technical experts dominate discussions or decision-making processes, other perspectives that could enhance problem-solving are overlooked.

Recognizing and addressing these challenges is essential for fostering balanced team dynamics. Teams must strive to integrate technical expertise into the broader framework of project goals and interpersonal collaboration. Leaders can play a key role by encouraging technical experts to share their knowledge in an accessible manner, facilitating cross-disciplinary understanding. For example, a team lead might organize knowledge-sharing sessions where developers explain their work in layperson's terms, helping non-technical team members appreciate its relevance and implications. This not only builds cohesion but also fosters a culture of mutual respect and learning.

Ultimately, technical expertise is a double-edged sword—it is both an enabler and a potential barrier within IT teams. By recognizing its strengths and mitigating its challenges, teams can harness technical proficiency as a unifying force rather than a source of division. This requires deliberate effort to integrate technical skills with interpersonal collaboration, ensuring that expertise enhances rather than detracts from team dynamics.

THE IMPORTANCE OF INTERPERSONAL SKILLS IN TEAM DYNAMICS

While technical expertise is critical to IT projects, interpersonal skills are the glue that holds a team together, enabling collaboration, conflict resolution, and collective progress. Interpersonal skills—such as communication, empathy, active listening, and adaptability—foster the human connections necessary for a group to function effectively. In the fast-paced and often high-pressure environment of IT, these skills ensure that team members can navigate challenges, share knowledge, and align their efforts toward common goals.

A key function of interpersonal skills is their ability to bridge gaps between diverse team members. IT projects frequently involve individuals from different disciplines, backgrounds, and levels of expertise. Without strong interpersonal dynamics, these differences can lead to miscommunication or misunderstandings. For example, a project manager might fail to convey a client's requirements in terms a developer can act on, resulting in wasted effort and frustration. Interpersonal skills, such as clear communication and active listening, help to translate diverse perspectives into actionable outcomes, ensuring everyone remains on the same page.

Interpersonal skills also play a vital role in conflict resolution. In any collaborative setting, disagreements are inevitable, whether about technical approaches, project priorities, or resource allocation. Teams that lack the ability to navigate these conflicts constructively risk creating an environment of tension and mistrust. On the other hand, individuals with strong interpersonal skills can address conflicts openly and respectfully, transforming disagreements into opportunities for growth and innovation. For instance, a team member who practices empathy can better understand a colleague's viewpoint, facilitating compromise and consensus.

Leadership amplifies the importance of interpersonal skills within team dynamics. Leaders set the tone for communication and collaboration, modeling behaviors that encourage openness, respect, and accountability. A team lead who recognizes and celebrates individual contributions fosters a sense of belonging, motivating team members to work cohesively. Conversely, a lack of interpersonal awareness in leadership can lead to disengagement and a fragmented team culture. Effective leaders leverage interpersonal skills to build trust, facilitate dialogue, and ensure that each team member feels valued.

In IT projects, where technical challenges can dominate the agenda, interpersonal skills often take a backseat—but their absence is deeply felt when team dynamics falter. By emphasizing interpersonal skills alongside technical expertise, teams can create an environment where collaboration thrives, challenges are addressed constructively, and shared goals are achieved. These skills are not merely "soft" attributes; they are essential components of successful, high-functioning teams.

IDENTIFYING IMBALANCES AND ADDRESSING SKILL GAPS

In IT teams, the interplay between technical expertise and interpersonal skills often reveals imbalances that can hinder collaboration and project success. These imbalances typically arise when a team overemphasizes one set of skills while neglecting the other. For example, a team composed entirely of highly technical individuals may struggle with effective communication, while a team rich in interpersonal skills might lack the technical proficiency needed to execute complex tasks. Identifying and addressing these disparities is essential for achieving a well-rounded and productive dynamic.

One way to identify imbalances is through careful observation of team interactions and performance. Patterns of miscommunication, recurring conflicts, or missed deliverables may signal gaps in interpersonal skills. Conversely, bottlenecks in technical tasks or over-reliance on a few specialists may indicate gaps in technical expertise. For instance, if project updates frequently require clarification or rework, it could point to a lack of communication skills among team members. Similarly, if technical challenges routinely delay progress, the team may need additional technical training or support.

Once imbalances are identified, addressing skill gaps requires a multi-pronged approach. For technical gaps, providing targeted training or pairing less experienced members with mentors can enhance the team's overall capability. Workshops, certifications, or cross-training sessions can help team members deepen their technical expertise and broaden their skill sets. For example, a team struggling with Agile processes might benefit from a Scrum Master certification program to improve their proficiency in managing sprints and deliverables.

Addressing interpersonal skill gaps often requires a more nuanced approach. Team-building activities, communication workshops, and one-on-one coaching can help individuals develop these critical skills. Leaders should foster an environment where open dialogue and feedback are encouraged, allowing team members to identify and address their own areas for growth. For example, if a developer struggles to explain their work to non-technical stakeholders, role-playing exercises or presentation training can build their confidence and communication skills.

Balancing these efforts is key to ensuring the team develops holistically. Leaders must avoid focusing exclusively on one area at the expense of the other. An ideal intervention plan integrates technical and interpersonal development, recognizing their interdependence. For instance, a coding workshop can be paired with a session on collaborative problem-solving to strengthen both technical and team dynamics simultaneously.

Iidentifying and addressing skill gaps is not a one-time effort but an ongoing process. As team members grow and projects evolve, new imbalances may emerge. Regular evaluations, such as feedback sessions or performance reviews, can help leaders stay attuned to these shifts. By proactively addressing skill gaps and fostering a culture of continuous improvement, teams can maintain a dynamic balance between technical expertise and interpersonal collaboration, paving the way for sustained success.

BUILDING TEAMS THAT EXCEL IN BOTH AREAS

Creating teams that excel in both technical expertise and interpersonal skills requires a deliberate and strategic approach. Such teams are not only capable of solving complex technical challenges but also thrive on collaboration, adaptability, and trust. Striking this balance ensures that projects move forward efficiently while maintaining a cohesive and supportive team culture. Achieving this synergy involves intentional hiring, skill development, and fostering a collaborative work environment.

The foundation of building balanced teams starts with hiring practices. Recruitment processes should assess both technical proficiency and interpersonal capabilities. While technical expertise is often easier to measure through tests and certifications, interpersonal skills require deeper evaluation. Behavioral interviews, role-playing scenarios, and group exercises can help identify candidates who possess qualities like empathy, communication, and adaptability. For instance, a coding test may be paired with a team-based problem-solving task to evaluate how candidates approach collaboration. This ensures that new hires not only bring the required technical knowledge but can also integrate effectively into the team.

Skill development is equally critical in cultivating a well-rounded team. Once individuals are onboarded, providing ongoing opportunities for professional growth ensures that both technical and interpersonal skills are continually enhanced. This might include offering technical training in emerging technologies alongside workshops on emotional intelligence, conflict resolution, or active listening. For example, a team learning a new programming framework could simultaneously participate in sessions on managing cross-functional collaboration, preparing them to handle the technical demands and the interpersonal complexities of their next project.

Leadership also plays a pivotal role in fostering excellence in both areas. Effective leaders model the balance they seek to cultivate in their teams. They demonstrate technical understanding while also prioritizing clear communication, empathy, and team-building. Leaders should provide regular feedback that acknowledges achievements in both domains, encouraging team members to develop holistically. For example, recognizing a developer for both solving a challenging bug and mediating a conflict between colleagues reinforces the value of balanced expertise.

Creating a collaborative environment is the final piece of the puzzle. Teams excel when they operate in an atmosphere of trust, respect, and open communication. This involves setting up processes and tools that facilitate seamless collaboration, such as regular check-ins, shared knowledge repositories, and transparent communication channels. Celebrating team achievements, hosting informal bonding activities, and creating psychological safety further enhance this dynamic. For instance, a retrospective meeting that encourages team members to share not only technical improvements but also interpersonal lessons learned fosters a culture of mutual respect and learning.

By integrating these practices, organizations can build teams that are not only technically competent but also highly collaborative and resilient. Such teams are well-equipped to tackle the multifaceted challenges of modern IT projects, ensuring both successful outcomes and a positive team experience. The result is a workplace where individuals feel empowered to contribute their best, both as experts in their field and as integral members of a cohesive team.

CASE STUDIES: SUCCESSFUL BALANCING OF SKILLS

Real-world examples highlight the importance of balancing technical expertise with interpersonal skills, demonstrating how this synergy drives success in IT projects. The following case studies illustrate how organizations and teams have leveraged both skill sets to overcome challenges and achieve exceptional outcomes.

Case Study 1: Transforming Cross-Functional Collaboration in a Fintech Startup

A fintech startup faced significant challenges in coordinating between its development and product management teams. The developers, highly skilled in coding and algorithm design, struggled to effectively communicate technical limitations to the product team, leading to unrealistic project timelines. Simultaneously, the product team's lack of understanding of technical nuances caused frustration among developers.

To address this, the company introduced cross-functional training sessions. Developers were taught basic product management principles, while the product team learned about coding workflows and constraints. Role-reversal exercises helped each team appreciate the other's challenges and perspectives. Additionally, communication workshops equipped team members with active listening and conflict resolution skills.

Within three months, project timelines became more realistic, and collaboration improved. Developers started contributing insights during product planning, while the product team adjusted their expectations and communicated changes more effectively. This balance of technical and interpersonal skills not only improved team morale but also accelerated the product development cycle, allowing the startup to launch a critical update ahead of schedule.

Case Study 2: Enhancing Stakeholder Communication in a Healthcare IT Firm

A healthcare IT firm undertaking a large-scale system upgrade faced persistent delays due to misaligned priorities between its internal IT team and external stakeholders, including hospital administrators. The IT team's technical reports were too complex for stakeholders to understand, while the stakeholders' vague requirements led to constant revisions.

The firm appointed a project liaison skilled in both IT systems and communication. This individual acted as a bridge, translating technical jargon into actionable insights for stakeholders and clarifying stakeholder feedback for the IT team. Regular workshops were also conducted to train the IT team in presenting their work clearly and listening actively to non-technical input.

As a result, communication between the two groups improved significantly. Stakeholders felt more involved in the process, and the IT team experienced fewer change requests. The project was completed within the revised timeline, and the system upgrade received praise for its seamless integration and user-friendly design.

Case Study 3: Building a Resilient Team in a Global E-commerce Company

A global e-commerce company operating across multiple time zones struggled with siloed work practices. While the technical teams excelled individually, the lack of interpersonal connection and shared understanding created inefficiencies and duplication of work.

To address this, the company implemented a team-building program emphasizing cultural sensitivity and collaboration. Virtual coffee chats, shared projects across regions, and leadership training in fostering inclusivity were introduced. These efforts encouraged team members to build rapport and trust, bridging cultural and interpersonal gaps.

Additionally, the company adopted collaborative tools like shared task boards and asynchronous communication platforms to align workflows. By emphasizing both technical excellence and interpersonal harmony, the organization transformed its team dynamics. Productivity increased, and employees reported higher job satisfaction, with stronger cross-regional bonds ensuring the smooth execution of global projects.

Case Study 4: Overcoming Skill Imbalances in a Government IT Project

In a government IT project, an over-reliance on a few senior developers created bottlenecks, while junior staff lacked the expertise to contribute meaningfully. This imbalance slowed progress and increased tension within the team.

To address the issue, the project lead introduced a mentorship program. Senior developers were paired with junior staff to provide on-the-job training and share knowledge. Simultaneously, leadership emphasized the importance of soft skills, such as teamwork and communication, through weekly workshops.

Over time, junior team members gained the confidence to handle more complex tasks, reducing the workload on senior developers. Enhanced communication within the team fostered a more inclusive environment, where ideas and concerns could be openly shared. The project ultimately met its deadlines, with a stronger, more balanced team emerging from the process.

These case studies underscore the transformative impact of balancing technical expertise and interpersonal skills. By addressing gaps and fostering synergy, teams can navigate challenges more effectively, drive innovation, and achieve sustainable success.

ACTIONABLE STEPS FOR LEADERS AND TEAM MEMBERS

Effectively balancing technical expertise with interpersonal skills requires intentional actions from both leaders and team members. These steps are designed to foster growth, improve collaboration, and ensure team dynamics are aligned with project goals.

Step 1: Conduct a Team Skill Assessment

Leaders should begin by evaluating the current balance of technical and interpersonal skills within the team. This can be achieved through self-assessment surveys, performance reviews, and peer feedback. Identify areas of strength and opportunities for improvement, both at the individual and team levels.

Team members can reflect on their own abilities, asking questions such as:

- Are my technical skills effectively contributing to the team's success?
- Am I communicating my ideas clearly and collaboratively? This self-awareness helps individuals pinpoint areas for personal development.

Step 2: Set Clear Expectations for Team Dynamics

Leaders need to define what a balanced team looks like and communicate those expectations clearly. Emphasize that both technical contributions and interpersonal interactions are equally valued. For instance, reward not just task completion but also effective collaboration, problem-solving, and mentorship within the team.

For team members, this means understanding their dual responsibilities. Beyond delivering technical outputs, they must actively participate in discussions, provide constructive feedback, and respect diverse perspectives.

Step 3: Provide Training and Development Opportunities

Investing in training programs is crucial. Leaders can organize workshops on technical upskilling and soft skills such as conflict resolution, emotional intelligence, and active listening. Encourage team members to attend external courses or certifications tailored to their needs.

Team members should take initiative in their development. For example, they can seek mentorship, participate in peer-led knowledge-sharing sessions, or use online platforms to improve skills they perceive as lacking.

Step 4: Foster a Culture of Collaboration and Feedback

Leaders should model and encourage open communication. Regular feedback sessions, one-on-one check-ins, and collaborative goal-setting meetings help maintain alignment. Establish norms where feedback is seen as a tool for growth rather than criticism.

Team members can contribute by practicing constructive feedback and being open to receiving it. They should also take the lead in fostering inclusivity by ensuring that quieter voices in the team are heard and valued during discussions.

Step 5: Leverage Tools to Enhance Team Dynamics

Leaders can introduce tools that facilitate better teamwork and communication. For instance, project management platforms like Trello or Asana can streamline task assignments, while communication tools like Slack or Microsoft Teams can keep conversations organized.

Team members should embrace these tools, using them to share updates, collaborate on tasks, and clarify responsibilities. Being consistent in their use helps minimize misunderstandings and enhances overall efficiency.

Step 6: Monitor Progress and Adjust Strategies

Leaders must regularly evaluate the effectiveness of their initiatives. Are team dynamics improving? Are interpersonal skills being applied to solve real-world challenges? Use metrics like employee engagement scores, project completion rates, and client feedback to gauge success.

Team members should also assess their own progress. Are they applying new skills effectively? Are they contributing more meaningfully to team discussions? Self-reflection combined with peer input ensures continuous growth.

Step 7: Celebrate Milestones and Successes

Acknowledging and celebrating successes reinforces positive behaviors. Leaders should recognize not only technical achievements but also instances of exceptional teamwork and collaboration. Public praise, rewards, and team-building events can motivate further improvement.

For team members, celebrating wins—both individual and collective—helps build camaraderie and a shared sense of purpose. Small gestures like thanking a teammate for their help or recognizing someone's interpersonal contributions can strengthen bonds within the group.

By following these steps, both leaders and team members can actively cultivate an environment where technical excellence and interpersonal skills complement each other, driving both individual growth and team success.

Tools for effective team communication

Effective team communication is the backbone of successful IT projects, where collaboration often spans diverse roles, technical disciplines, and organizational levels. Without clear and consistent communication practices, even the most skilled teams risk inefficiencies, misunderstandings, and missed deadlines. Tools designed specifically for structuring team interactions—such as meeting agendas, status updates, and feedback loops—are indispensable in bridging gaps, maintaining alignment, and fostering a culture of accountability and continuous improvement.

At their core, communication tools act as the scaffolding that supports the flow of information and ideas. Meeting agendas, for example, provide a clear framework for discussions, ensuring that all participants are prepared and that time is allocated efficiently. Status updates serve as a pulse check for team progress, enabling transparency and helping to identify potential roadblocks early. Feedback loops, meanwhile, create opportunities for team members to refine their processes, celebrate successes, and address interpersonal dynamics in a constructive manner. These tools don't just facilitate communication—they enhance its quality, transforming interactions into productive, goal-oriented exchanges.

In IT environments, where technical complexity and fast-paced project cycles are the norm, communication tools help mitigate common challenges. For instance, a structured agenda can prevent technical jargon from derailing meetings, while regular status updates keep team members on the same page amidst shifting priorities. Feedback loops ensure that lessons learned from past projects are integrated into future efforts, fostering growth and resilience within the team. These tools also help balance the needs of diverse team members, accommodating both highly technical contributors and those in client-facing or managerial roles.

Communication tools are not merely logistical aids but strategic enablers of team success. By providing clarity, promoting collaboration, and aligning expectations, they allow IT professionals to navigate complexity with confidence and agility. Teams that embrace these tools are better equipped to meet project demands, adapt to unforeseen challenges, and maintain strong relationships both within and outside their organizations. This section will explore how meeting agendas, status updates, and feedback loops can be harnessed to maximize team efficiency, cohesion, and project outcomes.

CRAFTING EFFECTIVE MEETING AGENDAS

A well-crafted meeting agenda is more than a simple list of topics—it is a roadmap that directs discussions, ensures productivity, and respects the time and energy of every participant. For IT teams managing complex projects, agendas serve as critical tools to maintain focus and clarity, especially in environments where cross-functional collaboration and diverse expertise are involved. Without a structured agenda, meetings risk devolving into aimless conversations, leading to confusion, frustration, and wasted resources.

The first step in creating an effective agenda is defining the meeting's purpose. Is the goal to solve a specific problem, align on project updates, or brainstorm new ideas? Articulating the objective helps determine the meeting's structure and prioritizes topics that align with the desired outcome. Each agenda should include actionable goals, such as finalizing a timeline, resolving a blocker, or clarifying stakeholder expectations. By focusing on results rather than mere discussions, teams can ensure that every meeting advances the project in meaningful ways.

Key components of a strong agenda include a clear title, a list of topics, time allocations for each item, and the desired outcomes for every discussion point. For example, an Agile sprint planning meeting might include sections for reviewing completed tasks, discussing new priorities, and addressing impediments, with specific time frames for each. Including time allocations encourages participants to stay on track and minimizes the risk of one topic dominating the entire session. Additionally, agendas should specify who will lead each segment, ensuring accountability and encouraging active participation.

Engaging the team in the agenda creation process fosters ownership and inclusivity. Inviting input on topics beforehand allows team members to highlight their concerns, ensuring that the meeting addresses relevant and pressing issues. Agendas can also be shared in advance, giving participants time to prepare and reducing the need for lengthy explanations during the session. However, flexibility is also important—while agendas provide structure, they should allow room for unanticipated but relevant discussions that arise naturally during meetings.

Effective meeting agendas are invaluable in IT projects, where time is often constrained, and collaboration is critical. By establishing clear objectives, structuring discussions, and encouraging active participation, agendas transform meetings into productive sessions that drive progress. As teams consistently use agendas, they develop a culture of purposeful communication, ensuring that every meeting is a step toward achieving project success.

STATUS UPDATES: KEEPING TEAMS ALIGNED

Status updates are vital for maintaining alignment and momentum in IT projects, serving as consistent touchpoints that connect team members, track progress, and address potential roadblocks. In a field where tasks often span multiple disciplines and time zones, these updates prevent silos and ensure that every contributor remains informed and engaged. When executed effectively, status updates are not just informational—they are tools for fostering transparency, accountability, and collaboration.

The primary purpose of a status update is to provide a snapshot of where the team stands relative to project goals. It allows individuals to share completed tasks, highlight ongoing work, and identify challenges requiring attention. For instance, in an Agile context, daily stand-up meetings serve as quick status updates, where team members briefly outline what they did yesterday, what they will do today, and what obstacles they face. These updates help synchronize efforts, ensuring that everyone is aware of dependencies and priorities.

Consistency is key to effective status updates. Regular updates—whether daily, weekly, or tied to specific project milestones—help establish a rhythm that keeps the team engaged and informed. The format of these updates can vary depending on the team's needs: they can be verbal (e.g., during meetings), written (e.g., via email or collaboration tools), or visual (e.g., dashboards in project management software). For example, a Kanban board updated daily provides a clear, at-a-glance view of tasks in progress, completed tasks, and backlog items, fostering transparency across the team.

A successful status update focuses on relevance and brevity. Team members should share information that directly impacts others or advances the project, avoiding unnecessary detail. Structured templates can help streamline the process, guiding contributors to include essential elements such as task progress, key metrics, and requests for support. For example, a simple template might prompt individuals to report on achievements, current priorities, and any blockers, ensuring that updates are comprehensive yet concise.

By integrating status updates into their workflows, IT teams can create an environment of trust and collaboration. These updates provide a platform for celebrating accomplishments, addressing challenges proactively, and making informed decisions about resource allocation and timelines. Moreover, regular updates empower teams to adapt quickly to changes, ensuring that they remain aligned and focused on delivering high-quality outcomes.

FEEDBACK LOOPS: CREATING A CULTURE OF CONTINUOUS IMPROVEMENT

Feedback loops are essential for fostering continuous improvement in IT teams, offering a structured way to reflect, adapt, and enhance performance. In the fast-paced, ever-changing environment of IT projects, feedback loops help teams identify what is working well and address areas of improvement promptly. By embedding these loops into team dynamics, organizations create a culture of learning and accountability that drives both individual and collective success.

The essence of an effective feedback loop lies in its cyclical nature: observe, assess, act, and reassess. This iterative process ensures that insights gained from past performance are applied to future efforts, enabling teams to evolve and refine their workflows. In an Agile framework, for example, retrospective meetings at the end of each sprint serve as formal feedback loops. Team members discuss achievements, identify bottlenecks, and propose adjustments for the next cycle. Such practices help teams avoid repeating mistakes and build on their strengths.

Establishing a culture of feedback requires psychological safety, where team members feel comfortable sharing honest observations without fear of judgment. Leaders play a critical role in setting this tone by encouraging open communication, actively listening, and demonstrating that feedback—whether positive or critical—is valued and acted upon. When leaders model receptive behavior, it fosters trust and motivates team members to engage in constructive dialogue.

Feedback loops can take many forms, depending on the context. Formal channels, like performance reviews or post-project evaluations, provide structured opportunities for in-depth discussion. Informal methods, such as one-on-one check-ins or quick follow-ups after meetings, create opportunities for real-time adjustments. Tools like anonymous surveys or digital suggestion boxes can also help gather feedback from individuals who may be hesitant to speak up in group settings.

The ultimate goal of feedback loops is to translate insights into actionable changes that enhance team performance and project outcomes. For example, if a retrospective reveals inefficiencies in communication during sprints, the team might implement a new tool or process to streamline updates. Regularly revisiting the feedback ensures that changes are effective and that the team remains on a path of continuous improvement.

By embracing feedback loops, IT teams cultivate a proactive and adaptive mindset. This commitment to reflection and growth not only improves project efficiency but also strengthens team cohesion, enhances morale, and establishes a foundation for long-term success in a competitive industry.

Case Studies: Communication Tools in Action

Real-world examples illustrate how effective use of communication tools can transform team dynamics and project outcomes in IT settings. These case studies highlight the impact of thoughtfully implemented strategies, providing actionable insights that other teams can replicate.

Case Study 1: Using Meeting Agendas to Revitalize Weekly Team Syncs
A software development team at a mid-sized tech company struggled with unproductive weekly sync meetings. Discussions often veered off-track, and critical issues were overlooked. The team leader introduced a structured meeting agenda template with clearly defined sections for updates, blockers, and action items. Each team member received the agenda beforehand and was encouraged to prepare their inputs.

The impact was immediate: meetings became shorter, more focused, and outcome-driven. Team members reported feeling more engaged, as their contributions were acknowledged and discussed systematically. Moreover, the structured approach ensured that no critical task slipped through the cracks, leading to a 15% improvement in sprint completion rates within three months.

Case Study 2: Leveraging Status Updates for Cross-Department Collaboration

In a multinational IT services firm, misaligned priorities between development and quality assurance teams led to delays in product releases. To address this, the project manager implemented a shared status update format in their project management tool, tailored to both teams' workflows.

Each department updated their progress daily, highlighting dependencies and roadblocks. Weekly review meetings provided a forum for clarifying misunderstandings and realigning goals. This transparent communication fostered greater collaboration and reduced miscommunication. Within two quarters, the team cut defect resolution time by 20% and met product release deadlines consistently.

Case Study 3: Feedback Loops in a DevOps Transition

A financial services company transitioning to a DevOps model encountered resistance from employees unfamiliar with the new processes. To address this, leadership established bi-weekly feedback sessions, where employees could share concerns and suggest improvements.

Using insights from these sessions, the company implemented targeted training sessions and adjusted workflows to align better with team capacities. Over six months, employee satisfaction scores improved by 30%, and the team achieved a 25% increase in deployment frequency. Feedback loops proved critical in easing the transition and building team confidence in the new system.

Case Study 4: Implementing Collaboration Tools for Remote Teams

A global IT consultancy firm with a distributed workforce struggled with maintaining effective communication across time zones. The introduction of a unified collaboration platform, integrating Slack for real-time chats, Asana for task management, and Zoom for virtual meetings, streamlined their communication efforts.

With clear guidelines for using each tool—such as reserving Slack for quick questions and Asana for task updates—teams reduced redundant communication. Monthly retrospectives revealed a 40% reduction in email traffic and a significant decrease in missed deadlines. Employees also reported feeling more connected despite geographical distances.

These case studies demonstrate the transformative power of communication tools when applied thoughtfully. By addressing specific challenges and tailoring tools to team needs, IT leaders can enhance efficiency, foster collaboration, and drive successful project outcomes.

IMPLEMENTATION GUIDELINES FOR TEAMS

Effectively integrating communication tools into team workflows requires a thoughtful, phased approach. Successful implementation ensures that tools serve as enablers rather than distractions, fostering collaboration, clarity, and productivity. The following guidelines outline best practices for deploying communication strategies and tools within IT teams.

Assess Team Needs and Challenges

Before introducing any tool or strategy, it is crucial to assess the specific communication needs and challenges of the team. Are meetings unstructured and inefficient? Are status updates inconsistent or redundant? Are team members struggling to provide or receive actionable feedback? Conducting surveys, interviews, or retrospectives can help identify pain points and establish clear objectives for implementation.

For example, a team grappling with remote communication challenges might prioritize adopting a collaboration platform that supports asynchronous updates. Conversely, a team struggling with meeting effectiveness might focus on structured agenda templates. Tailoring solutions to real issues ensures higher acceptance and relevance.

Choose the Right Tools for the Team

Not all communication tools are suitable for every team. The selection process should consider the team's size, complexity, and preferred working styles. For instance, small teams might benefit from simple tools like Trello or Google Workspace, while larger, cross-functional teams may require more robust platforms like Jira or Microsoft Teams.

When choosing tools, prioritize integration and ease of use. Tools that align with existing workflows and integrate with other software minimize disruption and ensure seamless adoption. Offering trial periods or pilot phases can also help teams evaluate tools in practice and refine their choices.

Establish Clear Protocols and Expectations

The most powerful tools can fall short without clear guidelines for use. Teams must define how and when specific tools or strategies should be applied. For example, outline expectations for meeting agendas, such as who creates them, when they are shared, and how follow-ups are tracked. Similarly, status update protocols should include frequency, format, and required details to keep everyone aligned.

Leaders should also communicate the purpose of each tool. For instance, Slack might be reserved for real-time discussions, while project management tools like Monday.com are used for task tracking. By clarifying boundaries and use cases, teams can avoid miscommunication and tool fatigue.

Provide Training and Resources

Introducing new tools or strategies often requires a learning curve. Leaders should invest in training sessions to familiarize the team with the functionalities and benefits of new systems. These sessions can include live demonstrations, Q&A opportunities, and follow-up resources like video tutorials or FAQs.

Additionally, offering support during the initial phase of implementation is critical. Designate a point person or "tool champion" to answer questions, troubleshoot issues, and gather feedback from team members. Encouraging peer-to-peer learning, where experienced users guide others, can also accelerate adoption.

Monitor Progress and Iterate

Implementation doesn't end with deployment. Teams should regularly review the effectiveness of communication tools and strategies through retrospectives or surveys. Metrics such as meeting duration, task completion rates, and employee satisfaction can provide valuable insights.

Based on feedback, refine processes and address emerging challenges. For example, if a tool is underutilized, identify barriers to adoption and adjust guidelines or training accordingly. Continuous improvement ensures that communication practices remain relevant and impactful.

Foster a Collaborative Mindset

Successful implementation relies not only on tools but also on a team's willingness to embrace change. Leaders should encourage open dialogue about communication practices and invite team members to share their ideas and concerns. Celebrating early successes—such as reduced project delays or improved meeting outcomes—can boost morale and reinforce commitment to new practices.

By following these implementation guidelines, IT teams can seamlessly integrate communication tools and strategies into their workflows. This structured approach ensures that communication enhancements lead to tangible improvements in productivity, collaboration, and overall team satisfaction.

Actionable Takeaways

Successful communication within IT teams requires the consistent application of practical strategies and tools. This final section provides clear, actionable steps for teams and leaders to implement immediately, ensuring communication enhancements that drive collaboration and project success.

Commit to Structured Communication Practices

Adopt standardized approaches to meetings, status updates, and feedback loops. Use pre-defined templates for meeting agendas to ensure every discussion has a clear purpose and outcome. Incorporate recurring status updates into your workflows, such as weekly standups or sprint reviews, to keep everyone aligned and informed.

Feedback should be integrated as an ongoing process rather than a sporadic activity. Establish mechanisms like anonymous surveys or one-on-one check-ins to encourage open and honest exchanges that foster improvement and team trust.

Invest in Training and Onboarding

Ensure all team members are equipped to use communication tools effectively. Schedule workshops to introduce the purpose and functionality of platforms like Slack, Jira, or Confluence, and provide documentation to support their learning. Onboarding new team members should include a comprehensive overview of the team's communication standards and expectations, helping them integrate seamlessly.

Regularly update the team on any new tools or practices introduced, emphasizing their benefits and providing opportunities for clarification. A well-trained team will adapt more quickly to changes and make better use of available resources.

Focus on Transparency and Clarity

Make transparency a cornerstone of team communication. Clearly define each team member's role and responsibilities, ensuring everyone understands their contributions to the project. Use shared dashboards or collaborative tools to make project updates visible and accessible in real time.

When discussing tasks or deliverables, avoid ambiguous language. Use concise and direct phrasing to eliminate misunderstandings, and confirm alignment by summarizing key points at the end of meetings or updates.

Measure and Reflect on Communication Effectiveness

Establish metrics to evaluate the impact of communication practices on team performance. Track indicators such as project completion times, employee engagement levels, or reduced miscommunications. Conduct regular retrospectives to gather team feedback on what's working and where improvements are needed.

Use these insights to refine your strategies, iterating on tools, protocols, or workflows to address new challenges or inefficiencies. Continuous assessment ensures communication practices evolve alongside the team's needs.

Cultivate a Culture of Inclusivity and Respect

Encourage active participation from all team members by creating an environment where every voice is valued. Rotate roles, such as meeting facilitators or note-takers, to ensure balanced involvement. Address conflicts or miscommunications promptly, using them as learning opportunities to strengthen team cohesion.

Emphasize respect for diverse perspectives, particularly in cross-functional or global teams. This fosters mutual understanding and improves collaboration, ensuring communication practices align with the team's unique dynamics.

Embrace Technology Thoughtfully

Select tools that fit the team's specific needs, avoiding unnecessary complexity or tool fatigue. Establish clear protocols for using platforms, such as distinguishing between synchronous and asynchronous communication. Periodically audit tools to ensure they remain relevant and effective.

Technology should enhance, not hinder, communication. Use it strategically to streamline processes, reduce redundancies, and empower team members to focus on their work rather than navigating complicated systems.

By implementing these actionable takeaways, IT teams can strengthen their communication practices, enhance collaboration, and achieve consistent project success. Each step is designed to empower teams to operate more effectively, fostering an environment where clarity, alignment, and mutual support thrive.

Chapter 3: Communicating with Stakeholders: Managing Expectations

In any IT project, stakeholders play a pivotal role in defining the trajectory and success of the endeavor. Stakeholders—ranging from project sponsors and business leaders to end-users and external clients—shape the goals, deliverables, and overall expectations of a project. Yet, their needs and priorities are often misunderstood or overlooked, leading to misaligned outcomes. Understanding stakeholder needs is not merely an initial project task; it is the foundation upon which the entire project rests. Failure to comprehend these needs can create gaps that ripple across every phase, from planning to execution.

When stakeholder needs are misidentified, projects suffer in multiple ways. Misalignment often results in wasted resources, such as time, budget, and personnel, being allocated to tasks or features that fail to address core priorities. For example, a development team might spend weeks perfecting a technical feature only to learn it does not align with the client's business objectives. Similarly, overlooked stakeholder concerns, such as compliance requirements or user experience preferences, can result in costly revisions and delays. This not only undermines the project team's credibility but also damages relationships with stakeholders, making future collaboration more challenging.

Moreover, stakeholders themselves may have conflicting interests, further complicating the process. For instance, a project sponsor may prioritize meeting tight deadlines, while end-users may demand additional functionality that extends development timelines. Without a clear understanding of these differing perspectives, project managers risk making decisions that satisfy one group while alienating another. A thorough and systematic approach to understanding stakeholder needs helps mitigate these conflicts by identifying common ground and ensuring that decisions are informed by a holistic view of the project's impact.

Beyond operational benefits, understanding stakeholder needs builds trust and fosters collaboration. Stakeholders who feel their perspectives are valued and incorporated into the project are more likely to remain engaged and supportive. Transparent communication about how their needs are being addressed reassures them that their priorities are guiding the project. This sense of partnership not only increases stakeholder satisfaction but also creates a foundation for long-term relationships that benefit both the project team and the organization. Recognizing stakeholder needs as a central component of strategic communication is therefore not just a practical necessity—it is a cornerstone of successful project management in IT consultancy.

STAKEHOLDER IDENTIFICATION AND ANALYSIS

Identifying and analyzing stakeholders is the first step toward establishing a solid communication framework in IT projects. This process begins by recognizing all individuals and groups with a vested interest in the project's outcomes, which often extends beyond the obvious decision-makers. Stakeholders can range from senior executives who allocate resources to end-users who interact with the final product daily. A comprehensive identification process ensures no critical perspective is overlooked, as even seemingly minor stakeholders can introduce significant roadblocks if their concerns are ignored. Mapping out the full spectrum of stakeholders is essential to addressing their diverse needs and maintaining alignment throughout the project.

Once identified, stakeholders must be categorized based on their influence and interest in the project. Tools like the Power-Interest Grid are invaluable for this purpose, helping project managers visually plot stakeholders along two axes: their level of authority and their degree of concern. This analysis enables prioritization, ensuring that high-power, high-interest stakeholders receive the most attention, while still maintaining clear communication with others. For instance, a CEO may require concise, high-level updates, while a department manager might need detailed explanations of how changes impact their team's workflow. By tailoring communication strategies to these categories, project managers can maximize the efficiency and relevance of their interactions.

Understanding stakeholder roles within the organizational ecosystem also plays a critical role in this analysis. Internal stakeholders, such as team members or departmental leads, often have specific operational concerns tied directly to the project's execution. In contrast, external stakeholders, like clients or regulatory bodies, may focus on compliance, market impact, or user experience. Differentiating these roles helps in addressing their unique priorities and in anticipating potential conflicts. For instance, an internal stakeholder might push for technical excellence, while an external stakeholder prioritizes cost-efficiency. Effective analysis equips project managers with the tools to mediate these competing demands constructively.

Equally important is the dynamic nature of stakeholder relationships over the course of a project. Stakeholders' priorities and levels of engagement may shift as the project progresses, necessitating regular re-evaluation. Early-stage stakeholders, such as financial sponsors, might become less involved after initial approvals, while end-users might emerge as key voices during testing and deployment. Ongoing analysis ensures that project managers remain responsive to these shifts, maintaining alignment and avoiding surprises. By taking a structured approach to stakeholder identification and analysis, IT professionals lay the groundwork for a communication strategy that is both inclusive and adaptive.

Gathering and Validating Stakeholder Needs

Gathering stakeholder needs is a nuanced process that goes beyond initial meetings or standardized requirements documents. It demands active listening, strategic questioning, and a deep understanding of the project's broader objectives. Often, stakeholders articulate their expectations in ways that reflect their immediate concerns rather than the full scope of their needs. For example, a department manager might request a feature to simplify workflow, but their underlying need could be increased productivity to meet organizational benchmarks. Capturing these underlying priorities requires a blend of technical expertise and emotional intelligence, ensuring that both explicit and implicit requirements are addressed.

A key method for gathering needs is direct engagement through interviews, workshops, and surveys. These forums allow stakeholders to articulate their concerns while providing project managers with an opportunity to clarify ambiguities. Structured techniques like brainstorming sessions or stakeholder journey mapping can uncover hidden needs and foster a shared understanding among diverse participants. For example, a workshop might reveal that while IT sees system performance as the top priority, end-users prioritize ease of navigation. Bringing these perspectives to light early prevents conflicts and ensures a more holistic approach to project planning.

However, gathering needs is only half the battle—validation is equally critical. Stakeholders often have incomplete or evolving understandings of their own requirements, and unverified assumptions can derail a project. Validation involves aligning stakeholder needs with the project's technical feasibility, budget, and timeline. Techniques such as prototyping, use case modeling, or requirements walkthroughs can bridge the gap between stakeholder expectations and practical realities. For instance, a prototype of a user interface can confirm whether the design meets user needs before full-scale development begins, reducing the risk of costly revisions later.

Feedback loops are indispensable in this process, ensuring that needs remain aligned as the project evolves. Regular check-ins with stakeholders provide opportunities to refine and revalidate their requirements based on changing circumstances or new insights. Additionally, creating clear documentation of validated needs, such as a requirements traceability matrix, ensures accountability and prevents scope creep. By rigorously gathering and validating stakeholder needs, project teams establish a strong foundation for both the technical success of the project and the satisfaction of all involved parties.

Managing Conflicting Priorities

Conflicting priorities among stakeholders are a common challenge in IT projects, arising from their diverse roles, goals, and perspectives. For instance, a project sponsor might prioritize adhering to tight deadlines to minimize costs, while end-users may focus on achieving a seamless, feature-rich experience. These competing interests, if unmanaged, can lead to delays, inefficiencies, and dissatisfaction. Effectively managing such conflicts requires a strategic approach that balances competing needs while keeping the project aligned with its overarching goals.

The first step in managing conflicting priorities is fostering transparency. Open communication allows stakeholders to understand not only their own priorities but also those of others involved in the project. This can often be achieved through facilitated discussions, where stakeholders are encouraged to express their concerns and listen to alternative perspectives. By providing a platform for mutual understanding, project managers can create a sense of shared ownership and collaboration, reducing the friction caused by perceived competition. For example, explaining how a feature delay might improve system stability can help stakeholders see the broader value of the trade-off.

Prioritization frameworks are invaluable tools for resolving conflicts systematically. Techniques such as the MoSCoW method (Must Have, Should Have, Could Have, Won't Have) or weighted scoring models help stakeholders rank priorities based on factors like impact, feasibility, and alignment with business objectives. By quantifying and categorizing requirements, these frameworks shift the discussion from subjective preferences to data-driven decision-making. For instance, a feature deemed "Must Have" by multiple stakeholders may take precedence, while less critical requests are deferred. Such methodologies not only clarify priorities but also provide a defensible rationale for difficult decisions.

Conflict resolution also benefits from a strong leadership approach. A skilled project manager acts as a mediator, balancing empathy with authority to navigate disputes. This involves not only listening to stakeholders' concerns but also having the courage to make decisive calls when necessary. In cases where priorities cannot be reconciled, escalating decisions to a steering committee or senior leadership can provide impartial judgment. The key is maintaining trust throughout the process by demonstrating that all viewpoints are considered and decisions are made in the project's best interest.

Finally, managing conflicting priorities is an ongoing process, not a one-time event. Stakeholder needs and project constraints often evolve, and new conflicts may emerge as the project progresses. Regular reviews and updates to the prioritization plan ensure continued alignment and adaptability. By approaching conflicts with transparency, structured methodologies, and proactive leadership, project teams can turn potential obstacles into opportunities for collaboration, ultimately driving the project toward a successful outcome.

TOOLS AND TECHNIQUES FOR STAKEHOLDER UNDERSTANDING

Effectively understanding stakeholders' needs and priorities requires the use of targeted tools and techniques that provide clarity and structure to the process. These tools facilitate the collection, analysis, and interpretation of information, enabling project teams to align their strategies with stakeholder expectations. By employing a combination of qualitative and quantitative methods, IT professionals can navigate complex stakeholder dynamics and ensure that their communication strategies are both precise and actionable.

One essential tool is the **Stakeholder Map**, which visually represents the relationships, influence, and interests of all involved parties. This map categorizes stakeholders based on their power and level of interest in the project, using frameworks like the Power-Interest Grid. For example, key decision-makers with high influence and interest—such as project sponsors—are placed in the "Manage Closely" quadrant, while less involved parties may fall under "Keep Informed." Such categorization helps prioritize efforts, ensuring that resources are focused on the stakeholders most critical to project success. The map also serves as a dynamic reference point that evolves as roles and priorities shift throughout the project lifecycle.

Interviews and Questionnaires are invaluable for gathering in-depth insights directly from stakeholders. One-on-one interviews allow for personalized discussions where stakeholders can elaborate on their goals, concerns, and expectations. Structured questionnaires, on the other hand, are useful for capturing a broad range of perspectives from larger groups in a standardized format. Questions should be carefully designed to elicit actionable information, such as "What specific outcomes do you expect from this project?" or "What risks do you foresee, and how would you prioritize addressing them?" Combining these techniques ensures a balance of qualitative richness and quantitative breadth.

For more collaborative exploration of stakeholder needs, techniques like **Workshops** and **Focus Groups** can be highly effective. Workshops bring stakeholders together to discuss project objectives, identify shared goals, and surface potential conflicts. These sessions often use tools such as brainstorming, affinity diagrams, or stakeholder journey mapping to foster engagement and uncover nuanced insights. Focus groups, typically smaller and more targeted, delve deeper into specific aspects of the project, such as usability or functionality. Both formats encourage active participation and help build consensus among diverse groups, laying a foundation for alignment and cooperation.

Incorporating digital tools such as **Survey Platforms** and **Analytics Dashboards** further enhances stakeholder understanding. Platforms like Google Forms or Typeform can streamline data collection, while dashboards aggregate responses, providing visual summaries of stakeholder feedback. These tools not only save time but also help identify trends and patterns that might be overlooked in manual analysis. For instance, recurring themes in survey responses could highlight a critical requirement shared across departments, prompting timely action.

By combining these tools and techniques, project teams can gain a comprehensive understanding of stakeholder expectations. This structured approach ensures that insights are both actionable and adaptable, equipping IT professionals to manage stakeholder relationships effectively and align project outcomes with organizational objectives.

Summarizing Stakeholder Needs for Communication

Summarizing stakeholder needs is a critical step in translating diverse priorities into actionable and cohesive communication strategies. This process involves distilling the collected information into clear, concise, and accessible formats that guide project decision-making and ensure alignment across all parties. An effective summary not only encapsulates the essence of stakeholder expectations but also serves as a reference point for ongoing communication, reducing misunderstandings and fostering collaboration.

The first task in summarizing stakeholder needs is **categorizing the information based on relevance and priority**. Grouping needs into thematic areas—such as technical requirements, business objectives, or user experience goals—creates a structured overview that is easier to analyze and share. For example, a software development project might categorize stakeholder inputs into system performance, security, and user interface design. This organization allows teams to identify overlaps, gaps, or contradictions within the data, enabling more focused discussions during subsequent meetings. Such clarity also ensures that summaries are targeted and avoid overwhelming stakeholders with unnecessary details.

Creating tailored **stakeholder briefs** is a practical way to ensure that each group's needs are communicated effectively. These briefs should highlight key priorities, expectations, and constraints for each stakeholder or stakeholder group, presented in a manner that resonates with their level of expertise and concerns. For instance, a technical team might receive a detailed summary with specifications and diagrams, while executives would be provided with a high-level report emphasizing strategic benefits and risks. Customization ensures that stakeholders feel their needs are understood and that the communication is relevant to their role in the project.

Visualization tools such as **charts, matrices, and dashboards** can further enhance the clarity of summaries. Tools like a requirements traceability matrix link stakeholder needs to specific project tasks, milestones, or deliverables, illustrating how priorities are being addressed. Dashboards, which aggregate real-time data, provide a dynamic view of progress and alignment with stakeholder expectations. These visual aids not only improve comprehension but also serve as living documents that can be updated as needs evolve, keeping all parties informed and engaged throughout the project lifecycle.

Finally, ensuring alignment involves presenting the summarized needs back to stakeholders for validation and feedback. A structured review process, such as a formal meeting or digital collaboration via platforms like Confluence or Microsoft Teams, allows stakeholders to confirm the accuracy of the summary and voice any concerns. This step reinforces transparency and builds trust, showing stakeholders that their input is valued and accurately represented. Moreover, it provides an opportunity to clarify any ambiguities, ensuring that all parties share a unified understanding of project priorities.

By methodically summarizing stakeholder needs, project teams establish a solid foundation for clear and consistent communication. This practice not only facilitates effective collaboration but also minimizes the risk of misalignment, ensuring that the project remains focused on delivering value to all stakeholders involved.

Techniques for presenting technical information in a clear and actionable way.

Effectively presenting technical information begins with a deep understanding of the audience. Technical professionals often face the challenge of communicating complex concepts to stakeholders who have varying levels of familiarity with the subject matter. Tailoring communication to the audience is essential to bridge this gap, ensuring that the message is both comprehensible and impactful. Without this adjustment, even the most brilliant technical solutions can be misunderstood, undervalued, or rejected entirely.

The diversity of stakeholders in IT projects is vast—ranging from executive decision-makers and project managers to end-users and external vendors. Each group has distinct priorities and varying degrees of technical expertise. Executives may focus on how a solution affects strategic goals or the bottom line, while end-users care about usability and performance. Recognizing these differences allows technical professionals to craft messages that align with stakeholder interests, using language, examples, and data that resonate with their audience. A one-size-fits-all approach, on the other hand, risks alienating key stakeholders or creating unnecessary confusion.

Tailoring communication also involves striking a balance between technical accuracy and accessibility. Overloading an audience with technical jargon or overly detailed explanations can obscure the key message, leading to frustration or disengagement. Conversely, oversimplifying technical information can undermine credibility, especially with stakeholders who possess advanced technical knowledge. The key lies in knowing the audience's baseline understanding and adapting the depth of the explanation accordingly. For instance, when discussing cloud migration with executives, the emphasis should be on cost savings and scalability, while a presentation to IT teams would focus on architecture, security, and implementation timelines.

Finally, tailoring communication enhances trust and collaboration. When stakeholders feel that their perspectives and concerns are acknowledged, they are more likely to engage in meaningful dialogue and support project objectives. This approach fosters an environment where technical professionals are not just seen as implementers of solutions but as partners who understand and address the broader goals of the organization. It also ensures that stakeholders leave discussions with a clear understanding of what is being proposed, how it aligns with their needs, and what steps they are expected to take moving forward.

By prioritizing tailored communication, technical professionals can transform complex data into compelling narratives that drive informed decision-making. This practice not only increases stakeholder buy-in but also lays the groundwork for successful project outcomes, ensuring alignment across all levels of the organization.

USING NARRATIVE TO CONTEXTUALIZE TECHNICAL CONCEPTS

The power of storytelling extends beyond novels or movies; it is an essential tool in the technical professional's arsenal. Narratives provide a framework for presenting technical information in a way that feels relevant and engaging, transforming abstract data into relatable and actionable insights. When stakeholders can see how a technical concept fits into a broader story—especially one that aligns with their goals—they are far more likely to understand, value, and act upon it.

At its core, using narrative to contextualize technical concepts means framing the information within a meaningful scenario or problem-solving journey. For example, instead of presenting a system upgrade as a series of technical improvements, the narrative might focus on how it will reduce customer complaints by 30% or prevent outages during peak usage. This shift in framing ties the technical details to a real-world impact, creating a compelling reason for stakeholders to engage with the information. Narratives also help humanize technical discussions by connecting them to the day-to-day experiences or concerns of the audience.

Effective narratives in technical communication follow a logical structure: context, challenge, resolution, and impact. The context sets the stage, explaining why the discussion is relevant (e.g., "Customer churn has increased by 15% due to slow response times"). The challenge introduces the technical problem or opportunity ("Our legacy system cannot scale to meet demand"). The resolution presents the proposed solution ("Implementing a cloud-based architecture will eliminate bottlenecks and improve response times"). Finally, the impact highlights tangible outcomes ("This change will enhance customer retention and add $2M to annual revenue"). This structured approach ensures stakeholders see not just what is being done but why it matters.

Additionally, storytelling in technical presentations bridges the emotional and intellectual divide. Facts and figures are essential, but alone, they can fail to inspire action. A well-crafted narrative engages the audience emotionally, making them care about the problem and its solution. For instance, describing a system's downtime in terms of lost revenue or frustrated customers resonates more deeply than simply stating the number of hours it was offline. Analogies, metaphors, or personal anecdotes can also be valuable narrative tools, helping stakeholders draw parallels between technical concepts and familiar experiences.

Finally, narratives make information memorable. While stakeholders might forget the specifics of a technical diagram or data table, they are more likely to recall a story about how the proposed solution prevented a competitor from outpacing the company. Memorable narratives not only improve comprehension but also empower stakeholders to articulate the value of a project to others, amplifying its support within the organization.

By embedding technical concepts within relatable, outcome-focused narratives, IT professionals can transcend the barriers of jargon and complexity. This approach ensures that stakeholders not only grasp the details but also feel invested in the solution, driving informed decisions and unified action.

SIMPLIFICATION WITHOUT OVERSIMPLIFICATION

Presenting technical information clearly requires a delicate balance: simplifying complex ideas so they are accessible to non-technical stakeholders without diluting the essential details that define their value. Oversimplification can lead to misunderstandings, diminish the credibility of the presenter, and risk decisions being made on incomplete or inaccurate information. On the other hand, excessive detail or technical jargon can overwhelm the audience, leaving them disengaged and confused. Achieving the right level of simplification involves clarity, precision, and an understanding of what truly matters to the audience.

The first step in this process is determining the key points of a technical concept that stakeholders need to know. This involves prioritizing the "why" and "what" over the intricate "how." For example, if explaining a new data security protocol to senior management, the focus should be on the outcomes—reduced risk, compliance with regulations, and cost savings—rather than the technical specifics of encryption algorithms. By understanding the audience's priorities and framing the discussion around their concerns, simplification becomes a tool for alignment rather than a reduction in technical depth.

One effective technique for simplification is the use of analogies or metaphors that translate technical concepts into everyday terms. For instance, comparing a system upgrade to renovating a house—where outdated wiring is replaced to handle modern appliances—can make the purpose and value of the change relatable. However, these analogies must be carefully chosen to avoid misrepresentation or introducing inaccuracies. A strong analogy clarifies a concept without replacing it, leaving room to layer in technical specifics if the audience requires more depth.

Visual aids also play a vital role in simplifying complex ideas. Charts, diagrams, and infographics can distill intricate processes into digestible visuals that stakeholders can grasp at a glance. For instance, a flowchart of a proposed software implementation plan can convey timelines and dependencies far more effectively than a textual explanation. However, the visual should be designed to complement the narrative rather than replace it—offering just enough detail to explain the concept while leaving space for further discussion if needed.

Finally, simplification should always allow for scalability. This means being prepared to adjust the level of detail based on audience questions or the evolving direction of the conversation. A layered approach works well: start with a simplified explanation, then build upon it with more granular details as needed. For example, an overview of cloud migration might begin with the benefits for performance and cost, with technical specifics about architecture or API integration introduced only if stakeholders express interest. This approach respects the diverse technical fluency of the audience while ensuring clarity for all.

Simplifying without oversimplifying is an exercise in empathy, precision, and adaptability. It is not about dumbing down information but about making it intelligible and actionable. By focusing on relevance, using illustrative tools, and remaining responsive to audience needs, technical professionals can ensure their messages are both accurate and accessible, building trust and driving informed decision-making.

Leveraging Visual Aids to Enhance Understanding

Visual aids are indispensable tools for translating complex technical information into comprehensible and engaging formats. By presenting data, processes, and concepts visually, they can convey clarity, highlight relationships, and anchor key points in the audience's memory. In stakeholder communication, where attention spans are limited and technical fluency varies widely, effective use of visual aids can bridge the gap between complexity and understanding, fostering better collaboration and decision-making.

One of the primary benefits of visual aids is their ability to simplify intricate systems and processes. Flowcharts, for instance, can map out workflows, showing how different components interact in a process. This is particularly useful in scenarios like illustrating the dependencies in a project timeline or demonstrating the flow of data between system components. Stakeholders who might struggle to follow a textual explanation of these dynamics can quickly grasp the overall picture through a well-designed diagram. The key is to prioritize simplicity and focus on the most relevant aspects of the process while avoiding clutter that could overwhelm the viewer.

Data visualization is another powerful technique for enhancing understanding. Charts, graphs, and heat maps can distill large datasets into digestible insights, making it easier for stakeholders to identify patterns, trends, or areas of concern. For instance, instead of presenting raw performance metrics for a server infrastructure, a line graph showing trends in uptime or a bar chart comparing before-and-after optimization results tells the story at a glance. To maximize impact, visuals should be designed with clear labels, intuitive color coding, and a layout that draws attention to the most critical data points.

Interactive visual aids, such as slide decks or dashboards, take this engagement further by allowing stakeholders to explore information at their own pace. In a presentation, incorporating clickable elements or layered views can cater to different audience preferences, providing high-level summaries for non-technical participants and drill-down options for those seeking deeper technical detail. Modern tools like Power BI or Tableau make it easy to create dynamic and responsive visualizations that adapt to real-time input, enhancing the audience's engagement and comprehension.

Lastly, the effectiveness of visual aids depends on their seamless integration into the communication strategy. They should complement the narrative rather than replace it, providing additional clarity and support. For example, a Gantt chart in a project update should align directly with the spoken explanation of milestones and deadlines. Visuals that contradict or distract from the verbal message undermine credibility and confuse stakeholders. It's equally important to test visual aids for accessibility, ensuring they are readable, colorblind-friendly, and suitable for various devices or formats.

By leveraging visual aids thoughtfully, IT professionals can transform dense or technical material into compelling, actionable insights. These tools not only make information more accessible but also enhance stakeholder confidence, demonstrating that the presenter has both a clear understanding of the material and the communication skills to convey it effectively. When used strategically, visual aids become more than just supplementary elements—they are essential components of impactful technical communication.

ENCOURAGING INTERACTION AND CLARIFICATION

Effective communication is a two-way process, and presenting technical information should never be a passive lecture. Encouraging interaction and clarification transforms a one-sided presentation into a collaborative dialogue, where stakeholders feel engaged and valued. When stakeholders are invited to ask questions, share concerns, and validate their understanding, the result is not only clearer communication but also stronger alignment and trust across all parties.

The first step in fostering interaction is creating an environment where stakeholders feel comfortable participating. This begins with setting expectations at the outset of a discussion or presentation, explicitly encouraging questions and feedback. For example, opening with a statement like, *"I want this session to be collaborative, so feel free to ask for clarification at any point,"* signals that engagement is both welcomed and expected. Additionally, adopting a conversational tone rather than a rigid, formal style can make technical content feel less intimidating and more accessible to a diverse audience.

Another effective technique is to integrate pauses and checkpoints into the presentation flow. After explaining a complex concept or sharing a key piece of data, pause to ask the audience for their thoughts or questions. For instance, saying, *"Does this approach make sense given our project goals?"* invites input without putting anyone on the spot. Checkpoints can also include brief recaps, such as summarizing a key point and asking for confirmation: *"Just to ensure we're aligned, this means X. Would you agree?"* These moments encourage dialogue and signal that the presenter values the stakeholders' perspectives.

Interactive tools can further enhance opportunities for clarification. Digital collaboration platforms like Miro, MURAL, or Microsoft Teams allow stakeholders to annotate documents, participate in polls, or provide live feedback during virtual presentations. These tools can be especially valuable for dispersed teams, ensuring everyone has a chance to contribute regardless of their location or time zone. In in-person settings, using whiteboards or sticky notes for brainstorming and gathering reactions can foster a hands-on and inclusive approach.

Finally, addressing questions and feedback effectively is critical for sustaining trust and engagement. Stakeholders may hesitate to ask questions if they fear their concerns will be dismissed or belittled. Responding to inquiries with patience and genuine interest, even when questions seem basic, demonstrates respect for the audience's varied expertise. If a question requires deeper exploration, it's better to acknowledge it and offer a follow-up discussion rather than deflecting it in the moment. For example, saying, *"That's a great point—let me gather more details and get back to you with a thorough answer,"* ensures the stakeholder feels heard and reassured.

Encouraging interaction and clarification is not just about making stakeholders feel involved; it's about ensuring mutual understanding and alignment. By actively engaging the audience, soliciting their input, and responding thoughtfully, technical professionals can transform presentations into collaborative problem-solving sessions. This approach not only enhances clarity but also builds stronger partnerships, ensuring that all stakeholders leave the conversation with a sense of shared purpose and confidence in the project's direction.

FRAMING INFORMATION FOR ACTION

Presenting technical information in a way that leads to actionable outcomes is a critical skill for IT professionals. Stakeholders are often inundated with details, but unless those details are framed within a clear path forward, they can become overwhelming or ineffective. Framing technical data for action requires a combination of clarity, prioritization, and a results-oriented mindset to ensure that stakeholders understand not only *what* the information means but also *what they should do about it*.

The first step in framing for action is to define the decision or task associated with the information upfront. Stakeholders are more likely to engage with the material when they know its purpose. For instance, instead of beginning with an exhaustive explanation of a system upgrade's technical specifications, the presenter might start by saying, *"This update will improve response times by 30%, but we need your approval on the rollout plan."* This approach establishes a clear objective and gives the audience context for interpreting the subsequent details.

Prioritization is equally essential in framing information for action. Not all data points carry equal weight, and it is the presenter's responsibility to highlight what is most critical. By organizing information into categories such as "must-know," "nice-to-know," and "future considerations," stakeholders can focus their attention on the most pressing issues. For example, during a project status update, emphasizing milestones achieved and the immediate next steps ensures that stakeholders are aligned on what has been accomplished and what requires their input or action next.

Action-oriented language is another powerful tool for driving clarity and engagement. Instead of presenting a static snapshot of the current state, technical professionals should phrase their insights in ways that suggest forward motion. For instance, instead of saying, *"The system has 5% downtime on weekends,"* they might frame it as, *"To address the 5% downtime, we recommend reallocating server resources during weekends. This change could reduce downtime by 70% within a month."* By framing data with clear recommendations and potential outcomes, the presenter guides stakeholders toward actionable decisions.

Lastly, supporting actionable framing with visual and written summaries reinforces clarity and accessibility. Infographics, decision trees, or one-page briefs can succinctly capture key points and associated actions, giving stakeholders a reference tool they can revisit after the meeting. For example, an infographic summarizing a security audit might include three sections: current risks, proposed mitigations, and a timeline for implementation. This format not only distills complex data but also provides stakeholders with an intuitive roadmap for addressing the issues.

Framing information for action transforms technical communication from mere reporting into a driver of decision-making and progress. By defining objectives, prioritizing data, using action-oriented language, and supporting the narrative with clear visuals, IT professionals empower stakeholders to move from understanding to implementation. This approach not only enhances communication but also builds momentum, ensuring that projects and initiatives advance with clarity and confidence.

Building trust through regular updates, transparent reporting, and responsive communication.

Trust is the bedrock of any successful collaboration, and its significance is magnified in stakeholder relationships within IT and consultancy projects. Stakeholders, who often have diverse expectations and varying levels of technical expertise, rely heavily on the project team's communication to feel confident in the project's trajectory. A lack of trust can lead to skepticism, resistance to decisions, and disengagement—hindrances that jeopardize not only project outcomes but also long-term professional relationships.

Building trust begins with establishing a track record of reliability. When project teams consistently meet deadlines, deliver quality work, and maintain open lines of communication, stakeholders naturally develop a sense of confidence. Each successful interaction, from a well-delivered presentation to a timely response to an inquiry, reinforces the perception that the team is competent and dependable. Trust, in this context, becomes an accumulation of positive experiences that reduce uncertainty and align expectations.

Transparency is another critical component of trust. Stakeholders need to believe that they are receiving the full picture, including both achievements and challenges. A team that is forthright about potential risks or setbacks, coupled with proactive strategies to address them, demonstrates integrity. Such openness encourages stakeholders to view the team as partners rather than gatekeepers, fostering a collaborative spirit. Transparency also ensures that decisions are made with a shared understanding of the project's status, reducing the likelihood of misalignment or surprises.

Equally important is the ability to adapt communication to stakeholder needs. Trust is not one-size-fits-all; it requires understanding the individual concerns and priorities of each stakeholder group. For instance, an executive stakeholder may prioritize high-level outcomes, while a technical stakeholder might value detailed insights. By tailoring communication to resonate with each audience, the project team shows respect for their perspectives and investment, strengthening the relational bond.

Ultimately, trust is not just a "nice-to-have" in stakeholder relationships; it is a strategic asset that underpins the success of the entire project. A foundation of trust minimizes friction, accelerates decision-making, and creates a collaborative environment where both the project team and stakeholders can work toward shared goals with confidence and mutual respect.

ESTABLISHING CREDIBILITY THROUGH REGULAR UPDATES

Credibility is the cornerstone of trust, and in stakeholder relationships, it is often built through the consistency and quality of updates. Regular updates serve as touchpoints that reassure stakeholders about the project's progress, address their concerns, and demonstrate the team's commitment to transparency and accountability. By establishing a rhythm of communication, project teams can foster a sense of reliability and professionalism, which are crucial in high-stakes IT and consultancy projects.

A structured approach to updates ensures that stakeholders remain informed without being overwhelmed. Updates should align with predefined communication plans, specifying their frequency, format, and content. For example, weekly progress emails or monthly status meetings provide predictable intervals for information sharing, allowing stakeholders to anticipate and prepare for these interactions. This regularity not only keeps stakeholders engaged but also reinforces the team's organizational competence, a key factor in establishing credibility.

The content of these updates must balance technical depth with accessibility. Stakeholders often have varied backgrounds, ranging from highly technical to business-focused. To accommodate this diversity, updates should be layered: high-level summaries for those seeking strategic insights, followed by detailed breakdowns for more technically inclined stakeholders. This approach ensures that the information is both relevant and digestible, reducing the risk of misunderstandings or perceived opacity.

Transparency in updates enhances credibility further. Stakeholders should not only hear about successes but also be informed of challenges, risks, or deviations from the plan. Acknowledging difficulties and presenting clear, actionable plans to address them demonstrates maturity and problem-solving acumen. Stakeholders are more likely to trust a team that openly discusses setbacks with solutions than one that only highlights achievements while concealing potential issues.

Finally, updates should invite stakeholder feedback, creating a two-way communication channel. Incorporating stakeholder input shows respect for their expertise and priorities while fostering a collaborative relationship. For instance, closing an update with questions like, "Are there additional concerns we should address?" or "Do these priorities align with your expectations?" signals openness and a commitment to mutual alignment. Over time, this habit of engaging stakeholders during updates solidifies the team's credibility and strengthens the overall project relationship.

By providing regular, transparent, and interactive updates, project teams not only keep stakeholders informed but also cultivate a reputation for dependability and professionalism. These efforts contribute significantly to building trust, ensuring stakeholder confidence in both the team and the project's trajectory.

THE POWER OF TRANSPARENT REPORTING

Transparent reporting is one of the most effective tools for fostering trust in stakeholder relationships. It transforms communication from a one-sided relay of information into a shared understanding of the project's realities, challenges, and opportunities. By making project data accessible and verifiable, transparent reporting reassures stakeholders that they are privy to the same truths as the project team, fostering a culture of honesty and collaboration.

Transparency in reporting begins with clarity. Reports should be free from unnecessary jargon, overly technical language, or obfuscation. The goal is to present data in a way that stakeholders with varying levels of expertise can comprehend and act upon. For example, instead of detailing raw metrics or complex technical processes, reports can use summaries, graphs, and key performance indicators (KPIs) to convey progress and highlight critical areas. Clear, accessible reporting demonstrates respect for stakeholders' time and ensures that all parties remain aligned on the project's status.

Another critical aspect of transparent reporting is its inclusivity. A comprehensive report doesn't just highlight successes—it also addresses challenges, risks, and areas of concern. For instance, if a project is falling behind schedule, stakeholders should be informed promptly and presented with mitigation strategies. This level of candor reinforces the project team's integrity and demonstrates a proactive approach to problem-solving. Stakeholders are more likely to trust a team that shares setbacks alongside solutions than one that withholds uncomfortable truths.

Consistency is also key to transparent reporting. Regularly scheduled reports—be they weekly dashboards, monthly progress reviews, or quarterly updates—establish a rhythm that stakeholders can rely on. Consistency builds confidence that no aspect of the project is being neglected and ensures that stakeholders are continually informed. Ad hoc reporting, while sometimes necessary, should complement rather than replace regular updates, ensuring that the flow of information remains predictable and reliable.

Finally, transparent reporting fosters a collaborative environment by inviting stakeholder input. When stakeholders are presented with open and honest information, they feel empowered to provide feedback, raise concerns, or contribute insights that can help guide the project's direction. For instance, a transparent report that highlights a potential risk could prompt stakeholders to offer resources or adjustments that mitigate the issue. This dynamic not only strengthens the relationship between the team and stakeholders but also enhances the project's chances of success.

Transparent reporting is more than a communication strategy—it is a trust-building mechanism that aligns stakeholders and teams around a shared vision of the project. By emphasizing clarity, inclusivity, consistency, and collaboration, transparent reporting ensures that stakeholders remain engaged and confident in both the project's direction and the team's capabilities.

Responsiveness: Ensuring Stakeholders Feel Heard

Responsiveness is a cornerstone of effective stakeholder communication, fostering trust and engagement by demonstrating that their concerns, questions, and feedback are valued and acted upon. In the fast-paced world of IT and consultancy projects, where priorities can shift rapidly, being responsive ensures that stakeholders remain confident in the project team's ability to adapt and address emerging needs. This practice not only strengthens relationships but also mitigates potential conflicts by fostering a culture of openness and mutual respect.

Responsiveness begins with timely acknowledgment. Stakeholders often raise issues or inquiries in moments of uncertainty or urgency. A prompt response, even if it's simply to confirm receipt and provide a timeline for a more detailed reply, conveys attentiveness and respect. For instance, if a stakeholder flags a concern about a delayed deliverable, acknowledging their message within hours rather than days reassures them that their input is being taken seriously. Such proactive communication reduces anxiety and creates a sense of reliability.

Equally important is the substance of the response. Stakeholders need clear, relevant, and actionable answers, not vague reassurances. For example, if a stakeholder questions a deviation in project scope, the response should include specific reasons for the change, its implications, and the steps being taken to address any associated risks. Providing comprehensive answers demonstrates a commitment to transparency and reinforces the perception of the project team as competent and trustworthy.

Responsiveness also involves active listening. Stakeholders should feel that their concerns are understood, not just addressed superficially. This requires paraphrasing their input, asking follow-up questions, and ensuring alignment before taking action. For instance, if a stakeholder raises a concern about resource allocation, a responsive team might say, "To clarify, you're concerned about the impact of shifting resources on the delivery timeline. Is that correct?" Such dialogue not only ensures accuracy but also makes stakeholders feel genuinely heard.

Responsiveness must extend beyond problem-solving to include proactive communication. This means not waiting for stakeholders to raise issues but actively checking in with them to gather input and provide updates. Regularly soliciting feedback—through surveys, one-on-one meetings, or collaborative workshops—demonstrates a commitment to their involvement in shaping the project. When stakeholders see their suggestions reflected in decisions, their confidence in the team deepens.

Finally, being responsive requires flexibility. Stakeholders often have diverse needs and expectations, which may sometimes conflict with existing plans. Responsiveness involves finding creative ways to address these concerns without compromising the project's integrity. For instance, accommodating a stakeholder's request for additional details in reports might involve creating a supplementary section in the next update, ensuring their needs are met while maintaining the document's broader purpose.

Responsiveness is a dynamic process that goes beyond merely reacting to stakeholder input—it's about creating an environment where stakeholders feel valued, understood, and empowered. By prioritizing timely acknowledgment, clear communication, active listening, and proactive engagement, project teams can foster trust, strengthen relationships, and ensure stakeholders remain confident in their ability to deliver successful outcomes.

Balancing Formality and Approachability in Communication

Striking the right balance between formality and approachability is vital when communicating with stakeholders. This equilibrium ensures that interactions maintain professionalism while fostering a sense of openness and trust. Whether the stakeholder is a senior executive, an external partner, or a team member with vested interests, the tone and style of communication play a critical role in shaping perceptions and driving collaboration.

Formality in communication conveys respect and competence. Using structured formats, professional language, and clear documentation reflects the project team's commitment to excellence and attention to detail. For instance, when delivering project updates, a well-organized presentation or report signals thoroughness and reinforces stakeholders' confidence in the project's progress. However, excessive rigidity in tone or overly technical language can alienate stakeholders, particularly those less familiar with the project's complexities. Striking a balance means adapting formal structures while ensuring accessibility and clarity.

Approachability, on the other hand, invites stakeholders to engage without hesitation. An approachable tone fosters a sense of collaboration and encourages stakeholders to voice concerns, ask questions, or provide feedback.

For example, incorporating conversational elements in meetings, such as asking open-ended questions ("What are your thoughts on this approach?"), can create an inclusive atmosphere. Similarly, acknowledging stakeholder contributions with phrases like "We appreciate your input" strengthens relationships by making them feel valued.

The context of the communication often dictates the balance between formality and approachability. A high-stakes presentation to a steering committee may lean towards formality, with a structured agenda, polished visuals, and precise language. In contrast, a one-on-one check-in with a stakeholder to discuss emerging concerns may call for a more approachable tone, emphasizing empathy and active listening. Recognizing the nuances of each interaction helps ensure the appropriate tone is employed.

To achieve this balance, consistency is key. Stakeholders should not experience drastic shifts in tone that create confusion or undermine trust. For example, maintaining a professional yet friendly demeanor across emails, meetings, and reports ensures stakeholders perceive the team as both competent and relatable. Additionally, personalizing communication—such as addressing stakeholders by name, referencing past interactions, or acknowledging their unique priorities—adds a layer of authenticity that bridges formality with warmth.

Finally, leveraging technology can aid in maintaining this balance. Platforms like email, Slack, or project management tools can be used to align tone with context. A formal email with detailed updates might be supplemented by a brief and conversational follow-up message on Slack, ensuring stakeholders receive both the necessary information and an invitation for dialogue. This dual-channel approach allows for precision and relatability to coexist effectively.

Balancing formality and approachability in stakeholder communication requires attentiveness to context, consistency in tone, and a genuine interest in fostering collaboration. By respecting stakeholders' roles while creating an inviting atmosphere for engagement, project teams can build relationships founded on both professionalism and trust, ensuring smoother interactions and more successful project outcomes.

Chapter 4: Bridging the Gap with Third-Party Teams

In modern IT projects, third-party collaborations have become a standard practice, driven by the need for specialized expertise, cost efficiency, and the flexibility to scale resources as required. Vendors, external consultants, and partner companies often bring unique skills and perspectives that can significantly enhance project outcomes. However, these collaborations also introduce complexities that can challenge even the most experienced teams. Understanding how to effectively navigate these relationships is critical to ensuring that the contributions of external parties align seamlessly with internal goals and objectives.

The role of third parties in IT projects is multifaceted, ranging from providing technical solutions to offering strategic advice or managing key components of a deliverable. This diversity in roles makes it essential to approach such collaborations with clear objectives and well-defined expectations. Without a structured framework, it is easy for miscommunication or misaligned priorities to disrupt project timelines or impact quality. For many organizations, the challenge lies in integrating these external teams into existing workflows without compromising efficiency or cohesion.

At the core of successful third-party collaboration is the establishment of mutual trust and respect. These partnerships often extend beyond contractual obligations and require an understanding of cultural, operational, and strategic differences. Companies that fail to invest in building strong relationships with their external collaborators may find themselves facing issues such as inconsistent deliverables, unmet deadlines, or even damaged reputations. Effective communication and transparency serve as the foundation for addressing these potential pitfalls and fostering an environment where all parties work towards shared success.

Additionally, third-party collaboration provides a valuable opportunity to reassess internal practices and discover innovative approaches. External teams can offer fresh perspectives that challenge entrenched habits or outdated methodologies, leading to growth and improved efficiency. When managed strategically, these partnerships not only enhance project outcomes but also enrich the organization's capacity to adapt to changing market demands. By recognizing both the opportunities and challenges inherent in these collaborations, organizations can position themselves for greater long-term success.

ESTABLISHING A STRONG FOUNDATION

The success of any collaboration with vendors, external consultants, or partner companies hinges on building a strong foundation at the outset. This foundation is rooted in mutual understanding, shared goals, and well-defined expectations. Without these elements, even the most well-intentioned partnerships can falter under the weight of misaligned priorities or vague responsibilities. Laying this groundwork is not just about signing contracts or drafting agreements; it is about creating a partnership framework that ensures clarity and fosters accountability from the very beginning.

Central to establishing this foundation is the clear definition of roles and responsibilities for all parties involved. Each collaborator must understand their specific contribution to the project, how their efforts align with the broader objectives, and the expectations for delivery. This clarity prevents duplication of work, reduces misunderstandings, and ensures that everyone remains focused on their designated tasks. A thorough kickoff process—where roles, timelines, and workflows are discussed in detail—sets the stage for a collaborative relationship where each participant knows their place in the bigger picture.

Contracts and service-level agreements (SLAs) play a pivotal role in formalizing this understanding, providing a documented reference point for responsibilities, deadlines, and performance standards. However, the effectiveness of these documents lies in their ability to go beyond legal formalities and serve as operational blueprints. A well-crafted agreement should not only outline deliverables but also address contingencies, escalation paths, and communication protocols. By anticipating potential challenges and embedding solutions into these foundational documents, organizations can mitigate risks and maintain alignment even when unexpected situations arise.

Another crucial aspect of building a strong foundation is onboarding third-party teams into the organization's culture, tools, and processes. External collaborators often bring their own methods and systems, which, if not aligned with internal practices, can create friction. A comprehensive onboarding process familiarizes these teams with the organization's workflow, communication platforms, and project goals, ensuring smoother integration.

This alignment fosters a sense of partnership, transforming what could be a transactional relationship into a cohesive collaboration that is prepared to tackle the project's complexities together.

BUILDING EFFECTIVE COMMUNICATION CHANNELS

Effective communication channels form the backbone of any successful collaboration with third parties, ensuring that information flows seamlessly between internal teams and external partners. Without clear and reliable communication mechanisms, misunderstandings can arise, delays can multiply, and the quality of deliverables may suffer. Establishing these channels early in the collaboration process is critical to fostering alignment and trust, especially in complex IT projects where precision and coordination are non-negotiable.

The first step in building effective communication channels is identifying the appropriate tools and platforms that suit the project's needs. With an array of options available, from email and instant messaging to project management software like Jira or Asana, it is important to choose tools that are both accessible and scalable. However, simply selecting tools is not enough; defining how and when they should be used is equally crucial. For example, instant messaging may work for quick clarifications, but critical updates or contractual discussions might require formal documentation through email or centralized project platforms. Setting these norms ensures consistency and reduces confusion across teams.

Regular and structured communication is another cornerstone of an effective strategy. Weekly check-ins, progress reviews, and milestone updates provide opportunities for all parties to stay informed and address issues proactively. These meetings should have clear agendas and objectives, with action items documented and shared afterward to ensure accountability. Additionally, creating an escalation protocol helps manage conflicts or delays efficiently, ensuring that concerns are addressed by the appropriate stakeholders without disrupting overall progress.

Equally important is the role of transparency and cultural sensitivity in communication. Teams from different organizations or geographical locations may have varying approaches to collaboration and feedback. Acknowledging these differences and encouraging open dialogue can prevent friction and build rapport. Clear, concise, and respectful communication not only minimizes the risk of misinterpretation but also cultivates a collaborative environment where all participants feel valued. By prioritizing the establishment and maintenance of effective communication channels, organizations lay the groundwork for partnerships that thrive on clarity, efficiency, and mutual understanding.

MAINTAINING ALIGNMENT THROUGHOUT THE PROJECT

Maintaining alignment between internal teams and third-party collaborators is an ongoing process that requires vigilance and adaptability. Projects involving vendors, external consultants, or partner companies often span extended periods and encounter shifts in priorities, resources, or external conditions. Without consistent efforts to ensure alignment, these changes can disrupt workflows, create confusion, and jeopardize deliverables. Effective alignment is not achieved through a one-time effort but through sustained communication, monitoring, and coordination throughout the project lifecycle.

One critical strategy for maintaining alignment is the regular review of goals and expectations. As projects evolve, initial objectives may need to be refined to reflect new realities, such as updated customer requirements, resource constraints, or technological advancements. Regularly revisiting the project's scope and milestones with all stakeholders ensures that everyone remains on the same page and that third-party collaborators can adjust their contributions accordingly. Scheduled alignment sessions, combined with clear documentation of any changes, serve as a safeguard against miscommunication or scope drift.

Another key factor is the consistent tracking of deliverables and performance metrics. Transparency in reporting progress allows both internal and external teams to assess whether they are meeting their commitments and staying aligned with overall objectives. Tools like dashboards or collaborative software can centralize this information, providing real-time visibility into task completion, dependencies, and potential bottlenecks. This approach fosters accountability while also making it easier to identify and address issues before they escalate.

Relationship management also plays a pivotal role in sustaining alignment. Collaboration is as much about interpersonal dynamics as it is about technical execution. Investing in the relationship with third-party teams—through regular touchpoints, acknowledgment of their contributions, and resolving conflicts with fairness—builds trust and mutual respect. These elements strengthen the partnership and ensure that external collaborators remain motivated and engaged in achieving shared goals.

Finally, adaptability is essential in maintaining alignment. No project proceeds exactly as planned, and unexpected challenges will inevitably arise. The ability to pivot quickly and realign efforts ensures that the project remains on track despite obstacles. Flexibility in methods, combined with a commitment to the project's overarching vision, allows both internal and external teams to navigate uncertainty effectively. By embedding these practices into the collaboration process, organizations can maintain alignment, enhance productivity, and drive project success from start to finish.

CONFLICT RESOLUTION AND RELATIONSHIP MANAGEMENT4

Conflicts are an inevitable aspect of any collaborative effort, particularly in projects involving third-party teams. Differences in priorities, misunderstandings, or unmet expectations can arise, threatening timelines, budgets, and trust. However, conflicts do not have to derail a project. When managed effectively, they can serve as opportunities to strengthen relationships and improve processes. Conflict resolution, paired with proactive relationship management, is essential for navigating challenges while maintaining productive partnerships.

The foundation of conflict resolution lies in addressing issues promptly and directly. Avoiding or delaying resolution efforts often allows tensions to escalate, making reconciliation more challenging. Open communication is the first step: ensuring all parties involved have the opportunity to voice their perspectives in a constructive and respectful manner. Facilitating discussions in a neutral setting and focusing on shared goals rather than individual grievances helps de-escalate tensions and steer conversations toward solutions.

Establishing a clear protocol for resolving disputes is equally important. These protocols might include predefined escalation paths, timelines for addressing grievances, and agreed-upon methods for arbitration or mediation. For example, minor disagreements can often be resolved through direct dialogue between team members, while more significant issues may require the involvement of project managers or other neutral third parties. A structured approach ensures fairness and prevents conflicts from consuming disproportionate time or resources.

Proactive relationship management plays a complementary role by reducing the likelihood of conflicts arising in the first place. Building rapport with third-party teams requires regular communication, transparency, and mutual respect.

Simple gestures, such as recognizing their contributions or seeking their input during decision-making, can foster goodwill and collaboration. Strong relationships create a foundation of trust, making it easier to navigate disagreements constructively when they do occur.

Additionally, cultural and organizational differences should be carefully navigated as part of relationship management. Third-party teams may come from diverse professional or geographical backgrounds, each with its own communication styles and expectations. Demonstrating cultural sensitivity and adaptability helps bridge these differences, ensuring that misunderstandings stemming from disparate norms are minimized. When conflicts are resolved thoughtfully and relationships are nurtured consistently, collaborations with third-party teams not only recover from challenges but also emerge stronger and more effective in the long run.

Managing dependencies, contracts, and deliverables through structured communication.

Clarifying and managing dependencies between internal teams and third-party collaborators is essential for a project's success, particularly in complex IT environments where each team's work impacts the next phase. Dependencies, whether they relate to resource availability, task sequencing, or technological requirements, shape the overall project timeline and can introduce significant risks if not addressed effectively. Establishing a clear understanding of these interconnections at the project's outset provides both a roadmap for execution and a buffer against unforeseen delays or misunderstandings. In an IT consultancy setting, where project components are often managed across different teams or vendors, recognizing and defining dependencies early can streamline collaboration and keep all parties on the same page.

One of the first steps in managing dependencies is thorough dependency mapping, which visually organizes and displays the interconnections between various tasks and responsibilities. This can take the form of charts or dependency grids that outline which teams rely on one another to complete critical tasks. By documenting these relationships, project managers create a resource that internal teams and third-party partners can refer to throughout the project. This mapping effort should also clarify each team's role within the broader project, helping all stakeholders understand how their work influences the final outcome and where they need to coordinate closely with other groups.

Proactive communication is crucial for maintaining alignment around dependencies. This involves establishing regular check-in points dedicated specifically to discussing dependency progress. Dependency-focused meetings provide a structured opportunity to assess whether timelines are holding or if adjustments are needed. In cases where a team identifies potential delays, these check-ins ensure that all impacted parties are informed promptly, enabling adjustments in related schedules or priorities. Such meetings serve as both a diagnostic tool and a preventive measure, helping teams quickly address issues before they escalate into larger problems that could derail timelines or reduce quality.

Finally, maintaining flexible yet structured protocols around dependency management is essential. Since project requirements may evolve, setting rigid timelines around dependencies can sometimes backfire. Instead, creating adaptable frameworks that allow for adjustments without compromising project integrity is vital. For example, leveraging project management software that allows real-time updates on task statuses and provides notifications of changes to dependencies can keep all teams in sync. Regularly revisiting dependency maps and adjusting them as needed reinforces a flexible, resilient approach to managing dependencies. By continuously refining and communicating about these interdependencies, teams can navigate the complexities of cross-functional collaboration more effectively, leading to a smoother project flow and enhanced final outcomes.

Defining and Maintaining Contracts as Communication Tools

Defining and maintaining contracts as communication tools is essential in structuring clear, reliable agreements with third-party vendors, consultants, and partners. In collaborative IT projects, contracts do more than outline service terms or deliverable timelines; they serve as foundational communication instruments that detail mutual expectations, roles, and responsibilities. A well-defined contract clarifies the project's scope and establishes benchmarks for deliverables, thereby preventing confusion as the project unfolds. By approaching contracts as living documents, project managers and IT consultants create a shared reference that guides both operational execution and strategic alignment over the project's duration.

Creating a robust contract starts with precise language that removes ambiguity around deliverables, timelines, resources, and roles. For instance, specifying details such as data sharing, reporting frequency, and quality standards provides a practical roadmap for both internal and external stakeholders. This clarity helps prevent misinterpretation and fosters a sense of accountability from all parties. Often, IT projects involve technical specifics that require additional context or explanation, and building these details into the contract ensures that each collaborator understands the project's requirements in depth. By embedding structured information in the contract, both internal teams and third-party vendors have a clear baseline against which they can track progress.

In addition to initial specifications, contracts must also account for contingency protocols and change management. IT projects, especially in consultancy settings, frequently encounter shifts in client requirements or external conditions that may impact timelines or deliverables. Including terms that outline procedures for revisiting or renegotiating parts of the contract under certain conditions enables teams to adapt flexibly without destabilizing the project. These provisions help avoid potential conflict by establishing a pre-approved framework for addressing scope changes. Structured communication protocols around contract amendments ensure that any updates are clearly documented and agreed upon by all parties, maintaining alignment as project demands evolve.

Furthermore, maintaining open, consistent communication about contract status and expectations is critical throughout the project's lifecycle. Periodic contract review sessions allow teams to assess whether all parties are meeting their commitments, addressing issues early before they escalate. These reviews can be a formal aspect of project management meetings, where team leads check that the agreed-upon standards are being met, and, if necessary, clarify any misunderstandings. Documentation from these reviews can then be attached to the contract as addendums, building a comprehensive record of accountability that holds each party responsible for their contributions. This iterative approach to contract maintenance turns the contract into a dynamic tool that supports ongoing alignment, transparency, and mutual trust.

Treating contracts as communication tools strengthens the foundational trust necessary for effective project execution. Well-managed contracts provide a reliable framework for collaboration that supports clarity, adaptability, and mutual respect. By fostering accountability through detailed, transparent contracts, project leaders and team members can create a culture of reliability, where each contributor understands their role and is empowered to communicate openly about progress or issues. This approach transforms the contract from a static document into an active part of project communication, promoting shared understanding, reducing risks, and setting the stage for successful, efficient collaboration.

CREATING AND MANAGING A STRUCTURED PROCESS FOR DELIVERABLES

Creating and managing a structured process for deliverables is a key element in ensuring that IT projects progress smoothly and meet expected outcomes. In collaborative environments where third-party vendors and external consultants are involved, establishing a well-defined approach to deliverables minimizes misunderstandings, aligns team efforts, and promotes accountability. To begin, it is essential to outline each deliverable clearly from the outset, including specific requirements, quality standards, and expected delivery dates. This approach sets precise targets, enabling internal teams and external collaborators to work in sync, guided by a shared understanding of the project's needs and timelines. By establishing this clarity upfront, teams lay the groundwork for effective coordination, reducing the likelihood of delayed or substandard outputs.

Managing deliverables requires more than just initial clarity; it also involves an organized tracking system to monitor progress at each stage. Project managers can implement tools and platforms—such as project management software or shared dashboards—that allow every stakeholder to view the current status of each deliverable in real-time. These tools serve as centralized communication hubs where tasks are broken down into actionable steps, deadlines are visible, and responsibilities are clearly assigned. Regular updates to the dashboard help team members stay informed, enabling swift intervention if a deliverable starts to fall behind schedule or requires additional resources. Structured progress reporting, such as weekly or bi-weekly check-ins, reinforces accountability by providing teams with a consistent rhythm for tracking advancement and resolving minor issues before they evolve into larger obstacles.

Another vital aspect of managing a structured deliverable process is establishing clear acceptance criteria and review procedures. Each deliverable should have predefined standards that indicate when it has been successfully completed and is ready for review. Acceptance criteria might include technical specifications, functionality checks, or quality benchmarks, depending on the project's goals and requirements. By making these standards transparent to all stakeholders, teams avoid discrepancies between expected and actual outcomes. Review procedures, whether conducted by project leads or external quality assurance teams, provide an additional layer of validation, ensuring that deliverables meet the required standards before they are formally handed over. This process not only helps uphold quality but also strengthens trust between internal teams and third-party partners, as each party can be confident in the reliability of the outputs.

An effective communication protocol is crucial to the deliverable process, especially for managing changes, delays, or dependencies that may impact completion timelines. When a deliverable requires an adjustment—whether due to resource constraints, shifting priorities, or unforeseen complications—project managers should initiate a structured communication sequence. This sequence might include notifying stakeholders of the change, discussing alternative timelines, and recording the adjusted parameters in a shared document or project tracking system. By handling changes in an organized, transparent manner, teams mitigate potential disruptions, keeping everyone aligned even as project demands evolve. Documenting these adjustments ensures that no detail is overlooked and that each party remains aware of current expectations and responsibilities.

A structured process for deliverables ultimately transforms collaborative projects into coordinated efforts where expectations are clear, progress is measurable, and quality is maintained. By prioritizing organization and transparent communication, project managers build an environment where internal teams and external partners can work seamlessly toward shared objectives. In the end, this structured approach to deliverables is not only a pathway to successful project completion but also a foundational practice that cultivates trust, accountability, and operational efficiency.

IMPLEMENTING STRUCTURED COMMUNICATION CHANNELS FOR DEPENDENCY, CONTRACT, AND DELIVERABLE MANAGEMENT

Implementing structured communication channels for managing dependencies, contracts, and deliverables is essential to the success of projects involving multiple stakeholders, especially when coordinating between internal teams and external vendors or consultants. Structured communication channels act as formalized pathways that ensure essential project details are consistently shared, updates are timely, and adjustments to contracts or deliverable timelines are clearly understood. By implementing these channels early in the project, teams set up a reliable infrastructure that minimizes the chances of miscommunication, which can lead to misaligned goals, missed deadlines, and strained relationships. Effective communication channels are instrumental in keeping project dynamics organized, establishing clear expectations for all parties, and reducing potential disruptions from issues related to dependencies or changes in scope.

Structured communication channels should be customized to suit the specific needs of each project phase and type of interaction. For example, dependencies require proactive communication to prevent bottlenecks; this might involve regular meetings where teams discuss dependencies that are upcoming or currently at risk. These check-ins should be held at predetermined intervals to address dependency-related issues before they become blockers to progress. Similarly, contracts necessitate clear communication to ensure that all parties are fully aware of their obligations, milestones, and any recent amendments. Setting up a dedicated communication pathway, such as a contract management platform or an online document repository, keeps contract-related conversations accessible and prevents misunderstandings. This focused approach to communication ensures that the right channels are in place for each aspect of project management, creating a streamlined system where dependencies, contractual commitments, and deliverables can be effectively overseen.

The use of both synchronous and asynchronous communication channels is crucial for handling the various facets of dependency, contract, and deliverable management. Synchronous methods, such as video calls and live meetings, are ideal for discussions requiring real-time feedback, such as initial project kickoff meetings, periodic reviews, or when addressing urgent issues. On the other hand, asynchronous communication—such as email updates, shared dashboards, or project management software—is invaluable for maintaining a record of discussions and keeping all team members informed without requiring immediate responses. Documenting communication in a shared space enables ongoing transparency and allows team members in different time zones or with varying schedules to remain up-to-date. This blend of communication styles ensures that project information is accessible, enabling teams to engage with information in a manner that best supports their workflow while fostering responsiveness and clarity.

In addition to regular updates, structured communication for managing dependencies, contracts, and deliverables must prioritize clarity and consistency. For dependency management, establishing specific formats for communicating requirements—such as standardized forms or templates—helps team members quickly understand what is needed and what impact delays or changes might have. For contract communication, periodic reviews are essential, providing an opportunity to address any questions, clarify obligations, and discuss any necessary amendments. Ensuring consistency in how these communications are documented and shared fosters a culture of reliability, where every stakeholder knows how to access and interpret key project information. Moreover, by defining standard operating procedures for each type of communication, the project manager builds a system that all contributors can follow with ease, which is particularly important in cross-functional teams where members may not be familiar with each other's processes.

Finally, structured communication channels also play a pivotal role in facilitating post-delivery assessments and feedback loops, which are vital for improving future project interactions and solidifying relationships with third-party teams. After the completion of a deliverable or fulfillment of a contract, structured communication enables a thorough review, helping identify areas for improvement in the collaboration process. Conducting these evaluations with transparency, often through documented feedback forms or retrospective meetings, allows both internal teams and external partners to reflect on what went well and what could be improved. By incorporating feedback into structured communication practices, project managers cultivate a continuous improvement mindset that not only benefits current projects but also strengthens long-term partnerships. Through clear, methodical communication channels, project teams can better navigate the complexities of managing dependencies, contracts, and deliverables, achieving a higher standard of collaboration and project success.

REVIEW AND CONTINUOUS IMPROVEMENT OF STRUCTURED COMMUNICATION PRACTICES

Reviewing and continuously improving structured communication practices is an essential final step to ensure that the processes in place remain effective, efficient, and adaptable to evolving project needs. As projects progress and stakeholders gain insights into what communication strategies work best, regular reviews enable teams to refine their approaches, keeping communication aligned with changing requirements, team dynamics, and technological advancements. Effective reviews often begin with structured feedback sessions, where team members, stakeholders, and third-party collaborators assess current communication practices and identify areas for enhancement. Gathering input from all relevant parties creates a comprehensive understanding of the strengths and gaps in the current system, providing a basis for meaningful improvements. This commitment to periodic assessment fosters a culture of responsiveness and adaptability, equipping project teams to proactively address issues and optimize their communication framework over time.

Continuous improvement of communication practices should prioritize addressing pain points or recurring challenges identified through feedback. For example, if teams frequently report delays in receiving critical updates from third-party vendors, project managers might implement additional communication checkpoints or automate reminders for deadline-based notifications. Likewise, if stakeholders express confusion over contract terms, creating clearer guidelines or using more accessible language in contract-related communications may resolve these issues. By targeting specific weaknesses highlighted during reviews, project teams can implement tailored solutions that directly enhance communication effectiveness. Addressing these areas not only improves the day-to-day operations of current projects but also strengthens the foundation for future collaborations, enabling smoother, more efficient communication workflows in the long term.

The process of refining communication practices also involves examining the tools and platforms used for maintaining structured communication. As digital tools continue to evolve, project managers should assess whether the current technology stack best serves the team's needs or if alternative solutions could streamline communication further. For instance, if project updates are currently managed through email chains, the team might benefit from transitioning to a centralized project management platform that offers better tracking and collaboration features. Regularly evaluating the efficacy of these tools can reveal opportunities to adopt more advanced technology, minimizing inefficiencies and reducing the risk of miscommunication. This proactive approach to tool optimization keeps communication systems modern, reliable, and well-suited to the demands of cross-functional and third-party team environments.

Finally, fostering a culture of continuous improvement in communication practices requires a clear, documented process for implementing changes and monitoring their impact. After adjustments are made based on feedback, the team should establish measurable goals for assessing whether the new communication practices are achieving desired outcomes. For example, improvements could be tracked through key performance indicators (KPIs) like response times, project milestone adherence, or feedback from stakeholders on communication clarity. Setting these metrics creates accountability and allows the project team to monitor progress objectively, ensuring that new practices contribute positively to project outcomes. Over time, this iterative approach reinforces a commitment to communication excellence, demonstrating that every adjustment is made with the intent of enhancing collaboration and fostering more successful project partnerships. By integrating continuous improvement into the fabric of their structured communication practices, project managers build a resilient framework that evolves alongside their projects and teams, consistently supporting project success in an ever-changing IT landscape.

Resolving conflicts and ensuring alignment between third-party teams and internal goals.

Recognizing common sources of conflict is essential in managing collaborations between internal teams and third-party entities. Understanding the typical areas where conflicts arise allows project leaders to anticipate challenges and implement proactive measures to prevent issues from escalating. A key source of conflict often stems from differing priorities and expectations. While internal teams may be focused on long-term goals or specific quality benchmarks aligned with company standards, third-party teams may prioritize timelines, cost efficiency, or their established workflows. These differing focus areas can result in misaligned efforts, where each side operates with a distinct set of assumptions that can lead to disagreements over resource allocation, project scope, or deadline feasibility.

Another frequent cause of conflict is the use of diverse project methodologies. In IT and consultancy projects, it's common for third-party teams to operate under frameworks like Agile or Scrum, which may emphasize iterative progress and flexibility. Internal teams, on the other hand, might rely on more traditional methodologies like PMP or Waterfall, which tend to follow a sequential and structured approach. These contrasting methodologies can result in friction around project pacing, feedback loops, and even expectations for deliverable revisions. For instance, Agile teams may expect constant adjustments, while those accustomed to Waterfall processes anticipate a more linear progression. Recognizing these methodology-based differences early on allows for smoother negotiation of processes and better preparation for potential misalignments.

Communication style differences also contribute significantly to conflicts. Third-party entities may have communication norms that differ from the internal team's standards, such as frequency of updates, preferred communication tools, and levels of detail in reporting. Miscommunication or lack of clarity around these norms can quickly lead to misunderstandings. For example, a third-party team may feel overwhelmed by what they perceive as micromanagement, while the internal team might feel frustrated by the third party's perceived lack of transparency. Acknowledging these differing styles and setting mutual expectations at the outset of the project helps prevent resentment and confusion later on.

Lastly, cultural differences and organizational hierarchies can influence interactions between internal and third-party teams. In multinational collaborations, team members from different cultural backgrounds may approach conflict, feedback, and decision-making differently. For example, some cultures might prioritize consensus and indirect feedback, while others favor direct communication and quick resolutions. Additionally, hierarchy can impact conflict dynamics; in some companies, decision-making is concentrated at higher levels, while others empower frontline employees with significant autonomy. Recognizing these organizational and cultural factors allows leaders to address potential challenges in communication and collaboration respectfully and effectively, fostering a working environment that minimizes friction and maximizes mutual understanding.

IMPLEMENTING A STRUCTURED CONFLICT RESOLUTION PROCESS

Implementing a structured conflict resolution process is essential in projects involving third-party teams, as it provides a reliable approach to addressing disagreements and maintaining alignment. By establishing a clear, systematic process, organizations can address conflicts swiftly and professionally, minimizing disruptions to project timelines and preserving relationships between internal and external stakeholders. The first step in this process should involve defining the rules and expectations for conflict resolution at the start of the project. This includes specifying when and how team members should raise concerns, ensuring all parties are aware of the process and can participate confidently and transparently when issues arise. By setting these expectations early, the team reduces the likelihood of unresolved issues and creates a foundation for constructive engagement.

An effective conflict resolution process must include defined roles and responsibilities to clarify accountability. Identifying who will facilitate discussions, make decisions, and ensure follow-through on resolutions prevents confusion and empowers team members to engage actively in conflict management. For instance, assigning a neutral facilitator—such as a project manager or an external mediator—can help ensure discussions remain impartial and focused on finding practical solutions. Additionally, defining roles for representatives from each team, particularly those with decision-making authority, ensures that solutions are actionable and reflect the priorities of both internal and third-party teams. This clarity reduces ambiguity and empowers each side to take ownership of conflict resolution.

Structured steps for resolving conflicts should also be formalized, including a clear escalation pathway. For instance, conflicts can first be addressed informally, with teams encouraged to discuss issues directly and collaboratively. If an issue remains unresolved, it can then be escalated to team leads or project managers, and finally, to senior leadership or a dedicated conflict resolution committee if necessary. This tiered approach ensures that conflicts are addressed at the lowest possible level, where solutions are often easier to reach. However, having a formalized escalation path ensures that unresolved conflicts receive the attention they need from those with higher authority, which can be crucial for maintaining project progress. By creating clear stages, the team reduces the risk of prolonged conflicts that might otherwise stagnate without intervention.

Lastly, documenting each step in the conflict resolution process ensures transparency and provides a record that can be reviewed and refined over time. This documentation should include summaries of issues discussed, agreed-upon solutions, and any follow-up actions required. Maintaining these records not only aids in accountability but also serves as a reference point for similar future conflicts. Patterns may emerge over time, highlighting recurring issues that could be addressed proactively. Regularly reviewing and updating the conflict resolution process based on these insights allows the team to continuously improve their approach, enhancing both current and future collaborations. Structured documentation and regular reviews create an adaptable process, ensuring the conflict resolution framework remains relevant to the unique dynamics of each partnership.

Fostering Alignment Between Internal and Third-Party Goals

Fostering alignment between internal and third-party goals is crucial for the successful collaboration of project teams. Effective alignment begins with a clear understanding of each team's objectives, expectations, and strategic priorities. Internal teams may focus on company-specific goals, quality standards, and deadlines, while third-party vendors or partners often prioritize deliverable completion, compliance with contractual terms, and maintaining efficient workflows to support multiple clients. To bridge these perspectives, it's essential to conduct a series of joint goal-setting meetings at the start of the project. These sessions should explore and clarify both parties' priorities, identifying where they overlap and where they diverge. Documenting and openly sharing these goals ensures that each team appreciates the other's objectives, laying the groundwork for collaboration rather than potential misalignment or misunderstandings later.

Aligning objectives is not a one-time task; it requires ongoing communication and regular check-ins to stay synchronized. Scheduled alignment meetings, or "syncs," should occur at key project milestones or whenever significant changes arise, allowing both parties to assess whether they remain on track with shared objectives. These syncs should include discussions on goal progress, emerging issues, and any necessary adjustments to initial plans. During these meetings, both teams should be encouraged to voice concerns and suggest modifications, fostering an environment where course corrections are seen as part of the natural project evolution rather than as setbacks. By making alignment part of the ongoing workflow, internal and third-party teams become more adaptable, ensuring that changes in one team's goals do not disrupt the overall project trajectory.

Building trust between internal and third-party teams is another critical component in sustaining alignment. Trust can be established by consistently following through on commitments, providing transparency in project updates, and openly sharing relevant information. For example, internal teams can share performance metrics, customer feedback, or end-user requirements that may influence the project's direction. This level of openness signals to third-party teams that they are valued partners, rather than simply service providers, and that their insights are integral to the project's success. Third-party teams, in turn, can reciprocate by offering insights from their areas of expertise, such as emerging industry trends or advanced technologies, that could benefit the project. This exchange helps reinforce a mutual respect that drives alignment beyond contractual obligations, encouraging both teams to work as cohesive units with a shared purpose.

Lastly, cultivating a sense of shared accountability is essential in keeping both teams invested in the alignment process. When both internal and third-party teams feel responsible for the project's outcomes, they are more likely to take initiative in resolving alignment issues and ensuring goal cohesion. A shared accountability framework can be established by assigning joint ownership over critical deliverables, which encourages cross-team collaboration and collective problem-solving. Additionally, setting up shared performance metrics—such as project timelines, quality benchmarks, or customer satisfaction scores—gives both teams a common standard to work toward. By making these metrics visible and regularly reviewed, both teams stay informed of their collective progress, fostering a sense of shared purpose that reinforces alignment even amid the dynamic challenges of the project. Through mutual goal setting, continuous communication, trust-building, and shared accountability, internal and third-party teams can stay aligned and drive project success in a coordinated and efficient manner.

Encouraging Open Communication and Transparency

Encouraging open communication and transparency is essential for fostering a collaborative relationship between internal teams and third-party partners. Transparency begins with clearly defined channels for sharing updates, challenges, and decisions, ensuring both parties are equally informed and involved in the project's progress. Establishing these channels early on prevents information silos, where critical updates are accessible only to one party, potentially leading to delays or misunderstandings. Effective channels for open communication include regular status meetings, shared project dashboards, and collaborative tools that give all team members real-time access to the latest information. By making communication straightforward and accessible, internal and external teams build a foundation of trust and collaboration that enables proactive responses to project needs and changes.

Open communication also entails creating a culture where team members feel comfortable discussing challenges and uncertainties. In high-stakes projects, internal and third-party teams might hesitate to share obstacles out of fear that it could impact perceptions of their expertise or reliability. However, fostering a safe space for open dialogue encourages teams to be transparent about potential setbacks or risks early on, allowing both sides to work together on solutions rather than scrambling to address issues after they become critical. Leaders on both sides should model transparency by openly discussing their own uncertainties or adjusting expectations when necessary. This openness reduces the likelihood of misaligned expectations, as all parties are aware of the project's true status and can make informed, collaborative decisions.

A culture of transparency extends to handling adjustments and feedback throughout the project. As projects evolve, both internal and third-party teams may encounter situations requiring modifications to initial plans or deliverables. Encouraging transparent communication around these adjustments—whether they involve shifting timelines, altering technical requirements, or adapting to new client demands—ensures that all stakeholders stay aligned with the project's current reality. When changes arise, both parties should share their perspectives on the potential impact of these modifications, including any constraints or concerns. This practice ensures that decisions are made with comprehensive input, balancing both teams' needs and fostering a collaborative approach to overcoming challenges.

Regular feedback loops strengthen transparency by allowing both internal and third-party teams to assess the quality and effectiveness of their collaboration continuously. Instituting feedback mechanisms, such as retrospectives at major milestones, anonymous surveys, or direct discussions with team leads, provides an ongoing opportunity to review communication practices, identify areas for improvement, and celebrate successes. These feedback sessions allow both teams to address any tensions or misunderstandings before they grow into significant issues. Moreover, feedback loops reinforce the commitment to mutual respect and transparency, as they demonstrate that both parties value open communication and are willing to adapt based on collective experiences. Over time, regular, transparent feedback helps refine the communication process, creating a collaborative environment where internal and third-party teams work seamlessly toward shared project objectives.

CULTIVATING A COLLABORATIVE CULTURE FOR CONFLICT RESOLUTION

Cultivating a collaborative culture for conflict resolution is a vital element in sustaining productive relationships with third-party teams. Building this culture starts with a commitment to seeing conflicts as opportunities for growth rather than disruptions. Both internal teams and external partners benefit from viewing disagreements as a chance to improve processes, clarify expectations, and ultimately enhance project outcomes. Leaders play a pivotal role in shaping this perspective by encouraging a mindset of curiosity and constructive problem-solving. When conflict arises, they can set a positive tone by guiding discussions toward shared goals rather than individual grievances, creating a sense that everyone is working on the same side to overcome obstacles. This approach not only improves conflict resolution but also strengthens the partnership by emphasizing mutual respect and shared purpose.

To embed this collaborative culture, it's essential to establish shared guidelines and principles for managing disagreements. By defining conflict resolution protocols in advance, both teams know what to expect when issues arise, reducing the tendency for conflicts to escalate. For instance, teams might agree on a structured escalation path where minor issues are addressed directly between team members, while more significant concerns are brought to a joint leadership discussion. These guidelines should prioritize open dialogue, empathy, and an unbiased assessment of the conflict's root causes. Encouraging both parties to approach conflicts with empathy—striving to understand the pressures and perspectives of others—helps humanize disagreements and reduces defensiveness. Documenting these protocols within the project framework reinforces their importance and provides a reference point for conflict resolution.

Active listening is another cornerstone of a collaborative culture, especially during conflict resolution. When team members feel genuinely heard, they're more likely to be open to compromise and less likely to harbor lingering frustration. Encouraging participants to listen without interrupting or formulating responses prematurely can lead to more nuanced discussions, as underlying concerns often come to light when individuals have the space to express themselves fully. Facilitators, whether from internal teams or third-party groups, can help by ensuring each voice is respected and by guiding conversations back to the key issues rather than allowing discussions to veer into personal or emotional territory. This level of structured listening fosters a collaborative environment that values understanding and empathy, which are instrumental in achieving lasting resolutions.

Empowering all team members to take ownership of conflict resolution promotes a proactive, rather than reactive, approach to collaboration. In a culture of collaborative ownership, everyone—from project leads to individual contributors—recognizes that they have both the right and the responsibility to address issues constructively. This empowerment can be encouraged through regular training sessions on conflict resolution skills, as well as open discussions about recent challenges and how they were addressed. When teams feel equipped to handle conflicts directly, they are less likely to avoid difficult conversations or rely on hierarchical escalation, leading to faster, more effective solutions. Additionally, this proactive culture builds confidence and accountability, as team members develop the skills to navigate disagreements without jeopardizing the relationship.

Recognizing and celebrating successful conflict resolution reinforces a collaborative culture and highlights the value of working through differences. Acknowledging instances where both internal and third-party teams have overcome disagreements to achieve project goals demonstrates the positive impact of effective conflict management. Whether through formal recognition in team meetings or informal acknowledgments in project updates, these moments emphasize that overcoming conflict can be a shared achievement, not a burden. This celebration of success encourages both parties to view future conflicts with optimism, knowing that they have a tested approach to resolving them. Over time, these practices create a resilient and collaborative partnership where conflicts are seen as manageable challenges, and both internal and third-party teams are aligned in their commitment to achieving project success together.

Chapter 5: Navigating Company Policies and Internal Communication Standards

Corporate policies and guidelines serve as the backbone of structured communication within organizations, particularly in IT projects where precision and clarity are paramount. These policies are formalized rules established to govern how teams interact, share information, and make decisions. Guidelines, on the other hand, translate these rules into actionable frameworks, offering practical steps for employees to follow. Together, they aim to create consistency across diverse teams and ensure that communication aligns with organizational values, industry standards, and project objectives. While they may seem bureaucratic, policies and guidelines are essential tools for driving efficiency and reducing ambiguity in complex projects.

One of the most critical roles corporate policies play is in setting clear expectations for communication. By defining protocols for interactions—whether through emails, meetings, or reports—organizations minimize the risk of misunderstandings. For instance, an email policy may dictate response times or specify how to format subject lines to ensure messages are prioritized correctly. Guidelines for meetings might require structured agendas and defined action items to enhance productivity. In IT projects, where multiple stakeholders often operate under tight deadlines, these standardized practices prevent miscommunication and help keep projects on track. Without these rules, teams risk falling into chaos, with unclear messages leading to delays, errors, or even conflict.

Corporate policies also ensure compliance with broader legal, regulatory, and ethical standards. Many IT projects operate in sectors governed by stringent regulations, such as healthcare, finance, or data protection. Adherence to policies like those governing data privacy (e.g., GDPR or HIPAA) is non-negotiable, as violations can result in significant fines or reputational damage. Policies in these contexts dictate how sensitive information is shared, stored, and documented, ensuring that communication remains secure and compliant. For IT professionals, understanding these requirements is crucial—not just for project success, but for safeguarding their organizations from legal risks and maintaining the trust of clients and stakeholders.

Importantly, corporate policies are not merely about imposing restrictions; they also act as enablers of collaboration and efficiency. By offering clear guidelines on how to document progress, escalate issues, or seek approvals, they streamline workflows and promote accountability. For example, a policy requiring weekly status updates might initially feel like extra work for team members. However, over time, it ensures that all parties—managers, clients, and team leads—remain aligned, reducing the likelihood of surprises or misunderstandings. When teams embrace these structures, communication becomes more predictable and effective, laying the groundwork for smoother project execution.

Understanding the role of corporate policies and guidelines is therefore essential for IT professionals. Far from being obstacles, these tools are designed to simplify processes, create alignment, and ensure that communication is both effective and compliant. By viewing them as resources rather than constraints, project managers and team members can unlock their full potential, using them to facilitate clarity, foster trust, and drive successful outcomes.

TYPES OF POLICIES RELEVANT TO IT COMMUNICATION

In the fast-paced and complex world of IT projects, various types of corporate policies play a critical role in shaping how communication unfolds within and across teams. These policies ensure that interactions are consistent, secure, and aligned with organizational standards, while also addressing the unique challenges posed by the technical nature of IT work. From safeguarding sensitive information to promoting efficiency in cross-functional collaboration, understanding the different types of policies that influence IT communication is essential for project success.

One of the most significant categories is data privacy and security policies, which govern how sensitive information is handled and communicated. In an age of increasing cyber threats and regulatory scrutiny, these policies ensure that IT professionals adhere to standards like the General Data Protection Regulation (GDPR), the Health Insurance Portability and Accountability Act (HIPAA), or other industry-specific frameworks. For example, a data-sharing policy may restrict the transmission of certain files over unsecured channels or mandate encryption for all email attachments containing confidential information. These policies not only protect organizational assets but also build client and stakeholder trust by demonstrating a commitment to data integrity.

Another crucial area is compliance and regulatory communication policies, which ensure that IT projects meet industry standards and legal requirements.

These policies often dictate how project updates, performance metrics, or financial reports are presented to external regulators or auditors. For instance, in financial services, communication policies might specify the format and frequency of compliance reports to meet the stringent demands of regulatory bodies. Adhering to these guidelines is non-negotiable, as even minor lapses in communication can result in hefty fines or reputational damage. By clearly defining how regulatory information should be documented and shared, these policies help avoid missteps and keep projects in good standing.

Internal communication policies and guidelines also play a vital role in fostering seamless collaboration within organizations. These policies standardize everyday interactions, such as meeting protocols, email etiquette, and the use of collaboration tools like Microsoft Teams or Slack. For example, a meeting policy might require detailed agendas to be shared in advance, ensuring that discussions remain focused and productive. Similarly, guidelines for email communication might include specific subject line formats or response time expectations to streamline correspondence. By establishing these norms, internal communication policies reduce misunderstandings, promote accountability, and help teams work more efficiently.

Lastly, hierarchy and approval policies influence the flow of information within IT projects. These policies define the levels of authority required to review or approve decisions, such as changes to project scope, budgets, or timelines. For instance, an IT project might have a policy requiring all scope changes to be approved by a steering committee, ensuring that critical decisions are thoroughly vetted. While these policies can sometimes slow down processes, they provide a necessary layer of oversight, preventing hasty decisions that could jeopardize project success. Understanding and adhering to these hierarchical structures is crucial for maintaining transparency and fostering trust among stakeholders.

Together, these policies create a framework for effective and secure communication in IT projects. By understanding the nuances of each type, IT professionals can navigate organizational expectations more confidently, ensuring that their communication aligns with both internal and external requirements. This alignment not only enhances efficiency but also strengthens the overall credibility of the project, paving the way for successful outcomes.

Challenges in Navigating Policies

While corporate policies and guidelines provide essential structure for communication within IT projects, they often present challenges that can impede their implementation. For IT professionals, balancing the rigid requirements of policies with the dynamic nature of projects can be a delicate task. Missteps in navigating these policies can lead to inefficiencies, strained relationships, or even project failure. Recognizing and addressing these challenges is crucial for fostering effective communication and achieving organizational goals.

One significant challenge is the complexity and volume of policies that IT professionals must navigate. Large organizations often have an extensive array of policies, ranging from data security and compliance to internal communication protocols. For IT projects, which may involve cross-departmental collaboration or external stakeholders, the sheer number of applicable guidelines can be overwhelming. This complexity can lead to confusion about which policies apply in specific situations. For example, team members may struggle to distinguish between general corporate communication policies and project-specific protocols, resulting in inconsistent practices or inadvertent non-compliance.

Another obstacle is resistance to policy adherence among team members and stakeholders. IT professionals often work with diverse groups, including technical experts, business stakeholders, and external vendors, each with their own communication styles and priorities. Policies, especially those perceived as overly rigid or time-consuming, may be met with resistance. For instance, requiring detailed documentation for every communication may frustrate team members focused on speed and efficiency. Similarly, external vendors might not see the value in following an organization's internal policies, leading to misaligned practices and potential conflicts.

Adapting policies to dynamic project needs poses an additional challenge. IT projects are inherently fluid, with priorities, timelines, and resources often shifting in response to new information or changing circumstances. Static policies can feel out of sync with this dynamic environment, creating friction when they hinder adaptability. For example, a policy requiring formal approval for every change request might delay critical decisions in an Agile project that thrives on iterative and rapid adjustments. Striking a balance between adherence to policy and the flexibility needed for project success can be difficult to achieve.

Lastly, there is the issue of inadequate training and communication around policies. In many organizations, policies are often disseminated as lengthy documents or through brief onboarding sessions, leaving employees with limited understanding of their practical implications. IT professionals may be unclear about how to apply certain guidelines to specific scenarios, especially when working on unique or high-stakes projects. This lack of clarity can result in inconsistent application, with some teams adhering strictly to policies while others inadvertently bypass them. Over time, such discrepancies can erode trust and efficiency within the organization.

Navigating these challenges requires a proactive approach that combines clear communication, ongoing training, and a willingness to adapt. Organizations must ensure that policies are not only well-defined but also accessible, relevant, and aligned with the realities of IT project work. By addressing these hurdles head-on, IT professionals can leverage policies as tools for success rather than viewing them as obstacles to be avoided.

BENEFITS OF POLICY-ADHERENT COMMUNICATION

Adhering to corporate policies in communication brings a range of significant benefits to IT projects and the organizations overseeing them. Far from being restrictive, these guidelines provide a foundation for consistency, accountability, and success in complex and often unpredictable environments. By fostering clear and structured communication, policy adherence enhances collaboration, reduces risks, and contributes to the overall effectiveness of IT teams and stakeholders.

One of the most immediate benefits of policy-adherent communication is the reduction of misunderstandings and errors. Policies establish clear expectations for how information should be shared, ensuring that all parties involved in a project receive accurate and consistent updates. For example, a policy requiring detailed meeting minutes and action items ensures that decisions are well-documented and accessible to everyone. This level of transparency minimizes the likelihood of miscommunication, which can lead to missed deadlines or poorly executed deliverables. For IT projects involving multiple teams or external vendors, this consistency is crucial for maintaining alignment and avoiding costly mistakes.

Another advantage lies in enhanced compliance with legal, regulatory, and ethical standards. Policies governing areas such as data protection, intellectual property, and financial reporting ensure that communication practices align with external requirements. For instance, adhering to policies related to GDPR or HIPAA protects sensitive data while meeting regulatory obligations. This not only safeguards the organization from fines and legal challenges but also bolsters its reputation among clients and stakeholders. Policy adherence demonstrates a commitment to ethical practices, which is increasingly valued in industries reliant on trust and transparency.

Policy-driven communication also promotes efficiency and accountability within IT projects. By providing standardized processes for reporting progress, escalating issues, or seeking approvals, policies eliminate ambiguity and streamline workflows. For example, a communication escalation policy may define exactly when and how team members should report critical project risks to higher management. This clarity allows teams to act decisively, ensuring that potential obstacles are addressed promptly. Furthermore, adherence to policies fosters accountability by assigning specific roles and responsibilities, reducing the likelihood of tasks being overlooked or duplicated.

Policy-adherent communication strengthens trust and credibility among stakeholders. When teams consistently follow established guidelines, it sends a signal of professionalism and reliability. Stakeholders, whether internal or external, are more likely to trust an organization that communicates predictably and transparently. For IT projects, where stakeholder buy-in is critical to success, this trust can make a significant difference in securing support, funding, or future opportunities. Policy adherence also reassures clients that the organization prioritizes quality and compliance, reinforcing long-term partnerships and repeat business.

In sum, adhering to corporate policies in communication offers a wealth of benefits that extend beyond individual projects. By reducing errors, ensuring compliance, increasing efficiency, and fostering trust, policy-driven communication creates a solid foundation for success in IT initiatives. Organizations that embrace and promote these practices not only enhance their operational effectiveness but also build a culture of accountability and excellence that supports sustained growth and innovation.

REAL-WORLD EXAMPLES AND CASE STUDIES

Real-world examples and case studies provide valuable insights into the impact of policy-adherent communication in IT projects, showcasing both its challenges and rewards. These narratives help illustrate how communication aligned with corporate guidelines can shape project outcomes, prevent critical failures, and build a foundation for long-term success. By examining real scenarios, IT professionals can better understand the practical applications of policy adherence and draw lessons to apply in their own environments.

One illustrative case is a global financial services firm that implemented strict data security policies to comply with GDPR regulations. During a large-scale IT infrastructure upgrade, the company mandated that all interdepartmental communication involving customer data follow specific encryption protocols. This included emails, shared files, and virtual meeting platforms. While some team members initially found the additional steps cumbersome, adhering to these policies ultimately prevented a major breach when a phishing attack targeted the project team. By ensuring that sensitive information was protected at every stage, the organization avoided both regulatory penalties and damage to its reputation, highlighting the value of security-focused communication policies.

Another example comes from a multinational tech company that faced challenges with vendor communication during the rollout of a new enterprise software solution. The organization's internal policies required all third-party interactions to be documented in a centralized collaboration tool. However, some external vendors resisted using the platform, preferring informal communication methods such as direct emails or verbal agreements. This misalignment led to delays in deliverables and confusion over project requirements. Recognizing the issue, the company reinforced its policy through targeted training sessions and added clauses to vendor contracts mandating adherence to the collaboration tool. As a result, communication became more streamlined, and the project progressed without further disruptions, underscoring the importance of policy-aligned practices in external collaborations.

A notable success story involves a healthcare organization implementing an electronic health record (EHR) system across multiple facilities. The project team adhered closely to communication policies that outlined escalation procedures for resolving interdepartmental conflicts. When disagreements arose between IT teams and medical staff regarding system functionality, the policy-mandated process facilitated structured discussions and timely resolutions. By adhering to the predefined guidelines, the organization avoided delays and ensured that all stakeholder concerns were addressed systematically.

This adherence not only kept the project on track but also fostered a collaborative environment, demonstrating how communication policies can bridge gaps between diverse groups.

Conversely, a cautionary tale highlights the consequences of disregarding policies. In a government IT project focused on modernizing public services, failure to follow communication protocols led to significant setbacks. The project's policies required that all updates to the project scope be formally approved by a steering committee. However, one team bypassed this requirement, implementing changes based on verbal agreements with a single stakeholder. When the changes resulted in budget overruns and delays, the lack of documentation made it impossible to pinpoint accountability or justify the decisions to senior management. This misstep emphasized the importance of adhering to established policies to maintain transparency and control.

These real-world examples illustrate the critical role that policy-adherent communication plays in IT projects. By following structured guidelines, organizations can mitigate risks, enhance collaboration, and ensure that projects meet their objectives. At the same time, these cases underscore the potential pitfalls of neglecting policies, serving as reminders of the value of consistency, clarity, and accountability in all aspects of communication.

ACTIONABLE TAKEAWAYS FOR IT PROFESSIONALS

For IT professionals, navigating corporate policies and communication standards is not just a matter of compliance—it is a strategic advantage that can drive the success of projects and careers alike. While understanding the theory behind these policies is important, applying them effectively requires practical, actionable steps. By adopting the following takeaways, IT professionals can align their communication practices with organizational policies while fostering collaboration and efficiency.

First, prioritize familiarity with key policies and guidelines. Every IT professional should dedicate time to understanding the corporate policies relevant to their role, from data security and compliance to communication protocols. Start by reviewing policy documents provided during onboarding or training sessions, and seek clarification on areas of ambiguity. For example, familiarize yourself with rules surrounding project documentation, escalation processes, and stakeholder reporting. Proactively staying informed about updates or changes to these policies ensures you remain compliant and reduces the risk of missteps during critical project phases.

Second, adapt communication strategies to integrate policy requirements seamlessly into daily workflows. This might involve incorporating policy-compliant tools and templates into routine practices. For instance, if your organization mandates that project updates follow a specific format, create a reusable template to save time while ensuring adherence. Similarly, leverage technology like collaboration platforms or automated reporting tools that align with corporate standards. Integrating these resources into your workflow can simplify compliance and improve the quality and consistency of communication.

Third, advocate for clarity and inclusivity in applying policies across diverse teams and stakeholders. IT projects often involve collaboration with external vendors, non-technical departments, or geographically dispersed teams, each of whom may interpret policies differently. Take the lead in ensuring that policies are communicated clearly and that all parties understand their responsibilities. For example, when working with external partners, provide an orientation on your organization's communication protocols or include specific policy requirements in contracts. A clear understanding of expectations minimizes confusion and fosters smoother collaboration.

Fourth, use policies as a tool for building trust and credibility with stakeholders. Demonstrating a commitment to policy adherence signals professionalism and accountability. For example, when delivering updates to stakeholders, reference applicable policies to highlight your alignment with organizational priorities, such as data privacy or project governance. Consistently following policies not only reassures stakeholders of your diligence but also positions you as a reliable leader capable of navigating complex organizational structures.

Finally, be proactive in identifying and addressing gaps between policy and practice. IT professionals are often on the front lines of spotting where policies may fall short in addressing real-world project needs. If a specific policy feels outdated or misaligned with agile project methodologies, raise the issue with leadership and propose refinements. For example, suggest revisions to escalation protocols to make them more flexible for time-sensitive decisions in Agile sprints. By offering constructive feedback, you contribute to the continuous improvement of communication standards while positioning yourself as a proactive and solutions-oriented team member.

By implementing these actionable strategies, IT professionals can turn corporate policies into enablers rather than obstacles. In doing so, they not only ensure compliance but also enhance their effectiveness as communicators and collaborators, ultimately driving better outcomes for projects and teams.

Strategies for aligning team practices with organizational standards.

In the fast-paced world of IT, where teams often juggle complex deliverables, competing priorities, and cross-functional collaborations, aligning team practices with organizational communication standards is not merely a procedural requirement—it is a strategic imperative. Effective alignment serves as a bridge between individual team operations and broader organizational objectives, ensuring consistency, clarity, and accountability in project execution. It is the foundation upon which successful communication, collaboration, and compliance are built.

When team practices deviate from organizational standards, the consequences can ripple across a project. Misaligned communication can lead to unclear expectations, inconsistent reporting, and inefficient workflows, all of which undermine trust with stakeholders. For example, a team that adopts its own ad-hoc approach to project updates might inadvertently exclude critical details required by corporate governance policies, leading to costly delays or compliance risks. Without alignment, even the most capable teams can find themselves at odds with organizational expectations.

However, aligning team practices with organizational standards is not about imposing rigidity or stifling creativity. Instead, it involves creating a cohesive framework that allows teams to operate efficiently while adhering to established guidelines. This balance is particularly important in IT environments, where teams often use flexible methodologies like Agile within organizations governed by more structured frameworks like ITIL or PMP. The key lies in customizing organizational standards to suit team dynamics without compromising the intent or integrity of the policies.

Alignment is about enabling teams to function as effective contributors to the organization's goals. It fosters a sense of shared purpose, streamlines communication across hierarchical and departmental boundaries, and provides teams with the tools they need to navigate complexities confidently. When achieved, alignment transforms policies from restrictive rules into empowering guidelines, helping teams work more cohesively while delivering consistent value to stakeholders and clients.

IDENTIFYING GAPS BETWEEN TEAM PRACTICES AND ORGANIZATIONAL STANDARDS

The first step in achieving alignment between team practices and organizational communication standards is to identify where misalignments exist. Gaps can emerge for various reasons, including the diversity of team workflows, unclear interpretation of policies, or the evolution of team practices that outpace updates to organizational guidelines. Recognizing these gaps is essential to bridge them effectively and ensure both compliance and operational efficiency.

One common source of misalignment arises from variations in team methodologies. For example, a software development team using Agile may prioritize rapid, informal communication through daily standups and instant messaging tools, while the organization's standards might require more structured reporting formats and documented approvals for key decisions. Without reconciling these differences, teams risk creating discrepancies that could lead to confusion or conflict during audits, stakeholder reviews, or cross-team collaborations.

Another challenge is incomplete or inconsistent adoption of organizational standards. Teams often adopt only parts of corporate guidelines that seem immediately relevant, overlooking critical components due to a lack of clarity or perceived irrelevance. For instance, a team may focus on meeting data security protocols for their deliverables but neglect to follow escalation procedures outlined in corporate communication policies, resulting in delays during crisis situations. Such partial adherence can weaken overall compliance and impact the project's success.

Identifying these gaps requires a deliberate and systematic approach. One effective method is to conduct policy audits, where teams compare their existing practices against organizational standards. This can involve reviewing documentation, communication workflows, and meeting procedures to pinpoint areas of divergence. Engaging team members in this process ensures that the evaluation considers both the policy requirements and the practical realities of day-to-day operations.

Additionally, feedback from stakeholders and collaborators can provide valuable insights into areas where team practices may be falling short of organizational expectations. External perspectives often reveal overlooked inconsistencies, such as inadequate stakeholder updates or missed opportunities to involve cross-functional teams in key decisions. Collecting this feedback through surveys, retrospectives, or project reviews can highlight specific issues that need to be addressed.

Identifying gaps is not about assigning blame or rigidly enforcing rules; rather, it is about understanding where misalignments occur and why. By doing so, teams can uncover opportunities to improve their practices, enhance communication, and ensure their operations are fully aligned with the broader objectives and standards of their organization.

CUSTOMIZING ORGANIZATIONAL STANDARDS TO FIT TEAM DYNAMICS

Organizational communication standards often serve as a guiding framework, outlining best practices and expectations for maintaining consistency across projects. However, these standards can sometimes feel too rigid or broad for the specific needs of individual teams. Customizing these guidelines to align with a team's unique dynamics is essential for fostering both compliance and operational efficiency. This balance ensures that standards enhance, rather than hinder, a team's productivity and creativity.

Every team operates within its own context, shaped by factors such as project complexity, technical expertise, and the interpersonal dynamics of its members. For example, a geographically dispersed IT team may rely heavily on asynchronous communication, while an on-site operations team might favor real-time discussions. Attempting to apply a one-size-fits-all communication policy to such varied scenarios can lead to frustration and inefficiencies. Customization allows teams to adapt these overarching policies into workflows and tools that suit their specific needs while maintaining alignment with organizational goals.

A practical approach to customization involves tailoring **reporting structures and communication tools**. For instance, if an organization mandates weekly status reports in a standardized template, an Agile team might integrate this requirement into their sprint review meetings, ensuring the information aligns with corporate expectations without disrupting their iterative process. Similarly, teams can use platforms like Slack, Jira, or Microsoft Teams to meet documentation requirements dynamically, automating parts of the process to save time and reduce manual effort.

Another key strategy is fostering **collaborative policy adaptation**. Teams and leadership should work together to interpret organizational standards in ways that address both compliance and practical application. For example, ITIL's communication guidelines might require extensive documentation for service incidents, but a team focused on rapid response could streamline this process by implementing concise yet compliant reporting formats. Involving team members in these decisions not only ensures practicality but also increases buy-in and adherence.

Customization should always prioritize the intent behind the standards rather than focusing solely on literal compliance. The goal is to create practices that uphold the principles of transparency, accountability, and effective communication while allowing for flexibility. By aligning organizational expectations with the realities of team operations, customization transforms static policies into dynamic tools that empower teams to achieve their objectives more effectively.

IMPLEMENTING TRAINING AND ONBOARDING PROGRAMS

Effective alignment of team practices with organizational standards begins with comprehensive training and onboarding programs. These initiatives are essential for equipping team members with the knowledge and tools they need to navigate corporate communication policies confidently and seamlessly integrate them into their workflows. Whether for new hires or existing employees, structured training ensures that everyone understands not only the requirements of these standards but also their relevance to day-to-day operations.

Training programs should start with a clear explanation of **organizational communication policies** and their objectives. Rather than presenting policies as rigid rules, framing them as enablers of project success fosters engagement and buy-in. For instance, emphasizing how adherence to specific documentation standards can prevent delays in stakeholder approvals or improve audit outcomes connects these guidelines to practical benefits. This approach helps team members see policies as integral to achieving their goals rather than as bureaucratic obstacles.

Beyond theoretical understanding, training should focus on **real-world application**. Simulations, case studies, and role-playing exercises can help team members practice applying communication standards in typical project scenarios, such as resolving conflicts with stakeholders or providing status updates in compliance with corporate templates. For example, an exercise could involve drafting a project report that balances technical detail with accessibility for non-technical stakeholders, reinforcing the importance of clarity and alignment with organizational expectations.

Onboarding programs for new team members should include a strong focus on communication standards to ensure a smooth transition into the organization's culture. A structured onboarding plan might provide new hires with resources such as policy guides, templates, and checklists, as well as mentorship from experienced colleagues. Pairing new employees with a seasoned "communication champion" within the team can accelerate their ability to adopt and implement standards effectively, while also fostering collaboration and knowledge sharing.

Continuous learning should be a cornerstone of any training initiative. Policies and practices evolve, particularly in dynamic IT environments where new tools and methodologies frequently emerge. Regular workshops, refresher courses, and updates on changes to organizational standards help teams stay informed and adaptable. Embedding feedback mechanisms into training programs also ensures they remain relevant and effective, as team members can voice challenges and suggest improvements to the training content.

By investing in well-designed training and onboarding programs, organizations can establish a strong foundation for aligning team practices with corporate communication standards. These efforts not only promote compliance but also empower teams to communicate more effectively, contributing to smoother operations and better project outcomes.

LEVERAGING TECHNOLOGY TO BRIDGE THE GAP

In modern IT environments, technology plays a crucial role in aligning team practices with organizational communication standards. As teams navigate the complexities of collaboration across geographies, time zones, and diverse roles, communication tools and platforms provide the necessary infrastructure to streamline workflows, ensure consistency, and promote adherence to corporate policies. By strategically leveraging technology, organizations can bridge the gap between individual team practices and broader organizational standards.

One of the primary benefits of technology is its ability to standardize communication processes. Tools like Jira, Confluence, or Trello can help enforce uniform reporting and documentation practices across teams. For example, an organization might implement templates for status updates or incident reports directly within these platforms, ensuring that all team members follow the same format and meet the required level of detail. By embedding organizational standards into everyday tools, compliance becomes an integral part of team operations rather than an additional task.

Technology also facilitates real-time communication and collaboration, which is especially critical in dynamic IT projects. Platforms such as Microsoft Teams, Slack, and Zoom enable teams to coordinate instantly while offering features like shared channels, task tracking, and searchable histories that align with corporate guidelines. For instance, by setting up structured communication channels (e.g., "Project Updates" or "Incident Escalations"), organizations can ensure that critical information is shared in the correct context and remains accessible for future reference.

Another powerful use of technology is automating compliance and oversight. Many tools now offer workflow automation features that can help teams adhere to organizational standards effortlessly. For example, automated reminders for meeting deadlines, approval requests, or policy compliance reviews can minimize human error and reduce the administrative burden on team members. Integration between tools, such as syncing tasks from Jira to calendar applications, further enhances productivity while maintaining alignment with organizational expectations.

Moreover, technology supports data-driven monitoring and feedback. Analytics dashboards in tools like Power BI or custom reporting systems can track communication metrics such as response times, documentation completeness, and stakeholder engagement. These insights enable organizations to identify gaps, recognize patterns, and provide targeted interventions to improve alignment. For example, if a team consistently misses deadlines for project reports, managers can use data to address the issue proactively through training or process adjustments.

While technology offers immense potential, its implementation must be deliberate and tailored to the organization's needs. Overloading teams with too many tools or features can lead to inefficiencies and resistance. Instead, organizations should focus on adopting platforms that integrate seamlessly into existing workflows and address specific communication challenges. With the right tools and strategies in place, technology becomes a powerful enabler of alignment, empowering teams to communicate effectively while adhering to organizational standards.

Monitoring and Continuous Improvement

Aligning team practices with organizational standards is not a one-time effort—it requires ongoing monitoring and a commitment to continuous improvement. This approach ensures that communication practices remain effective, relevant, and adaptable to changing organizational needs or project dynamics. By embedding mechanisms for evaluation and refinement, organizations can sustain alignment while fostering a culture of accountability and growth.

Monitoring begins with establishing key performance indicators (KPIs) for communication practices. These might include metrics such as the timeliness and accuracy of updates, adherence to reporting formats, or stakeholder satisfaction with communication processes. For example, an IT team might track the percentage of status reports submitted on time or the resolution time for queries escalated through established communication channels. By quantifying these aspects, organizations gain objective insights into how well teams are complying with communication standards.

Regular feedback loops are essential for identifying areas of improvement. Feedback from stakeholders, team members, and clients provides valuable qualitative data on the effectiveness of current practices. For instance, if stakeholders report frequent confusion over technical updates, it may signal the need for clearer documentation standards or additional training. Encouraging open dialogue about challenges also empowers teams to share insights and propose solutions, fostering a collaborative approach to improvement.

Organizations should also leverage technology to automate aspects of monitoring and reporting. Tools like Jira, Slack, or Microsoft Teams can generate logs of communication activity, such as meeting attendance, task updates, or file sharing. These records help managers assess compliance without imposing additional administrative burdens on the team. Advanced analytics platforms can aggregate this data into actionable insights, identifying trends or bottlenecks that may not be immediately apparent.

Continuous improvement involves more than addressing current gaps—it requires a forward-looking perspective. Organizations should periodically review and update their communication standards to reflect evolving needs, such as new project methodologies, technologies, or regulatory requirements. For instance, as hybrid and remote work models become more prevalent, policies may need to adapt to emphasize asynchronous communication and virtual collaboration tools. Engaging teams in these updates ensures their practicality and encourages ownership of the refined processes.

Celebrating successes is another crucial component of continuous improvement. Recognizing teams or individuals who excel in aligning with communication standards reinforces positive behaviors and motivates others to follow suit. For example, highlighting a team's innovative approach to bridging stakeholder communication gaps can inspire similar practices across the organization. This recognition not only enhances morale but also demonstrates the tangible benefits of effective communication.

By prioritizing monitoring and continuous improvement, organizations can maintain alignment between team practices and organizational standards in a dynamic environment. This commitment to evolution ensures that communication remains a powerful tool for achieving project success while fostering adaptability and resilience within teams.

CASE STUDIES AND EXAMPLES

Exploring real-world scenarios helps contextualize how teams can align their practices with organizational standards effectively, revealing both challenges and solutions. Case studies and examples illustrate how organizations have implemented strategies to enhance communication and overcome obstacles, offering practical lessons for IT professionals.

Case Study 1: Implementing Standardized Reporting in an Agile Environment

A multinational software development company faced significant challenges in aligning its Agile team practices with the company's reporting standards. Teams worked independently using varied formats for sprint reports, causing confusion for senior management and stakeholders who needed consistent updates. To address this, the company introduced a centralized reporting template integrated into its Jira system. Each team was required to complete specific fields at the end of each sprint, covering key performance metrics, achievements, and blockers.

The transition initially met resistance, as teams perceived the new system as an additional burden. However, after a series of workshops emphasizing how the standard format would streamline decision-making and improve transparency, adoption improved. Within six months, stakeholders reported higher satisfaction with project updates, and teams found that the new process reduced the time spent on follow-up questions and clarifications. This example highlights the importance of both standardization and change management in aligning practices.

Case Study 2: Bridging Communication in a Remote IT Support Team
A global IT support team struggled with inconsistent communication when transitioning to a remote work model. Different time zones and communication platforms led to delayed responses and misaligned priorities. To address this, the company rolled out a unified communication policy that included clear guidelines on using tools like Microsoft Teams and Slack. It established a shared communication calendar with overlapping working hours for critical discussions and introduced automated workflows for assigning and tracking tickets.

These measures significantly improved response times and task completion rates. Employees noted that the structured approach reduced misunderstandings and provided clarity on expectations. The organization also conducted quarterly reviews to refine the communication policy, incorporating employee feedback to ensure its relevance and effectiveness.

Example: Adapting Corporate Policies to Project-Specific Needs
In another instance, a consulting firm managed a large-scale digital transformation project for a retail client. The client's strict corporate policies required extensive documentation for each deliverable, which the consulting team initially found cumbersome. To bridge this gap, the team adapted the client's documentation standards into a streamlined process using collaborative tools like Confluence and DocuSign. By creating pre-approved templates and automating approvals for repetitive tasks, the team maintained compliance while minimizing the administrative load.

This example underscores the importance of flexibility and innovation in applying organizational standards without compromising efficiency or project outcomes.

These case studies and examples demonstrate that aligning team practices with organizational standards is not without challenges but is achievable with thoughtful implementation. They highlight key lessons, such as the need for clear communication, adaptable processes, and regular review mechanisms, which IT professionals can apply to their contexts.

Leveraging tools and platforms to streamline communication and documentation.

In today's IT-driven world, tools and platforms are not just accessories but essential enablers of effective communication and documentation. They have transformed the way teams collaborate, making it easier to bridge gaps between geographically dispersed members, align with organizational standards, and maintain transparency with stakeholders. These digital solutions have evolved to address the complexities of modern IT projects, providing structured approaches to handle everything from daily updates to long-term deliverables.

Communication tools, such as Slack and Microsoft Teams, have redefined how information flows within and across teams. They allow for real-time messaging, video calls, and file sharing, ensuring that no detail is overlooked. Similarly, documentation platforms like Confluence and SharePoint offer centralized repositories where all project-related information is stored, tracked, and updated in real-time. These tools reduce the risk of miscommunication and ensure that critical information is readily available to all relevant stakeholders.

The importance of tools extends beyond operational efficiency—they also support compliance with organizational policies and standards. For instance, platforms can be configured to enforce naming conventions, approval workflows, or version control, ensuring that documentation meets both internal and external requirements. By automating mundane tasks and providing structured formats for communication, tools free up valuable time for IT professionals to focus on problem-solving and innovation.

However, the adoption of these tools is not without challenges. Teams must navigate issues like tool fatigue, over-complication, or resistance to change. A well-thought-out strategy is essential to ensure that the selected tools genuinely enhance productivity and do not become a source of frustration. This chapter explores the critical role that tools and platforms play in facilitating effective communication and documentation, providing IT professionals with the knowledge to choose, integrate, and leverage them successfully.

SELECTING THE RIGHT TOOLS FOR THE JOB

Choosing the appropriate tools for communication and documentation is a critical step in streamlining workflows and aligning team practices with organizational standards. The success of any IT project often hinges on the seamless exchange of information and the clarity of documentation. However, not all tools are created equal, and selecting the wrong one can lead to inefficiencies, frustration, and miscommunication. The key lies in identifying tools that address specific team needs while fitting into the broader organizational framework.

To begin, understanding the purpose each tool serves is essential. Communication tools such as Slack or Microsoft Teams are ideal for real-time discussions, quick updates, and collaborative brainstorming sessions. On the other hand, platforms like Jira and Trello specialize in project management, allowing teams to track tasks, monitor progress, and assign responsibilities. For documentation, tools like Confluence and SharePoint provide centralized, searchable repositories that ensure all team members and stakeholders can access up-to-date information at any time. Recognizing these distinct functionalities can help teams create a well-rounded toolkit.

Compatibility and integration are equally important factors to consider. The best tools work seamlessly with existing systems and platforms, reducing the need for manual data transfers or duplicated efforts. For instance, a project management tool that integrates with a communication platform can automatically notify team members about task updates, ensuring everyone stays informed. Additionally, tools should be scalable, accommodating the team's growth and increasing complexity of projects over time without requiring disruptive changes.

Ease of use and user adoption play significant roles in tool selection. Even the most feature-rich platform can fail if it is overly complex or lacks intuitive navigation. Conducting pilot tests, gathering feedback from team members, and involving end-users in the selection process can ensure that the chosen tools align with both technical requirements and user preferences. This collaborative approach not only boosts adoption rates but also fosters a sense of ownership among team members, making them more likely to fully leverage the tools.

Selecting the right tools for the job is more than a technical decision—it is a strategic investment in a team's ability to communicate effectively, document thoroughly, and succeed in delivering IT projects. By evaluating needs, prioritizing integration, and focusing on user experience, teams can build a toolkit that empowers them to achieve their goals with efficiency and clarity.

INTEGRATING TOOLS INTO TEAM WORKFLOWS

Selecting the right tools is only the first step; their real value lies in how effectively they are integrated into daily workflows. Tools that remain underutilized or disconnected from the team's core activities can hinder productivity rather than enhance it. Successful integration ensures that tools become a natural extension of the team's processes, streamlining communication, improving collaboration, and fostering adherence to organizational standards.

The first step in integration is mapping tools to specific workflows. Each tool should have a defined purpose within the team's operational framework. For example, project management platforms like Jira can be aligned with task tracking and sprint planning, while communication tools like Slack can serve as a hub for instant updates and discussions. Defining these roles prevents overlap and confusion, ensuring that team members know where to turn for particular tasks or information.

Automation plays a crucial role in embedding tools into workflows. Most modern platforms offer features like automated notifications, recurring reminders, and workflow triggers that eliminate repetitive manual tasks. For instance, integrating Jira with Slack can send real-time updates about task assignments or status changes, keeping everyone informed without requiring constant manual input. Similarly, documentation tools like Confluence can be configured to generate reminders for periodic updates or approvals, ensuring compliance with organizational standards.

Consistency is key to successful integration. Establishing standardized practices for using tools—such as naming conventions, folder structures, or protocols for updates—ensures that all team members interact with the platforms in a unified manner. Clear guidelines prevent inefficiencies and make it easier for new team members to onboard. Additionally, regular check-ins to review tool usage can help identify gaps or inefficiencies and provide opportunities for refinement.

Lastly, effective integration requires leadership and advocacy. Team leaders or designated champions can guide the adoption process, provide training, and address challenges. By modeling proper usage and demonstrating the benefits of the tools, leaders encourage their teams to embrace the platforms as indispensable parts of their workflow. Integration is not a one-time effort but an ongoing process that evolves alongside team dynamics and project demands.

By thoughtfully integrating tools into workflows, teams can unlock their full potential, turning them into powerful assets for communication, documentation, and project success. This deliberate approach ensures that technology serves as a facilitator rather than a barrier, driving efficiency and alignment across all aspects of IT operations.

PROMOTING TOOL ADOPTION ACROSS TEAMS

Introducing new tools into a team's workflow is not merely a technical process; it is a cultural and behavioral challenge. Even the most advanced and well-suited platforms can face resistance if team members do not see their value or find them difficult to use. Promoting tool adoption requires a strategic approach that combines education, engagement, and ongoing support to ensure the tools become an integral part of team operations.

The foundation of successful adoption lies in clear communication about the *why* behind the tools. Team members need to understand how the new platform will make their work easier, enhance collaboration, or reduce inefficiencies. Highlighting specific pain points—such as missed deadlines, fragmented updates, or inaccessible documentation—and showing how the tool addresses these issues can create a compelling case. Positioning the tool as a solution rather than an imposition fosters enthusiasm rather than resistance.

Training and onboarding are crucial steps in the adoption process. Customized training sessions tailored to different roles within the team can help ensure that everyone—from project managers to developers—understands how to leverage the tool for their specific needs. For example, project managers may focus on advanced reporting features, while team members might prioritize task tracking and communication capabilities. Hands-on workshops, step-by-step guides, and access to ongoing support resources can further solidify comfort with the platform.

Championing early adopters within the team can also accelerate adoption. These individuals can serve as ambassadors, demonstrating best practices and showcasing the benefits of the tool in real time. Early adopters can help bridge the gap between initial skepticism and full-scale adoption by acting as resources for their peers, answering questions, and troubleshooting minor issues. Their visible success with the tool can inspire others to follow suit.

Finally, promoting adoption is an iterative process. Gathering feedback regularly from team members is essential for identifying obstacles, refining workflows, and ensuring the tool meets its intended goals. Simple feedback mechanisms, such as surveys or focus groups, can uncover areas for improvement or highlight features that require more emphasis during training. Addressing this feedback promptly shows the team that their input is valued and builds trust in the tool and its benefits.

Promoting tool adoption is about more than implementing new software; it is about fostering a culture of collaboration and efficiency. By aligning the tool with team needs, providing robust support, and continuously adapting based on feedback, teams can seamlessly incorporate these platforms into their daily workflows and realize their full potential.

MAINTAINING CONSISTENCY THROUGH TEMPLATES AND AUTOMATION

Consistency is the cornerstone of effective communication and documentation in IT teams, and achieving it requires structured approaches that minimize human error and streamline repetitive processes. Templates and automation are invaluable tools for embedding uniformity into team workflows, ensuring that information is presented clearly, actions are executed reliably, and organizational standards are consistently met.

Templates serve as predefined frameworks that simplify the creation of recurring documents and communication artifacts. For instance, a status update template might include sections for key accomplishments, current challenges, and next steps, ensuring that all updates follow the same structure regardless of who prepares them. Similarly, templates for meeting agendas, project plans, or stakeholder reports standardize the way critical information is shared. This not only saves time but also enhances clarity, as stakeholders know exactly where to find the details they need.

Automation complements templates by reducing manual effort in repetitive tasks. Many tools, such as Jira, Confluence, or Microsoft Teams, offer automation features that can trigger actions based on predefined rules. For example, a project management platform can automatically generate weekly status reports using data already entered by team members, or send reminders to update documentation before key milestones. Such automation eliminates the risk of missed deadlines or overlooked details while freeing team members to focus on more strategic activities.

The integration of templates and automation also strengthens adherence to organizational standards. Predefined formats ensure that documentation complies with company policies, such as branding guidelines or reporting protocols, without requiring team members to memorize every detail. Automated workflows can include checkpoints to verify compliance, such as flagging incomplete fields or routing documents for approval. These built-in safeguards reduce the burden on individuals while maintaining high-quality outputs.

Finally, the use of templates and automation fosters scalability as teams grow or projects become more complex. New team members can quickly adapt to established practices by using templates as guides, and automated processes can handle increased workloads without requiring additional resources. Over time, these tools not only enhance efficiency but also create a sense of stability, enabling teams to manage communication and documentation consistently even under pressure.

By leveraging templates and automation, IT teams can maintain a unified approach to communication and documentation, ensuring that outputs are both efficient and aligned with organizational standards. This proactive strategy minimizes variability, maximizes productivity, and creates a foundation for sustained success in dynamic project environments.

REAL-WORLD SCENARIOS: TOOLS IN ACTION

The practical impact of communication and documentation tools is best understood through real-world scenarios, where their implementation has directly influenced project outcomes. These examples illustrate how teams can leverage platforms to address common challenges, streamline workflows, and deliver results that align with organizational expectations.

Scenario 1: Managing Cross-Functional Team Communication with Slack and Jira

In a large-scale IT infrastructure migration project, teams faced the challenge of coordinating efforts across development, testing, and operations departments.

Misaligned communication led to duplicated work and missed deadlines. By integrating Slack with Jira, the teams established a system where Slack channels were mapped to project tasks in Jira. Automated notifications informed team members of updates, while pinned templates for incident reporting in Slack ensured consistent information sharing. The integration reduced confusion, increased accountability, and shortened the feedback cycle between departments, keeping the project on track.

Scenario 2: Documentation Consistency in Global Teams Using Confluence

A multinational IT consultancy firm struggled with maintaining consistent documentation practices across geographically dispersed teams. Regional offices often created reports in varying formats, complicating stakeholder reviews and decision-making. Introducing Confluence as a centralized documentation platform resolved these issues. The firm developed universal templates for project charters, meeting minutes, and risk assessments, ensuring all teams adhered to the same standards. Automated workflows in Confluence routed documents to appropriate reviewers based on project phase, ensuring that critical approvals were never delayed. This approach unified documentation practices and enhanced stakeholder trust in the firm's deliverables.

Scenario 3: Enhancing Stakeholder Engagement with Microsoft Teams

In an Agile software development project, the client's stakeholders complained about a lack of visibility into sprint progress. The project team addressed this by creating a dedicated Microsoft Teams workspace with embedded Power BI dashboards. The dashboards provided real-time insights into task completion, team velocity, and potential bottlenecks. Weekly sprint reviews were conducted using Teams' video conferencing and shared meeting agendas stored in OneNote. This solution not only increased stakeholder satisfaction but also allowed the team to proactively identify and resolve risks, improving overall project performance.

Scenario 4: Automating Compliance Reporting with ServiceNow

An organization managing IT operations under strict regulatory requirements faced difficulties in producing timely compliance reports. Manually compiling data from various systems was time-consuming and prone to errors. By implementing ServiceNow's automation capabilities, the organization created workflows that pulled data from monitoring tools, flagged potential non-compliance incidents, and generated formatted reports ready for review. This streamlined process reduced reporting time by 40%, ensured accuracy, and freed up resources for other critical tasks.

These real-world scenarios underscore the transformative potential of communication and documentation tools when applied strategically. By understanding specific challenges and tailoring tools to address them, IT teams can achieve greater efficiency, foster collaboration, and meet both project and organizational goals with confidence.

Challenges and Pitfalls in Tool Implementation

While leveraging tools for communication and documentation can significantly enhance IT workflows, the process of implementing these tools is often fraught with challenges. Missteps during selection, deployment, or adoption can lead to inefficiencies, wasted resources, and team frustration. Understanding these challenges and the pitfalls to avoid is essential for ensuring a smooth transition and maximizing the benefits of these platforms.

One common challenge is *poor tool alignment with organizational needs*. IT teams may select tools based on their popularity or surface-level features without fully evaluating whether they meet the team's specific requirements. For instance, a tool designed for Agile workflows might fall short in environments that follow ITIL or PMP methodologies. This mismatch can lead to dissatisfaction among users, underutilization of the tool, and wasted investment. To avoid this, a thorough needs assessment and stakeholder input are critical during the selection process.

Another issue is the *lack of user training and support*, which can result in resistance to adoption. Team members often struggle to integrate new tools into their daily routines, especially if the platform is complex or requires a steep learning curve. Without adequate training, they may revert to familiar but inefficient methods, such as relying on email or manual spreadsheets. This pitfall emphasizes the importance of providing comprehensive onboarding programs, clear documentation, and accessible support channels to ease the transition and foster confidence in the tool.

Over-reliance on tools without addressing underlying communication issues is another frequent pitfall. A tool cannot resolve systemic problems like unclear roles, weak leadership, or cultural barriers. For example, introducing a task management system will not eliminate misunderstandings if team members are not aligned on priorities or goals. Effective implementation requires addressing these foundational issues first, ensuring that the tool enhances rather than replaces robust communication practices.

The risk of *tool fatigue* is also significant, especially in IT environments where multiple platforms are often used simultaneously. Teams may struggle to manage a proliferation of tools, leading to information silos, duplicated effort, and confusion over which platform to use for specific tasks. For example, when a team uses Slack for discussions, Jira for task tracking, and SharePoint for documentation, lack of integration can hinder productivity. Choosing tools that integrate seamlessly and consolidating redundant platforms can alleviate this challenge.

Finally, *insufficient leadership support* can undermine tool implementation efforts. If managers and leaders fail to champion the tool or lead by example, team members may perceive it as a low priority. This can result in inconsistent usage and ultimately, the failure of the initiative. Leaders must actively promote the tool's benefits, participate in its use, and ensure alignment with broader organizational objectives to encourage widespread adoption.

By recognizing these challenges and proactively addressing them, IT teams can mitigate the risks associated with tool implementation. A well-planned approach, combined with ongoing evaluation and adjustment, ensures that tools truly enhance communication and documentation rather than becoming obstacles to success.

TOOLS AS ENABLERS OF SUCCESS

When effectively implemented, communication and documentation tools act as powerful enablers of success for IT teams. Far beyond their technical capabilities, these tools streamline collaboration, foster transparency, and ensure alignment between team efforts and organizational objectives. By integrating tools strategically, IT professionals can overcome common project challenges and unlock new levels of efficiency and performance.

One of the primary ways tools enable success is by *enhancing visibility across projects and teams*. Platforms like Jira, Asana, or Microsoft Teams create centralized repositories of information where team members and stakeholders can easily track progress, monitor milestones, and identify bottlenecks. This transparency fosters accountability, as everyone involved has a clear understanding of their roles and responsibilities. For example, when managing a complex software rollout, tools that provide visual dashboards and real-time updates reduce misunderstandings and keep everyone aligned on objectives.

Additionally, tools serve as *bridges across geographical and cultural divides*. In today's increasingly globalized workforce, teams often span multiple time zones and cultural backgrounds, which can lead to communication gaps. Collaborative tools like Zoom, Slack, and Confluence help overcome these barriers by enabling asynchronous communication, real-time updates, and shared documentation spaces. Features such as automatic meeting transcription or translation further support inclusivity and ensure that critical information is accessible to everyone.

Tools also act as *buffers against human error in documentation and record-keeping*. Manual processes are prone to mistakes, which can lead to costly missteps in IT projects. Platforms like ServiceNow or Trello incorporate automation features to streamline routine tasks, such as assigning responsibilities, generating status reports, or sending reminders. These automated workflows ensure consistency and accuracy, freeing team members to focus on more strategic activities while minimizing the risk of errors.

Beyond project management, tools enable *scalable knowledge sharing and institutional memory*. IT projects generate vast amounts of information, from technical specifications to lessons learned. Without proper tools, this knowledge can become siloed or lost over time. Platforms like SharePoint or Notion preserve institutional knowledge by offering structured, searchable repositories. Teams can easily access documentation, training materials, or past project reports, fostering continuous improvement and innovation.

Finally, tools empower teams to *adapt quickly to changing circumstances*. In dynamic IT environments, where priorities and deliverables can shift rapidly, agile tools allow teams to pivot without losing momentum. Features such as drag-and-drop task reassignments, real-time notifications, and customizable workflows make it easier to respond to new requirements or emerging risks. For instance, during a critical incident, IT teams can leverage tools like PagerDuty to coordinate responses efficiently, ensuring minimal downtime and faster resolution.

By leveraging these capabilities, communication and documentation tools transform from passive utilities into strategic assets that drive IT success. When selected thoughtfully and integrated seamlessly into workflows, these tools empower teams to navigate complexity, maintain alignment, and deliver results that exceed expectations.

Chapter 6: Connecting with the End Customer

In IT projects, the gap between technical teams and non-technical customers is a persistent challenge. While technical experts focus on the precision and intricacies of their work, customers prioritize outcomes, business impact, and usability. This divergence in priorities and communication styles often leads to misunderstandings, frustration, and, in some cases, project delays or failure. For customers, technical jargon can feel like an impenetrable wall, leaving them disengaged from critical discussions about their own projects. For IT teams, translating their work into layperson-friendly terms may seem unnecessary or even reductive, yet it is crucial to ensure alignment and satisfaction.

The disconnect stems from fundamentally different ways of viewing the same project. IT professionals may emphasize efficiency, scalability, or security, assuming these priorities are self-evident. However, customers are more likely to value how these deliverables translate into tangible benefits, such as saving money, improving customer experiences, or increasing revenue. Without clear communication, even the most technically sound deliverables can be met with skepticism or dissatisfaction simply because their value isn't understood. As a result, bridging this divide is not merely about simplifying language; it's about reshaping the narrative to focus on outcomes that resonate with the customer.

The communication divide becomes especially pronounced during high-stakes moments in a project, such as major updates, deliverable handovers, or problem-solving sessions. A misstep in these moments can have cascading effects, eroding trust and weakening the partnership between the IT team and the customer. Customers may feel sidelined, as though decisions are being made without their input or understanding. In turn, IT professionals may grow frustrated with what they perceive as unrealistic demands or constant questioning. This cycle of miscommunication, left unaddressed, can undermine even the most robust technical solutions.

Yet, this divide is not insurmountable. With deliberate effort and strategic communication, IT teams can build a bridge between their technical expertise and the customer's needs. The key lies in prioritizing clarity, relevance, and empathy. Translating technical deliverables into customer-friendly terms is not about "dumbing down" the content but about reframing it to focus on what matters most to the customer. This chapter delves into the strategies and techniques IT professionals can use to master this critical skill, turning a potential point of friction into a foundation for trust and collaboration.

UNDERSTANDING THE CUSTOMER'S PERSPECTIVE

Effective communication begins with understanding the customer's perspective—what they value, what concerns them, and how they interpret the progress and outcomes of an IT project. Customers are not typically interested in the technical processes or intricate details that go into creating deliverables; their focus lies on the practical implications and the impact on their goals. They want to know how the deliverables will solve their problems, improve their workflows, or help them achieve business success. Recognizing this mindset is critical for tailoring communication that resonates and builds confidence.

From the customer's viewpoint, technical terminology can be intimidating or confusing, leading to feelings of exclusion from the decision-making process. For example, when an IT consultant explains that a project delay is caused by "load balancing issues with the database cluster," a non-technical customer may find it difficult to grasp the significance or urgency of the problem. Instead, what they need to hear is a straightforward explanation of the issue's impact: "We're making adjustments to ensure your system can handle high traffic without disruptions." This shift in language makes the information relevant and actionable, aligning with their perspective.

Another key element of the customer's perspective is the desire for predictability and transparency. Customers often feel uneasy about the uncertainty inherent in IT projects, where deliverables may evolve and timelines may shift. They want clear communication that addresses these concerns proactively, such as outlining how potential risks will be managed and what safeguards are in place. Acknowledging their need for stability and demonstrating a commitment to minimizing disruptions fosters trust and reassures them that their priorities are understood and respected.

Understanding the customer's perspective also means recognizing the diversity of stakeholders involved. Within any organization, different individuals may have unique concerns based on their roles. For example, a financial manager might focus on budget implications, while an operations leader may prioritize the usability and scalability of the solution. To effectively communicate with all stakeholders, IT professionals must consider these varying viewpoints and tailor their messaging accordingly. This approach not only ensures clarity but also positions the IT team as a collaborative partner invested in the customer's success. By seeing the project through the customer's eyes, IT professionals can create a shared vision, paving the way for meaningful dialogue and stronger relationships.

TECHNIQUES FOR SIMPLIFYING TECHNICAL CONCEPTS

Simplifying technical concepts for customers requires not only clarity in language but also an understanding of how to frame information in ways that resonate with non-technical audiences. The goal is to bridge the knowledge gap between the technical complexities of IT deliverables and the practical, results-oriented concerns of the customer. Achieving this involves deliberate strategies to make technical information accessible without sacrificing accuracy.

One effective technique is the use of analogies and metaphors. Comparing complex IT systems or processes to familiar, everyday concepts can help customers grasp abstract ideas. For example, explaining a firewall as the "security guard" of a system, or describing cloud storage as a "digital filing cabinet," allows customers to form intuitive connections. These analogies not only make the concepts easier to understand but also build confidence in their ability to engage in discussions about the project. Care must be taken, however, to ensure the analogies are accurate and do not oversimplify to the point of misrepresentation.

Visual aids are another powerful tool for simplifying technical concepts. Diagrams, flowcharts, and infographics can present information in a more digestible format, breaking down processes into visual steps that clarify relationships and workflows. For instance, rather than explaining the intricacies of a data migration process in text-heavy detail, a consultant can use a visual timeline that highlights key stages—preparation, transfer, testing, and deployment. This not only simplifies communication but also enhances engagement, as visual content is often easier to retain and reference.

The structure of explanations also plays a critical role in simplifying technical ideas. IT professionals should adopt a top-down approach, starting with high-level overviews before diving into details. This ensures that customers first understand the "big picture" and its relevance to their goals. For instance, when discussing a new software feature, begin by describing its overall purpose—such as improving productivity or automating routine tasks—before elaborating on the underlying technology. This progression mirrors how people naturally process information, making it easier for customers to follow and engage.

Finally, prioritizing plain language over technical jargon is crucial. While specialized terms may be unavoidable in internal team discussions, they can alienate customers who lack technical expertise. Replacing terms like "latency optimization" with "making the system faster" or "scalable architecture" with "designed to handle growth" shifts the focus from the mechanics to the outcomes. This approach keeps the conversation customer-centric, emphasizing what the deliverables will achieve rather than how they are built. By combining these techniques, IT professionals can create a communication style that demystifies complexity, fosters understanding, and strengthens their relationships with customers.

STRUCTURING THE COMMUNICATION

Effective communication with customers goes beyond the content of the message; it requires thoughtful structuring to ensure clarity, engagement, and alignment with the customer's needs. A well-organized approach helps convey technical deliverables in a way that is logical, accessible, and actionable, allowing customers to follow the narrative and make informed decisions. Structuring communication is as much about what is said as it is about when and how it is presented.

The first step in structuring communication is to establish a clear purpose at the outset. Before diving into technical explanations, it is important to outline the objective of the interaction. Whether the goal is to present progress, resolve concerns, or propose solutions, defining this purpose ensures that both parties are aligned from the beginning. For example, beginning a conversation with, *"Today, we'll review the system upgrade plan and ensure it aligns with your operational goals"* sets the stage for a focused discussion. This approach also helps customers understand the relevance of the technical information being shared, reducing the likelihood of confusion or disengagement.

Organizing the content in a logical sequence is equally essential. Start with a high-level summary that provides an overview of the deliverable, followed by detailed breakdowns of its components, and conclude with actionable next steps. This structure mirrors the natural flow of comprehension: understanding the big picture first, then grasping specifics, and finally identifying the practical implications. For instance, when discussing a software deployment plan, begin with the overarching benefits, then detail each phase—testing, rollout, and maintenance—and finish with the timeline and customer responsibilities. This progression not only simplifies the information but also makes it easier for customers to contextualize their role in the project.

Another critical aspect of structuring communication is segmenting information into manageable parts. Long-winded technical explanations can overwhelm customers, especially if they are presented in one continuous stream. Breaking the discussion into smaller, focused sections—such as addressing one feature or functionality at a time—helps maintain attention and ensures each element is understood before moving on. Additionally, allowing for pauses or inviting questions after each section creates a two-way dialogue, reinforcing understanding and engagement.

Concluding the communication with a summary and actionable steps is a vital component of an effective structure. A brief recap of the main points reinforces key takeaways, ensuring that the customer leaves with a clear understanding of what was discussed. Following this with specific, next steps provides direction and clarity. For example, after explaining a deliverable, concluding with, *"We will finalize testing by the end of this week, and you will receive an update on deployment schedules next Monday,"* leaves no ambiguity about what comes next. By structuring communication with these principles, IT professionals can transform complex discussions into streamlined, customer-friendly exchanges, fostering trust and driving project success.

PRACTICAL TOOLS AND METHODS

Effectively translating technical deliverables into customer-friendly communication requires more than just verbal skills; it demands the use of practical tools and methods that facilitate clarity, engagement, and understanding. These resources bridge the gap between the technical and non-technical worlds, ensuring that customers not only grasp the information but also feel confident in its value and implications for their objectives. Employing these tools strategically can make the difference between a successful project update and a conversation fraught with misunderstandings.

One of the most effective tools for simplifying technical communication is the use of visual aids. Charts, graphs, and diagrams can distill complex data into digestible visuals that are easier for customers to comprehend. For instance, when presenting the progress of a project, a Gantt chart can provide a clear timeline of completed and upcoming phases. Similarly, flowcharts are invaluable for explaining processes like system integrations or troubleshooting workflows, allowing customers to visualize the sequence of actions and outcomes. By reducing reliance on lengthy explanations, these visuals make the technical content more accessible and engaging.

Slide decks are another versatile medium for structuring and simplifying communication. A well-designed slide presentation provides a narrative framework, allowing technical deliverables to be broken down into concise, visually supported segments. Effective slides avoid overwhelming the customer with too much detail, instead focusing on key points, supported by brief text, icons, and images. For instance, when discussing a software update, the slide deck could include a slide summarizing benefits (e.g., improved speed, enhanced security), followed by slides detailing how these improvements align with the customer's operational goals. This approach ensures that technical discussions are not only comprehensive but also retain customer interest.

Interactive demonstrations or prototypes are particularly valuable when discussing deliverables with a high degree of complexity. Allowing customers to engage with a simplified version of the product or process—whether through a live demo, a clickable prototype, or a mock-up—creates a tangible experience that bridges the gap between abstract concepts and real-world application. For example, during the development of a custom dashboard, providing a working prototype where the customer can click through features allows them to see firsthand how it meets their requirements. This hands-on experience often prompts insightful feedback, fostering collaboration and alignment.

Collaboration platforms and documentation tools also play a significant role in enhancing communication with customers. Tools like Confluence, Jira, or Microsoft Teams offer centralized spaces for sharing updates, tracking deliverables, and maintaining transparency throughout the project lifecycle. For instance, creating a shared dashboard that includes progress metrics, pending tasks, and notes from prior discussions ensures that all stakeholders have access to the same information. This not only reduces the risk of miscommunication but also encourages proactive customer involvement.

Ultimately, the combination of these tools and methods ensures that communication is not only informative but also engaging and actionable. By integrating visual aids, structured presentations, interactive prototypes, and collaborative platforms, IT professionals can provide their customers with a robust understanding of technical deliverables. This approach enhances satisfaction, builds trust, and lays the groundwork for long-term partnerships.

CASE STUDIES AND REAL-WORLD EXAMPLES

Illustrating concepts through real-world examples and case studies provides a compelling way to communicate technical deliverables to customers. Concrete scenarios offer clarity, helping customers see how theoretical deliverables translate into practical applications. These narratives not only enhance understanding but also build trust by demonstrating competence and a track record of success. By grounding technical concepts in relatable experiences, IT professionals can bridge the gap between abstract deliverables and their tangible value.

Consider a software development project for a healthcare client aiming to streamline patient record management. While technical deliverables like API integrations and database migration may sound complex to the client, framing these within the context of a case study makes the value clear. For example, the IT team could share an anecdote about a previous project with a similar scope: "In our last engagement with a mid-sized clinic, we implemented a similar system. The result was a 30% reduction in record retrieval times and a 20% improvement in data accuracy within six months." Such examples provide context, showing not just what is being delivered but the outcomes that can be expected.

Real-world examples are particularly effective when introducing innovative technologies or methodologies unfamiliar to the customer. For instance, in projects involving machine learning, clients may struggle to grasp the specifics of algorithm training or data preprocessing. Referring to a case study where machine learning was used to predict equipment failures in a manufacturing plant could illuminate the potential impact: "By analyzing equipment usage data, we reduced downtime by 40% in a similar facility. This predictive approach could be adapted to your needs to achieve similar efficiency gains." By grounding abstract technology in relatable scenarios, IT teams can foster understanding and excitement about the deliverables.

Case studies also provide opportunities to showcase problem-solving and adaptability, which are critical to building customer confidence. If a project faced challenges—such as delays in data availability or changes in scope—sharing how these were resolved demonstrates reliability. For instance, in a project involving the migration of legacy systems for a retail client, the team could highlight how unforeseen data inconsistencies were addressed: "During the migration, we encountered discrepancies in legacy data formats. By developing a custom data transformation tool, we ensured compatibility with the new system without delays." Sharing such experiences reinforces the team's capacity to manage uncertainties effectively, alleviating potential customer concerns about similar challenges.

Additionally, presenting case studies that align with the customer's industry can enhance their relevance and impact. Customers are more likely to engage when they can directly relate the deliverables to their specific operational context. For example, when implementing cloud solutions for a logistics company, referencing a successful cloud deployment for another logistics client allows the customer to see parallels. They gain insight into how similar solutions improved route optimization or enabled real-time shipment tracking, making the deliverables both credible and aspirational.

By integrating case studies and real-world examples into discussions, IT professionals can transform technical deliverables into relatable narratives. These stories connect abstract concepts to tangible outcomes, helping customers envision the benefits and fostering alignment between technical goals and business objectives. Furthermore, this approach builds trust, demonstrates expertise, and sets the stage for long-term collaboration.

ACTIONABLE TAKEAWAYS

Bridging the gap between technical jargon and customer comprehension requires not just thoughtful preparation but a set of consistent practices that ensure clarity and alignment. Actionable takeaways serve as quick-reference guidelines to simplify communication, reinforce customer understanding, and maintain satisfaction throughout the project lifecycle. Below, we explore these principles in detail.

Tailoring Language to the Customer's Understanding

To communicate effectively, it is essential to match the complexity of your language to the customer's technical aptitude. Using overly intricate explanations can alienate non-technical stakeholders, while oversimplifying may cause misunderstandings. Striking the right balance ensures your message resonates and supports decision-making.

Start by gauging the customer's familiarity with technical concepts during initial conversations. For example, if the customer represents a highly specialized team, technical depth may be welcomed. Conversely, in discussions with non-technical executives, analogies or simplified explanations can make concepts more digestible.

A practical way to test clarity is to paraphrase your message after delivering it. Asking the customer to restate their understanding can reveal gaps in communication. Additionally, developing a glossary of project-specific terms or creating a knowledge repository tailored to the customer's team can offer ongoing support. By continuously refining your language to align with the customer's understanding, you lay the groundwork for mutual trust and confidence.

Connecting to Customer Goals and Pain Points

Every communication should tie directly to the customer's overarching objectives or immediate concerns. Technical deliverables, while significant, only matter to the customer insofar as they resolve a problem or achieve a desired outcome. Demonstrating this connection transforms abstract details into actionable benefits.

Start by framing explanations with a direct link to project goals. For instance, if a software update enhances system security, lead with how it reduces risks or compliance concerns, rather than detailing the algorithmic intricacies. Aligning updates with the customer's priorities ensures they see the value behind each step, which fosters engagement and satisfaction.

This customer-centric approach extends to addressing pain points proactively. For example, if a customer has previously experienced delays in similar projects, consistently addressing timelines and mitigation strategies in your updates shows empathy and builds confidence in your processes. Tailoring communication in this way strengthens the customer's investment in the project's success.

Using Visual Aids and Examples

Visual aids and concrete examples transform abstract technical details into relatable, comprehensible insights. Humans process visual information faster than text, making diagrams, infographics, and interactive dashboards invaluable tools for effective communication.

Consider using flowcharts to explain workflows, timelines to illustrate progress, or mockups to preview the user experience. These visuals can serve as focal points during presentations, making it easier for customers to grasp complex processes and ask informed questions. For instance, in a meeting about a cloud migration project, presenting a before-and-after system architecture diagram can clearly illustrate the benefits of the change.

Similarly, practical examples grounded in the customer's domain resonate more effectively than abstract explanations. If discussing data analytics, framing it around how insights will impact the customer's sales forecasting or inventory management creates an immediate connection. Combining visuals with examples rooted in the customer's experience bridges technical gaps and builds comprehension.

Encouraging Questions and Feedback

Clear communication is a two-way street. Actively inviting questions and feedback not only ensures customer understanding but also fosters collaboration and trust. It allows you to identify areas of confusion early, address concerns, and reinforce the customer's role as a key stakeholder in the project.

Establishing a feedback-friendly environment begins with signaling openness during every interaction. Phrases like, *"Let me know if this aligns with your expectations"* or *"Does this address your main concern?"* encourage dialogue. Building pauses into presentations or updates for questions also ensures customers have time to process information and respond.

Follow up on questions promptly with clear, actionable answers, ensuring your responses further clarify project direction. Additionally, documenting feedback and providing a summary after discussions demonstrates accountability and helps track evolving customer needs. By prioritizing feedback, you strengthen mutual understanding and project alignment.

These actionable takeaways, when applied consistently, serve as a robust framework for ensuring that communication remains customer-focused, transparent, and impactful. Tailoring language, connecting to goals, leveraging visual aids, and fostering dialogue not only manage expectations effectively but also nurture long-term customer satisfaction.

Effective communication with customers is more than just ensuring clarity—it is about fostering trust, setting realistic expectations, and delivering a seamless collaborative experience. The principles and actionable steps outlined earlier serve as the cornerstone of translating technical deliverables into language the customer can understand and appreciate. However, successful communication extends beyond clarity.

The next critical aspect is managing customer expectations in a way that not only ensures satisfaction but also mitigates potential misunderstandings or conflicts. This involves proactive communication, consistent alignment of deliverables with agreed-upon objectives, and the ability to adapt messaging based on evolving project dynamics. By doing so, IT professionals can balance technical precision with the human element of customer relationships.

As we move forward, we will delve into the strategies, methodologies, and real-world applications of managing customer expectations. This section will explore the intricacies of maintaining transparency, navigating changing priorities, and ensuring that the customer remains both informed and engaged throughout the project lifecycle. Building on the foundation of clear communication, expectation management becomes the bridge to enduring satisfaction and project success.

Managing customer expectations and ensuring satisfaction through clear communication.

Clear expectations are the backbone of a successful customer relationship in any IT project. When stakeholders understand the scope, timeline, and deliverables from the outset, it reduces the risk of misunderstandings, dissatisfaction, or scope creep. Yet, many IT professionals underestimate the importance of this initial stage, often assuming that technical documents or contractual agreements alone suffice. Setting the stage for clear expectations requires intentional communication tailored to the customer's perspective and rooted in mutual understanding.

At the heart of this process is a commitment to transparency. Customers, especially those with limited technical expertise, often feel overwhelmed by the complexities of IT projects. Addressing this early means simplifying technical jargon and focusing on the "why" behind decisions. For example, instead of saying, "The integration will use a RESTful API," framing it as, "This method will ensure seamless communication between your systems, reducing delays and enhancing efficiency," shifts the conversation toward outcomes rather than methods. Such framing builds confidence and ensures the customer feels included in the decision-making process.

Equally important is setting boundaries around what the project will and will not deliver. This involves walking customers through the agreed-upon scope with a focus on deliverables that address their specific pain points. A well-structured kick-off meeting can be instrumental here. For instance, using visual aids like project roadmaps, milestones, and timelines allows customers to see how each phase contributes to their goals. These tools not only clarify expectations but also create a sense of partnership, as customers can visualize their role in the process.

Finally, establishing channels for ongoing dialogue is crucial. Even with the clearest initial agreements, IT projects evolve as new challenges or opportunities arise. Early discussions should include protocols for addressing change requests, unexpected delays, or additional requirements. For instance, clarifying how modifications will impact the timeline or cost ensures customers are not blindsided later. This proactive communication fosters trust and ensures that both parties feel equipped to navigate uncertainties together.

Setting the stage for clear expectations is not a one-time task but the foundation of a dynamic, evolving relationship. When customers are well-informed, engaged, and confident in the plan from the beginning, it sets a positive tone for the project and paves the way for satisfaction and collaboration throughout.

THE ROLE OF TRANSPARENT COMMUNICATION

Transparency is the cornerstone of any successful relationship, particularly in IT projects where the complexity and technical nature of deliverables can create significant barriers to understanding. Transparent communication bridges this gap, ensuring that customers are not only informed but also confident in the processes and decisions that drive a project's success. It transforms a potentially fraught collaboration into a partnership built on trust and shared objectives.

At its core, transparency involves sharing information openly and proactively. For IT professionals, this means going beyond merely updating the customer on project milestones. It includes explaining the reasoning behind technical decisions, outlining potential risks, and being candid about challenges as they arise. For example, if a delivery deadline is at risk due to unforeseen technical hurdles, informing the customer immediately and presenting a plan for resolution demonstrates integrity. This openness helps prevent frustration and allows customers to feel involved rather than blindsided.

Transparency also entails managing customer expectations about outcomes. In many IT projects, customers may not fully grasp the technical limitations or the potential impact of requested changes. Clear, honest communication about what is feasible within the project's scope can prevent misunderstandings later. For instance, when a client requests a feature that may delay the timeline or exceed the budget, articulating the trade-offs in simple terms—such as how this impacts their primary objectives—enables them to make informed decisions.

Another critical component of transparency is documentation. Well-maintained records of communications, decisions, and updates act as a reference point for all parties, reducing ambiguity. Providing customers with access to shared platforms like project dashboards or progress tracking tools ensures they can monitor progress in real-time. These tools give customers visibility into the workflow, helping to demystify processes and foster a sense of control.

Finally, transparent communication is not just about sharing information; it's also about encouraging dialogue. Effective IT professionals create an environment where customers feel comfortable asking questions, voicing concerns, or seeking clarification. Regular check-ins or feedback sessions provide structured opportunities for this exchange, ensuring that customers remain aligned with the project's trajectory. This two-way communication reinforces trust, as customers perceive the IT team as approachable and invested in their success.

The role of transparent communication extends far beyond the functional aspects of a project. It sets the tone for collaboration, strengthens the relationship between IT teams and their customers, and minimizes the risk of conflict or dissatisfaction. By embracing transparency as a guiding principle, IT professionals not only enhance project outcomes but also build enduring trust with their clients.

Aligning Expectations to Reality

One of the most critical yet challenging aspects of managing customer relationships in IT is aligning expectations to the realities of technical limitations, timelines, and resource constraints. Misaligned expectations can lead to dissatisfaction, strained relationships, and even project failure. To bridge this gap, IT professionals must employ a combination of strategic communication, proactive planning, and empathetic listening.

The process begins with understanding the customer's vision for the project. Customers often articulate their needs in broad, aspirational terms without understanding the technical intricacies or constraints involved. An IT professional's role is to distill these aspirations into actionable goals while identifying potential hurdles. For example, a customer may envision a seamless integration of multiple complex systems, but the IT team may foresee compatibility issues or extended development timelines. By outlining these challenges early and clearly, the IT team helps the customer ground their expectations in what is technically achievable.

Proactively communicating trade-offs is another essential component of aligning expectations. IT projects often involve balancing factors like cost, quality, and speed. When customers request features or changes that stretch project constraints, it's crucial to explain how these decisions impact the overall delivery. For instance, adding a new feature might extend the timeline or require additional resources. Framing these conversations in terms of the customer's priorities—such as "delivering on time" or "maximizing functionality"—helps them make informed choices and align their expectations accordingly.

Regular progress updates are a vital tool for maintaining alignment throughout the project lifecycle. While initial discussions set the tone, ongoing communication ensures that expectations evolve with the project. Weekly or bi-weekly check-ins can clarify shifting priorities, address unforeseen challenges, and keep both parties synchronized. These updates should focus not only on what has been accomplished but also on what lies ahead, providing customers with a clear roadmap and context for upcoming decisions.

Empathy is indispensable in managing customer expectations. IT professionals must acknowledge the customer's perspective, particularly when delivering disappointing news. For example, if a key deliverable is delayed, it's not enough to state the facts; explaining the reasons behind the delay and expressing a shared commitment to the project's success can soften the blow. Customers are more likely to remain understanding and cooperative when they feel their concerns are being respected and addressed.

Finally, aligning expectations to reality is not a one-time task but an ongoing effort. As projects unfold, new variables can emerge, requiring adjustments to plans and priorities. By fostering a collaborative mindset, where the customer is treated as a partner rather than an end-user, IT professionals can ensure that expectations remain realistic and adaptable. This approach not only safeguards the project's success but also reinforces trust, making the customer more likely to view challenges as manageable obstacles rather than insurmountable failures.

Aligning expectations to reality is a nuanced balancing act that combines technical expertise with emotional intelligence. It requires IT professionals to act as both educators and collaborators, helping customers navigate complex landscapes while staying focused on achievable outcomes. By investing in this alignment process, IT teams set the stage for smoother execution, higher satisfaction, and stronger relationships.

Managing Feedback and Iterations

Feedback is the lifeblood of any successful IT project. It provides critical insight into customer satisfaction, allows for realignment of goals, and fosters a sense of collaboration. However, managing feedback—especially in iterative cycles—requires thoughtful planning, clear communication, and a structured process to avoid scope creep, delays, or miscommunication. Ensuring that customer input leads to meaningful improvements without derailing the project is a delicate balance that IT professionals must master.

The first step in managing feedback is setting clear parameters for its collection. Customers should know when and how they can provide input, whether through scheduled review meetings, digital surveys, or dedicated feedback portals. By establishing these boundaries upfront, the IT team ensures that feedback is both actionable and timely. For instance, during the prototype review phase, asking customers to assess specific features rather than offering broad, unstructured input keeps the discussion focused and productive.

Active listening plays a critical role in interpreting feedback effectively. Customers often express concerns or dissatisfaction without pinpointing the technical issues behind them. For example, a client might say, "The interface feels slow," which could indicate problems ranging from server performance to user experience design. IT professionals must ask probing questions to clarify the root cause, such as, "Can you describe when you experience delays?" or "Which specific functions feel less responsive?" By seeking context, the team can identify actionable insights rather than making broad assumptions that may lead to unnecessary changes.

Balancing customer desires with technical feasibility is essential during iterations. Not all feedback can or should be implemented, particularly if it conflicts with the project's timeline, budget, or broader goals. In such cases, IT professionals need to explain why certain suggestions may not be practical, providing alternative solutions where possible. For instance, if a customer requests a feature that would delay the project significantly, the team could propose a simpler version for the current release while planning the full implementation for a future update. Framing decisions as trade-offs rather than outright rejections helps maintain trust and collaboration.

Transparency during the iteration process is crucial for building customer confidence. IT professionals should communicate what feedback has been addressed, what changes are in progress, and what remains out of scope. Using tools like change logs, annotated prototypes, or visual roadmaps allows customers to track how their input shapes the project. This not only validates their role in the process but also minimizes frustration by managing their expectations about what can realistically be achieved within each iteration.

A structured approach to closing feedback loops ensures that iterations remain efficient and purposeful. After implementing changes based on customer input, it is essential to seek confirmation that these adjustments meet their expectations. Simple follow-up questions like, "Does this new feature address your concerns?" or "Are there additional refinements you'd suggest?" reinforce a collaborative environment and demonstrate a commitment to continuous improvement. If the feedback indicates further issues, the cycle can continue with clear boundaries to prevent endless revisions.

Managing feedback and iterations is both an art and a science, requiring technical expertise, strategic communication, and emotional intelligence. By approaching the process with structure and empathy, IT professionals can ensure that customer input enhances the project without compromising its goals. Effective feedback management not only leads to better deliverables but also strengthens the relationship between the IT team and the customer, fostering a partnership built on mutual respect and shared success.

CONFLICT RESOLUTION THROUGH COMMUNICATION

Conflicts are an inevitable part of any project, particularly in the high-stakes, fast-paced world of IT. Whether due to differing priorities, misunderstandings, or unforeseen challenges, disputes can arise between customers and IT professionals at any stage. Effectively resolving these conflicts requires clear, empathetic, and proactive communication, ensuring that disagreements do not derail the project but instead lead to stronger collaboration and mutual understanding.

The foundation of conflict resolution lies in identifying the root cause of the disagreement. In many cases, conflicts stem from misaligned expectations, unclear deliverables, or miscommunication about project progress. For instance, a customer might express frustration over a delayed feature, believing it was deprioritized, when in reality, technical challenges extended the timeline. IT professionals must listen actively to uncover these underlying issues, asking clarifying questions such as, "Can you share your understanding of this feature's status?" or "What specific concerns do you have about the current timeline?" This not only helps in diagnosing the problem but also demonstrates a genuine commitment to addressing the customer's concerns.

Once the root cause is identified, the next step is to acknowledge the customer's perspective. Validating their concerns—even if they stem from a misunderstanding—helps de-escalate tension and fosters a sense of trust. For example, responding with, "I can see how this delay impacts your goals, and I want to ensure we resolve this together," conveys empathy while setting a collaborative tone. Avoiding defensive or dismissive language is critical, as it can exacerbate the conflict and damage the relationship.

Proactive problem-solving is the core of effective conflict resolution. IT professionals should present solutions that address the customer's concerns while remaining aligned with project constraints. For instance, if a customer is unhappy with the functionality of a delivered module, the team might offer to conduct a joint review session to clarify requirements and outline feasible adjustments. Transparency about the trade-offs involved—such as the impact on the timeline or budget—ensures that the customer has realistic expectations and feels included in the decision-making process. Providing multiple options, when possible, empowers the customer to choose the path that best meets their needs.

Maintaining open and structured communication channels is essential for preventing minor disagreements from escalating into major conflicts. Regular check-ins, status updates, and opportunities for feedback create a platform for addressing potential issues early. For example, using collaborative tools like shared project dashboards or setting up bi-weekly alignment meetings can keep both parties informed and aligned. These proactive measures not only mitigate the risk of conflicts but also reinforce a partnership-oriented approach, where both customer and IT team work towards shared objectives.

In situations where the conflict cannot be resolved immediately, it is important to establish a temporary resolution that prevents the project from stagnating. For instance, agreeing on a short-term compromise—such as delivering a minimally viable version of a disputed feature—allows progress to continue while the larger issue is addressed. Documenting these interim agreements ensures accountability and provides a reference point for follow-up discussions.

Finally, learning from resolved conflicts can strengthen future communication practices. Conducting a retrospective analysis—either internally or with the customer—can reveal valuable insights about what led to the disagreement and how similar situations can be avoided. For example, if unclear documentation contributed to a misunderstanding, implementing more rigorous review processes or standardized templates can prevent recurrence. Sharing these lessons transparently with the customer further demonstrates a commitment to continuous improvement and reinforces trust.

Conflict resolution through communication is not just about resolving disputes; it is an opportunity to build stronger relationships and enhance collaboration. By approaching conflicts with empathy, structure, and a solutions-oriented mindset, IT professionals can turn challenges into opportunities for growth and success. The ability to navigate disagreements effectively ensures not only the smooth progression of the project but also the cultivation of a partnership rooted in mutual respect and shared achievement.

ENSURING SATISFACTION THROUGH PROACTIVE MEASURES

Customer satisfaction in IT projects is not merely about delivering a completed product; it is about providing an experience that reflects reliability, transparency, and commitment. Satisfaction is cultivated not by reacting to issues as they arise but by anticipating needs and implementing proactive measures that prevent misunderstandings and build trust throughout the project lifecycle. A proactive approach demonstrates to customers that their priorities are valued and their concerns are addressed before they materialize.

One of the most effective proactive measures is establishing clear communication protocols from the outset. This involves setting expectations for how updates will be delivered, how questions will be addressed, and how decisions will be documented. For example, agreeing on a schedule of weekly or bi-weekly progress meetings ensures consistent engagement and prevents the customer from feeling out of the loop. Providing a project roadmap or timeline with detailed milestones further enhances transparency and reassures customers that their goals are being systematically addressed.

Anticipating potential challenges and addressing them early is another hallmark of proactive customer satisfaction. IT professionals, with their technical expertise, are often aware of potential roadblocks or risks long before they impact deliverables. By informing customers of these risks and discussing mitigation strategies, teams can prevent surprises and demonstrate foresight. For instance, if a particular integration with a third-party system is known to have compatibility issues, bringing this to the customer's attention early and offering alternative solutions ensures confidence in the team's ability to manage complexities.

Regularly soliciting feedback throughout the project is essential for maintaining alignment and satisfaction. Instead of waiting for formal review phases, IT professionals should create multiple opportunities for the customer to provide input. Techniques such as iterative design reviews, user acceptance testing sessions, and informal check-ins encourage customers to voice their preferences and concerns. This continuous feedback loop not only helps in refining the deliverables but also reinforces the customer's sense of involvement and ownership in the project.

Proactive measures also include going beyond the customer's stated requirements to identify unspoken needs or opportunities for added value. For instance, if the IT team recognizes that automating a process will save the customer significant resources in the long term, suggesting this enhancement—even if it falls outside the original scope—can strengthen the customer relationship. While such suggestions should be presented as optional and with full transparency regarding costs or timeline adjustments, they position the team as thoughtful and invested in the customer's success.

Training and knowledge-sharing initiatives further contribute to long-term customer satisfaction. Once deliverables are completed, customers often require guidance to maximize the value of the IT solution. Providing comprehensive documentation, conducting training sessions, or offering on-demand support options ensures that the customer feels confident using the technology. This proactive approach minimizes post-deployment frustrations and fosters a positive perception of the overall experience.

In addition to technical considerations, building a rapport with customers is an equally important proactive measure. Personalizing communication, acknowledging the customer's organizational culture, and celebrating milestones together help humanize the relationship. For example, recognizing when a key deliverable aligns with a significant business event for the customer demonstrates attentiveness and care. Simple gestures such as congratulating the customer on reaching a milestone or delivering a user-friendly summary of project achievements can leave a lasting impression.

Evaluating satisfaction during and after the project provides critical insights for future improvements. Conducting satisfaction surveys, gathering testimonials, or holding wrap-up meetings to review what went well and what could have been improved creates a culture of continuous enhancement. These evaluations should be approached as opportunities to refine processes and address lingering concerns, ensuring that customers leave with a positive impression, even if challenges arose during the project.

Proactively ensuring satisfaction requires IT professionals to blend technical expertise with emotional intelligence and strategic foresight. By staying ahead of potential issues, inviting collaboration, and prioritizing customer success, teams can create an environment where satisfaction is not left to chance but intentionally built into every aspect of the project.

Evaluating and Enhancing Satisfaction

Customer satisfaction in IT projects is not static—it evolves throughout the project lifecycle. Effective evaluation and enhancement practices enable IT professionals to not only measure satisfaction at various stages but also use insights to refine their processes for future success. The process involves gathering feedback, analyzing outcomes, and acting on findings in a way that builds trust and strengthens customer relationships.

The first step in evaluating satisfaction is to establish clear metrics that align with the customer's goals. These metrics may vary depending on the nature of the project but typically include factors like deliverable quality, adherence to timelines, responsiveness to feedback, and perceived value of the solution. Quantitative tools such as satisfaction surveys or rating scales can provide measurable insights, while qualitative approaches like interviews or focus groups capture more nuanced feedback. The key is to ensure that these evaluations reflect the customer's perspective, not just the team's internal benchmarks.

Timing is crucial when assessing satisfaction. Interim evaluations conducted during the project allow for real-time course corrections. For instance, if mid-project feedback reveals dissatisfaction with communication frequency, adjustments can be made immediately to improve engagement. Post-project evaluations, on the other hand, offer a comprehensive view of the customer's experience and help identify overarching trends. By soliciting feedback at multiple points, IT teams demonstrate a commitment to continuous improvement and an interest in the customer's voice.

Analyzing the feedback collected is the next critical step. This involves identifying patterns and correlations that provide actionable insights. For example, recurring feedback about delays in communication may point to a need for more streamlined updates or better use of project management tools. Positive feedback, such as appreciation for intuitive design features, can highlight best practices worth replicating. It is essential for IT professionals to approach feedback analysis objectively, viewing criticism as an opportunity for growth rather than a personal judgment.

Enhancing satisfaction goes beyond addressing immediate concerns; it involves proactively implementing changes that prevent similar issues in the future. This could mean refining documentation processes, updating communication protocols, or revisiting training methods for the customer-facing team. Sharing these improvements with customers reinforces the team's dedication to delivering a superior experience. For example, if a customer expressed difficulty understanding technical deliverables, the team might create a new template for future projects, incorporating clearer language and visual aids, and inform the customer of this initiative.

Another vital aspect of enhancing satisfaction is fostering a collaborative feedback culture. Customers should feel empowered to provide input without hesitation, knowing that their suggestions will be taken seriously and acted upon. Creating a system for tracking and addressing feedback transparently—such as maintaining a feedback log with status updates—ensures that no concern is overlooked. When customers see their feedback leading to tangible improvements, their trust in the IT team deepens.

Using evaluation data to celebrate successes strengthens customer relationships and builds morale within the IT team. Sharing positive feedback with both the customer and internal stakeholders acknowledges the team's efforts and reinforces practices that contributed to the project's success. For instance, if a customer highlights exceptional communication during a challenging phase, the team can analyze what worked well and replicate those strategies in future projects.

The process of evaluating and enhancing satisfaction is an ongoing commitment that extends beyond the completion of a single project. By systematically measuring outcomes, learning from feedback, and continually refining their approach, IT professionals can build lasting relationships with customers. This not only ensures satisfaction with current deliverables but also positions the team as a trusted partner for future collaborations, creating a cycle of mutual success and continuous growth.

Building long-term relationships with clients by delivering consistent and transparent updates.

Consistency in communication forms the backbone of long-term client relationships, especially in the IT sector, where projects often involve intricate technical details and significant uncertainties. Clients rely on regular updates to feel informed and confident about the project's progress, and the absence of such communication can create confusion, anxiety, and even mistrust. By delivering updates consistently, IT professionals position themselves as dependable partners who value the client's time, investment, and objectives.

Consistency reduces uncertainty by creating a predictable communication rhythm. When clients know to expect updates at regular intervals, they feel reassured that the project is under control, even if challenges arise. This predictability helps mitigate the perception of risk that is often inherent in IT projects, particularly those involving cutting-edge technology or large-scale implementations. A consistent communication strategy demonstrates professionalism, reliability, and attention to detail, all of which contribute to the client's confidence in the team's abilities.

Equally important, consistent communication reinforces the alignment between the project's progress and the client's expectations. Without regular updates, clients may develop unrealistic assumptions about timelines, deliverables, or outcomes, potentially leading to dissatisfaction or conflict. By maintaining a steady flow of accurate information, IT professionals can manage expectations proactively, reducing the likelihood of unpleasant surprises. This approach ensures that clients feel engaged and valued as active participants in the project.

Beyond maintaining trust, consistency in communication fosters accountability. Regular updates provide a structured opportunity to discuss achievements, address challenges, and outline the next steps. This not only keeps the team focused but also allows clients to track the value they are receiving at each stage. When communication falters or becomes sporadic, clients may question the team's competence or commitment, undermining the relationship. In contrast, consistent communication demonstrates a clear commitment to transparency and collaboration.

Ultimately, consistent communication establishes the foundation for a strong, long-term partnership. It creates an environment of trust and reliability, making clients more likely to turn to the same team for future projects. In an industry as competitive as IT, where word-of-mouth and reputation often dictate success, the benefits of consistent communication extend far beyond the immediate project. It positions IT professionals as trusted advisors rather than just service providers, ensuring sustained collaboration and mutual growth over time.

Transparency as a Foundation for Trust

Transparency is the cornerstone of building trust in any client relationship, particularly in the IT industry, where projects are complex and outcomes can sometimes feel intangible to clients. When clients are provided with clear, unvarnished insights into the project's progress, challenges, and decision-making processes, they are more likely to feel confident in the team's integrity and capability. Transparency not only strengthens trust but also creates an environment conducive to collaboration and long-term partnership.

One of the primary ways transparency fosters trust is by addressing uncertainty head-on. IT projects often involve unforeseen technical hurdles, changing requirements, or shifts in timelines. When these occur, teams that openly communicate the situation, the implications, and the proposed solutions demonstrate respect for the client's role as a stakeholder. This approach helps prevent frustration or skepticism, as clients are more willing to accept challenges when they feel they are being handled honestly and effectively.

Another critical aspect of transparency is the clear articulation of roles, responsibilities, and limitations. For example, explaining the boundaries of a project's scope or detailing the rationale behind certain technical decisions ensures that clients understand both the possibilities and constraints of the work. By aligning expectations with reality from the outset, IT professionals can avoid miscommunications that may lead to disappointment or conflict. Transparency here doesn't mean overwhelming clients with technical jargon but rather presenting information in a way that is accessible, relevant, and actionable.

Transparency also involves keeping clients informed about metrics and milestones. Regularly sharing performance data, budget updates, and progress reports provides clients with a tangible sense of advancement. Visual tools such as dashboards or status charts can enhance this process, offering real-time insights into the project. When clients see measurable progress, they are reassured that their investment is being managed responsibly, which in turn deepens their trust in the team's capabilities.

Lastly, transparency invites a culture of mutual respect and shared problem-solving. By involving clients in critical discussions and openly seeking their feedback, IT professionals demonstrate that they value the client's perspective and expertise. This collaborative approach not only builds trust but also helps identify creative solutions to challenges. Clients who feel that their voice is heard and respected are more likely to view the team as a true partner rather than just a service provider.

In the long term, transparency strengthens the professional bond between IT teams and their clients. It establishes a foundation of reliability and respect that supports not only the successful completion of current projects but also the potential for future collaborations. Transparency, when practiced consistently and thoughtfully, transforms client relationships into enduring partnerships built on mutual understanding and trust.

STRUCTURING UPDATES FOR CLARITY AND RELEVANCE

Effectively structured updates are crucial in maintaining client engagement and confidence throughout an IT project. In a field where technical complexities can be overwhelming, the way updates are communicated can make the difference between confusion and understanding, frustration and satisfaction. Structuring updates to emphasize clarity and relevance ensures that clients not only stay informed but also feel that their needs and priorities are being addressed.

To begin, updates should be tailored to the client's knowledge level and goals. Clients are often not as familiar with technical jargon or detailed project methodologies as the IT team. Therefore, updates should be written or delivered in straightforward, accessible language, focusing on the aspects that are most meaningful to the client. For instance, instead of diving into intricate code changes, highlight the outcome of those changes, such as improved functionality or a solved issue that aligns with the client's objectives. This approach respects the client's time and keeps the communication focused and effective.

A well-structured update also follows a logical flow, making it easier for clients to process and understand the information. A standard structure might include the following elements: a brief summary of the current status, key accomplishments since the last update, any challenges or risks encountered, and the next steps. Starting with a concise summary ensures that the most critical information is immediately accessible, while the detailed sections provide further context for those who wish to delve deeper. This layered approach allows clients to engage with the update at their preferred level of detail.

Including visual elements like charts, graphs, or dashboards can significantly enhance clarity. Visuals provide an immediate snapshot of progress, timelines, or issues, making complex data more digestible. For instance, a Gantt chart can visually display the project timeline, showing completed, ongoing, and upcoming tasks. A status indicator (e.g., green, yellow, red) can quickly signal overall project health. These tools allow clients to grasp the essentials at a glance while offering deeper insights for those who need them.

Relevance is another cornerstone of effective updates. Each communication should align with the client's interests and concerns. This means emphasizing how recent developments impact their goals, timelines, or budgets. For example, if a feature launch is delayed, the update should explain not only the reason but also how this will affect the overall project and what measures are being taken to mitigate the impact. Demonstrating that the team is proactive in managing challenges reassures clients of their commitment and expertise.

Updates should be delivered at consistent intervals, aligning with the agreed-upon communication cadence. Whether weekly, biweekly, or aligned with Agile sprints, regular updates create a predictable rhythm that clients can rely on.

Consistency reinforces the perception of reliability and professionalism, which are critical in fostering long-term relationships.

By structuring updates with clarity and relevance, IT teams can transform routine communications into powerful tools for building trust, managing expectations, and demonstrating value. This practice not only keeps clients informed but also positions the team as transparent, organized, and client-focused—qualities that are essential for successful and lasting collaborations.

TOOLS AND PLATFORMS FOR EFFECTIVE UPDATES

In the digital age, tools and platforms are indispensable for delivering consistent, transparent, and effective updates to clients. With IT projects often involving complex tasks, multiple teams, and tight deadlines, choosing the right tools can simplify communication, enhance understanding, and foster long-term relationships. Leveraging technology not only streamlines the process but also ensures that updates remain professional, timely, and accessible.

A key tool in effective updates is a project management platform. Platforms like Jira, Trello, Asana, or Microsoft Project offer centralized hubs where clients can view progress in real time. These platforms often include features like task boards, timelines, and automated notifications, which allow clients to monitor key milestones without waiting for scheduled meetings. For example, a client can log in to see how many tasks have been completed, which are in progress, and any blockers affecting deadlines. Such transparency not only builds trust but also reduces the need for repetitive inquiries, freeing up time for both the client and the team.

For collaborative and visually rich updates, presentation and dashboard tools such as Microsoft Power BI, Tableau, or Google Data Studio can be particularly effective. These tools allow teams to transform raw data into engaging visual reports, including charts, graphs, and infographics. Instead of wading through lengthy written reports, clients can quickly grasp project trends, performance metrics, or risk areas. For instance, a dashboard displaying color-coded status indicators (e.g., green for on track, yellow for minor delays, red for critical issues) immediately communicates project health at a glance.

Email platforms remain a cornerstone of client communication, especially for formal updates or reports. Tools like Microsoft Outlook or Gmail can be enhanced with scheduling and tracking features, ensuring that updates reach clients on time and allowing teams to monitor whether emails have been opened. Attaching concise, professional update templates or linking to interactive dashboards ensures that email communications are clear, actionable, and engaging.

For teams working across time zones or with geographically dispersed clients, video conferencing and collaboration tools like Zoom, Microsoft Teams, or Google Meet provide an invaluable way to deliver updates in person—or as close to it as possible. These tools facilitate direct conversations, where clients can ask questions, clarify concerns, and receive immediate responses. Coupled with screen-sharing features, they also allow teams to present complex concepts or visuals, enhancing understanding and fostering a collaborative spirit.

Finally, shared document repositories like Google Workspace, SharePoint, or Dropbox ensure that clients have ongoing access to key documents, update logs, and project files. These platforms reduce the risk of miscommunication by keeping all relevant materials in one easily accessible location. For example, an IT team might upload a weekly status report to a shared folder, ensuring that the client always has the latest information without needing to request it.

While tools and platforms are powerful enablers of effective updates, it's important to select those that align with both the team's capabilities and the client's preferences. Overloading clients with multiple tools can lead to confusion or "tool fatigue," detracting from the very clarity these tools aim to provide. Instead, focus on integrating a small number of versatile, user-friendly platforms that address the project's specific needs.

By thoughtfully utilizing modern tools and platforms, IT teams can elevate the quality of their updates, making them more efficient, engaging, and impactful. These tools not only enhance the delivery of updates but also reinforce the team's commitment to transparency, professionalism, and client satisfaction—cornerstones of building lasting relationships.

Turning Updates into Collaborative Opportunities

While updates are traditionally viewed as a one-way channel for sharing information, reframing them as collaborative opportunities transforms them into dynamic, interactive engagements. Collaborative updates invite clients to become active participants in the project, deepening their sense of ownership and fostering a stronger partnership. This approach not only strengthens the client-team relationship but also drives better project outcomes by integrating diverse perspectives.

At the heart of collaboration during updates is a dialogue-driven approach. Rather than simply presenting progress reports or action items, the team can design updates to include discussions on challenges, brainstorming solutions, and seeking feedback. For instance, instead of reporting that a particular module is behind schedule due to unforeseen complexities, the team might open the floor for the client's insights on reprioritizing features or adjusting timelines. This fosters mutual problem-solving, showcasing the team's openness and agility while valuing the client's input.

Collaboration during updates also helps align expectations. Clients often have evolving priorities based on external pressures or market demands. Structuring updates as a space to discuss these changes ensures that the project remains aligned with the client's goals. For example, an update meeting could include a segment where the team asks about any shifts in business needs or regulatory requirements. By integrating these discussions, the project remains flexible, responsive, and centered on delivering value.

Leveraging interactive tools and methods enhances the collaborative nature of updates. Tools like Miro or MURAL allow for real-time brainstorming and visual collaboration during update meetings. Similarly, shared action logs or live documents enable the team and client to co-create and refine project priorities. For instance, during a sprint review in an Agile project, a shared digital board could be used to jointly identify and prioritize the next set of tasks, giving the client a direct role in shaping the workflow.

Regular updates can also serve as a platform for knowledge exchange. IT teams often possess deep technical expertise, while clients bring industry-specific insights and operational needs. Updates that blend these perspectives enrich the project's direction. For instance, the team might explain how a new feature addresses a technical challenge, while the client can provide input on how end-users are likely to interact with the feature. This mutual sharing ensures that technical deliverables are not only robust but also practical and user-friendly.

Collaboration during updates builds trust and transparency, as it demonstrates the team's willingness to engage the client beyond surface-level reporting. When clients see their ideas influencing decisions or recognize their feedback being implemented, it creates a sense of partnership rather than a transactional relationship. This, in turn, fosters long-term loyalty and goodwill.

It's crucial, however, to set boundaries and structure for collaborative updates. While client participation is valuable, it's the responsibility of the IT team to guide these sessions effectively, ensuring they remain productive and focused. Clear agendas, time-boxed discussions, and well-defined objectives prevent collaborative updates from veering into unstructured debates or extended deliberations.

Turning updates into collaborative opportunities shifts the narrative from simply informing clients to actively engaging them in the project's journey. This not only strengthens the relationship but also results in deliverables that are more aligned, innovative, and impactful. By embracing collaboration as a core element of the update process, IT teams can create a dynamic and empowering environment where both parties work as partners toward shared success.

HANDLING SETBACKS WITH INTEGRITY

In any IT project, setbacks are inevitable. These can range from minor delays in deliverables to significant technical failures or misalignments in expectations. While challenges are a natural part of complex initiatives, how a team addresses these setbacks is what defines the strength and resilience of its relationship with the client. Handling setbacks with integrity is not only about finding solutions but also about fostering trust, credibility, and long-term partnership.

Transparency is the cornerstone of managing setbacks with integrity

Clients appreciate honesty over obfuscation, even when the news is unfavorable. The first step is to acknowledge the issue promptly, providing a clear and concise explanation of what went wrong, why it happened, and its potential impact on the project. Avoiding blame or downplaying the situation fosters a collaborative environment where both parties focus on solutions rather than assigning fault. For example, if a software deployment is delayed due to unforeseen integration issues, admitting the misstep and explaining the technical details demonstrates accountability and expertise.

Integrity also requires a proactive approach to resolution. When setbacks occur, clients expect more than an explanation—they want a clear path forward. The team should outline the steps being taken to address the problem, along with revised timelines or resource adjustments. Presenting multiple options and involving the client in choosing the most viable path strengthens their confidence in the team's ability to recover. For instance, if a feature implementation exceeds the estimated timeline, offering alternatives such as phased delivery or temporary workarounds keeps the project on track while accommodating the client's priorities.

Empathy plays a vital role in maintaining trust during setbacks. Clients often feel the pressure of delays or failures acutely, especially when these setbacks impact their business operations or customer relationships. Acknowledging their frustrations and demonstrating a genuine commitment to resolving the issue fosters goodwill. Phrases like "We understand how important this is for your team, and we are fully committed to resolving it as quickly as possible" convey empathy and dedication, transforming what could be a strained interaction into a constructive dialogue.

Setbacks also present an opportunity to demonstrate adaptability and resilience. Clients value teams that can pivot effectively in response to challenges. This might mean reallocating resources, bringing in additional expertise, or revisiting project priorities. Communicating these efforts clearly reassures clients of the team's ability to handle adversity with competence and professionalism. For example, if a critical vendor fails to deliver on time, the IT team could outline steps to source an alternative provider while minimizing project disruption, emphasizing their commitment to the client's success.

Documenting the setback and its resolution is equally important. This ensures that both the team and the client have a shared understanding of what occurred and how it was addressed. A post-mortem report or summary meeting can highlight lessons learned, preventing similar issues in the future. This approach not only demonstrates accountability but also positions the team as a partner focused on continuous improvement.

Finally, rebuilding confidence after setbacks is crucial. Even after an issue is resolved, lingering doubts may affect the client's perception of the project or team. Consistent communication, exceeding expectations in subsequent deliverables, and celebrating milestones together can help restore confidence. For instance, after successfully overcoming a delay, emphasizing the project's on-track progress in subsequent updates reinforces the team's reliability and commitment.

Handling setbacks with integrity transforms challenges into opportunities to strengthen client relationships. By being transparent, proactive, empathetic, and solution-oriented, IT teams can turn difficult moments into demonstrations of their professionalism and reliability. This not only resolves the immediate issue but also leaves a lasting impression of trustworthiness and partnership.

Reinforcing Long-Term Value Through Updates

Building lasting relationships with clients requires more than delivering results—it demands a consistent demonstration of the ongoing value a team brings to the partnership. Updates are not just about communicating progress but about reinforcing the broader benefits of collaboration and aligning deliverables with the client's evolving objectives. By framing updates in a way that underscores long-term value, IT teams can position themselves as indispensable partners rather than just service providers.

Start by connecting updates to the client's strategic goals. Every communication should emphasize how the current work aligns with and supports the client's long-term objectives. This approach transforms updates from routine status reports into strategic discussions. For example, instead of merely stating that a data migration is 80% complete, the update should highlight how this progress enables the client to transition to a more scalable infrastructure, ultimately supporting their growth targets. This narrative ensures that clients see the work's significance beyond its immediate scope.

Another crucial aspect is to highlight cumulative achievements over time. Individual milestones, while valuable, gain greater impact when framed within the context of broader project goals. Summarizing progress in quarterly or annual reviews can demonstrate how various accomplishments have built toward substantial outcomes. For instance, detailing how iterative improvements to a customer relationship management (CRM) system have directly contributed to increased user adoption and better customer retention reinforces the tangible value delivered through the team's efforts.

Use updates to proactively identify and address future opportunities. A forward-looking approach signals a vested interest in the client's success beyond the current project. Updates should include insights on emerging trends, potential areas for optimization, or upcoming risks that the team has identified. For example, an IT team supporting a retail client might provide updates on how analytics tools are driving insights but also suggest integrating predictive modeling to anticipate future customer needs. This not only reinforces the team's value but also positions them as thought leaders invested in the client's continuous improvement.

Equally important is the ability to translate technical achievements into relatable business outcomes. While clients may appreciate the technical intricacies of a system upgrade or a successful API integration, they are more likely to value the tangible benefits—cost savings, operational efficiencies, or improved customer satisfaction. For instance, an update on optimizing cloud storage usage could be framed as a reduction in operating expenses, freeing up resources for other strategic initiatives. This approach ensures that clients understand how technical advancements directly impact their organizational success.

Consistency in delivery reinforces trust and reliability. Regular updates—delivered on time and with predictable structure—signal a commitment to transparency and accountability. Clients come to rely on these updates as part of their decision-making process. For example, a biweekly dashboard update that consistently tracks key performance indicators (KPIs) assures the client that progress is being monitored and managed effectively. Consistency also allows teams to address concerns promptly, further strengthening the relationship.

Finally, end each update with a reminder of partnership value. Whether through a summary of contributions, a reflection on mutual successes, or a vision for future collaboration, ending on a positive note reinforces the long-term potential of the relationship. A simple statement like "This milestone is another step toward achieving your broader goal of digital transformation" ties the update to a larger narrative, reminding the client of the team's ongoing dedication to their success.

By using updates to reinforce long-term value, IT teams ensure that clients see the full scope of their contributions, not just as short-term problem solvers but as strategic partners driving sustained growth and innovation. This approach solidifies trust, enhances satisfaction, and lays the foundation for a lasting relationship.

Evaluating the Effectiveness of Updates

Delivering consistent and transparent updates is essential, but their ultimate value hinges on how effectively they achieve their purpose—fostering understanding, trust, and alignment between teams and clients. Evaluating the impact of updates ensures that communication is not only frequent but also meaningful, actionable, and relevant. Through continuous assessment and improvement, IT teams can refine their approach, reinforcing their value as strategic partners.

Start with client feedback as the primary metric. Direct input from the client is the most reliable way to assess whether updates meet their expectations. This feedback can be gathered through informal conversations, structured surveys, or periodic review meetings. For instance, asking whether updates are timely, clear, and aligned with their priorities can uncover gaps in communication. A client might indicate that while technical details are appreciated, they prefer more emphasis on business outcomes—a signal to adjust the focus of future updates.

Analyze engagement levels to gauge effectiveness. A well-constructed update should prompt questions, foster dialogue, and encourage collaboration. Low engagement, such as clients skipping meetings, providing minimal responses, or delaying sign-offs, may indicate that updates are not resonating. Tracking attendance at update presentations, monitoring follow-up actions, or evaluating response times to shared documents can reveal whether the updates are engaging or falling flat. These signals highlight areas for improvement, whether in format, frequency, or content.

Measure the alignment between updates and project goals. Effective updates should directly reflect the project's progress toward agreed-upon deliverables and strategic objectives. Regularly comparing the content of updates with the project plan ensures that communication remains on track. For example, if updates consistently report activities rather than outcomes, the client might struggle to connect the work being done to their broader goals. By focusing on outcomes and providing measurable progress against key milestones, updates become a more powerful tool for maintaining alignment.

Evaluate the clarity and accessibility of the communication. Updates should be easily understood by a non-technical audience while still conveying critical information. Tools such as readability tests, peer reviews, or even mock presentations to a neutral party can help determine whether the message is clear and compelling. If clients frequently ask for clarification or seem confused about certain aspects, this is a red flag that the updates need simplification. Using plain language, visual aids, or concise summaries can enhance clarity and ensure the message is accessible.

Leverage retrospective meetings to assess update quality. As part of broader project evaluations, retrospectives offer a structured way to reflect on the effectiveness of communication. These sessions can include discussions about what aspects of updates worked well, what caused confusion, and how the process can be improved. For example, a retrospective might reveal that weekly updates were too frequent, leading to redundancy, or that key metrics were missing, leaving clients uncertain about progress. Such insights guide adjustments to enhance future communication.

Monitor the outcomes linked to updates. The effectiveness of updates can also be measured by their tangible impact on decision-making, project progress, and client satisfaction. If updates consistently lead to timely approvals, smooth handoffs, or resolved concerns, they are serving their purpose well. Conversely, delays or misaligned expectations suggest a need to refine the process. For instance, if a delay occurred because a client misunderstood the technical implications of a decision, it might indicate that updates need more contextual explanation or visual support.

Establish a culture of continuous improvement. Evaluating updates is not a one-time activity but an ongoing process. By creating a feedback loop where clients and team members can share suggestions regularly, IT teams ensure that their communication evolves alongside project needs. For example, introducing a quarterly "communication review" meeting can help identify patterns and implement changes incrementally. This proactive approach reinforces the team's commitment to excellence and fosters stronger client relationships.

Through thoughtful evaluation and iterative improvement, IT teams can transform routine updates into a dynamic and impactful element of their client relationships. Effective updates not only convey progress but also demonstrate accountability, build trust, and ensure that communication remains a cornerstone of project success.

CASE STUDIES AND REAL-WORLD EXAMPLES

Case Studies and Real-World Examples

Examining case studies and real-world scenarios brings theoretical principles to life, providing practical insights into the impact of consistent and transparent updates on client relationships. These examples illustrate the challenges faced, the strategies employed, and the outcomes achieved, offering a roadmap for navigating similar situations in diverse IT environments.

Case Study 1: Navigating Misaligned Expectations in an ERP Implementation

A multinational manufacturing company embarked on a complex ERP implementation to streamline its supply chain. Early in the project, communication issues arose when clients expressed dissatisfaction with the perceived lack of progress, despite significant backend work being completed.

To address this, the IT team restructured their updates. Instead of providing highly technical reports that emphasized system configurations, they began framing updates around client-relevant milestones, such as data migration progress, user training schedules, and anticipated process improvements. These updates were supplemented with dashboards displaying clear, visual progress indicators.

The result was a noticeable shift in client perception. As updates became more relatable and aligned with their goals, trust was restored. The project ultimately achieved its objectives within the revised timeline, and the client credited the enhanced communication approach as a key factor in the turnaround.

Case Study 2: Building Trust in a Cloud Migration Project
A mid-sized financial services firm sought to migrate its infrastructure to a cloud environment to improve scalability and security. With a history of delayed IT projects, the client was initially skeptical about timelines and deliverables.

The IT consultancy managing the project prioritized transparency from the outset. Weekly updates highlighted progress, identified risks, and detailed mitigation strategies. A dedicated portal allowed the client to track deliverables in real time, ensuring there were no surprises. When a critical delay arose due to a third-party vendor, the IT team proactively communicated the issue, outlined the impact, and presented an adjusted timeline.

This approach not only reassured the client but also strengthened their confidence in the consultancy. By delivering updates that were honest, detailed, and solutions-oriented, the team fostered a long-term partnership. The client later engaged the same consultancy for additional projects, citing their transparent communication as a key differentiator.

Case Study 3: Collaborative Problem-Solving During a Mobile App Development
A healthcare startup partnered with an IT firm to develop a patient engagement mobile app. Midway through the project, it became clear that the client's initial requirements lacked clarity, leading to scope creep and potential cost overruns.

Recognizing the risk to the relationship, the IT team turned their updates into collaborative sessions. They introduced interactive workshops where updates were presented as a two-way dialogue, allowing the client to refine requirements in real time. Prototypes and mockups were integrated into these sessions, providing a tangible way for the client to visualize progress and adjust expectations.

This iterative approach not only resolved the immediate scope issues but also deepened the client's involvement. By empowering the client to shape the project's direction, the IT firm demonstrated flexibility and commitment, resulting in a successful product launch and a highly satisfied client.

Case Study 4: Crisis Management in a Cybersecurity Breach
An e-commerce company experienced a major cybersecurity breach, prompting an emergency response from their IT partner. The situation was high-stakes, with reputational and financial risks at play.

The IT team implemented hourly updates during the initial response phase, ensuring the client was informed of every development. They used plain language to explain technical findings, provided visual timelines for containment and recovery, and involved the client in key decisions.

Post-crisis, the team delivered a comprehensive incident report, including a root cause analysis and recommendations for future prevention. The transparency and frequency of updates during the crisis not only mitigated the client's anxiety but also reinforced their trust in the IT partner. The client later expanded their contract, citing the firm's exemplary communication during the breach.

Real-World Example: Adopting Agile in a Traditional Organization
A traditional manufacturing company transitioning to an Agile framework faced significant cultural resistance. The IT team introduced bi-weekly sprint reviews to update stakeholders on progress and gather feedback. These sessions were designed to be inclusive, using non-technical language and showcasing results through demos rather than written reports.

The regular, transparent updates helped demystify Agile for the stakeholders and demonstrated its value through visible progress. Over time, this approach not only facilitated the successful adoption of Agile but also strengthened relationships with key stakeholders, who began championing the framework within the organization.

Insights from Case Studies

These examples demonstrate that consistent and transparent updates are not a one-size-fits-all solution. They must be tailored to the project's context, the client's needs, and the relationship dynamics. Whether addressing misaligned expectations, navigating crises, or fostering collaboration, effective updates serve as a linchpin for successful client relationships. By drawing lessons from real-world scenarios, IT professionals can refine their communication practices to build trust, enhance satisfaction, and achieve long-term success.

ACTIONABLE TAKEAWAYS AND TOOLS

Building enduring client relationships requires a structured approach to delivering consistent and transparent updates. While principles like trust, clarity, and collaboration form the foundation, translating these into actionable practices demands a combination of disciplined communication habits and effective tools. This section provides practical insights and methods to enhance client communication through actionable takeaways and tested tools.

One of the most critical aspects of client communication is ensuring that updates consistently address the client's priorities and needs. Updates should be customer-centric rather than project-focused, reframing milestones in terms of how they benefit the client's goals. For example, instead of stating that "Module X is 70% complete," framing it as "The core feature requested for improving user experience is nearing completion and will be ready for testing next week" makes the update more meaningful. Each communication should reflect an understanding of the client's objectives, reinforcing the value of the project and the collaboration.

Consistency in the timing and delivery of updates is another vital factor. Setting a predictable schedule for updates—whether weekly reports, bi-weekly check-ins, or monthly reviews—establishes a cadence that clients can depend on. Predictability builds trust, as clients are assured of regular insights into progress and any emerging challenges. Regularity also reduces unnecessary back-and-forth communication and minimizes client uncertainty, fostering a professional image of reliability. This structured approach works best when paired with an established format that ensures key elements, such as progress summaries, risks, and next steps, are covered in every update.

The choice of communication platforms and methods significantly affects the clarity and impact of updates. Visual tools like charts, Gantt timelines, and dashboards help convey progress in an easily digestible manner, particularly for clients unfamiliar with technical details. Collaborative platforms, such as Trello or Jira, provide clients with real-time access to project status, creating transparency and fostering inclusivity. While written reports are essential for detailed documentation, combining them with periodic verbal presentations—such as video calls or face-to-face meetings—allows for richer dialogue and instant feedback. This multi-channel strategy caters to diverse client preferences and strengthens engagement.

Transparency, particularly during setbacks, plays a critical role in maintaining trust. Clients value honesty over attempts to mask or minimize challenges. When delays or issues arise, it is vital to communicate them promptly, along with a detailed plan to address the problem. This not only demonstrates accountability but also reassures the client that the project remains on track despite obstacles. For example, sharing that a delivery timeline has been impacted due to unforeseen circumstances, followed by an actionable recovery plan with revised deadlines, reinforces both integrity and a commitment to success.

Evaluating the effectiveness of updates is equally important to ensure that communication remains impactful. Soliciting client feedback on the frequency, content, and format of updates allows adjustments that align with their preferences. For example, some clients may prefer concise summaries supplemented by in-depth reports, while others may value more interactive discussions. Regular feedback loops demonstrate a willingness to adapt and prioritize the client's experience, further strengthening the relationship.

By combining client-centric communication, predictable schedules, and the appropriate tools, IT professionals can deliver updates that not only inform but also engage and reassure clients. The cumulative effect of these efforts is the cultivation of trust and a perception of value that extends beyond project completion.

Chapter 7: Managing Deliverables: Communication as a Control Mechanism

.Deliverables are the tangible outcomes of any project, and their clarity often determines the success or failure of an IT initiative. In the high-stakes environment of large-scale IT projects, where multiple teams and stakeholders converge, ambiguous deliverables can derail progress, increase costs, and erode trust. For stakeholders, clear deliverables offer a roadmap to measure success, while for teams, they provide actionable targets to focus their efforts. However, in practice, defining deliverables with precision remains a significant challenge. Many projects falter due to vague agreements or misaligned interpretations of what needs to be achieved.

The absence of clarity often stems from varying perspectives among stakeholders. For instance, business leaders may prioritize outcomes tied to customer experience, while IT professionals focus on the technical feasibility of deliverables. Without a shared understanding, these differences can result in friction, delays, and unmet expectations. Additionally, as IT projects frequently evolve due to changing requirements or unforeseen constraints, ambiguous deliverables make it difficult to adapt without conflict. Therefore, the foundation of successful project communication lies in explicitly defining deliverables from the outset and revisiting them regularly to maintain alignment.

Moreover, clarity in deliverables directly impacts the dynamics of collaboration within and across teams. When everyone involved in the project has a unified vision of what constitutes success, coordination becomes smoother, and accountability is easier to establish. On the other hand, unclear deliverables often lead to redundant efforts, inefficiencies, and the dreaded "scope creep," where projects spiral out of control due to poorly defined boundaries. Clarity acts as a safeguard, ensuring that all participants operate under consistent assumptions and focus their resources on the agreed objectives.

Clarity in deliverables is not just about reducing confusion; it is a critical element of risk management in IT projects. Ambiguity introduces risks at every stage of the project lifecycle, from planning to execution and delivery. By establishing well-defined deliverables, project managers can identify potential issues early, set realistic timelines, and ensure that the outcomes meet stakeholder needs.

This chapter explores how to achieve this clarity, providing frameworks and strategies to align teams and stakeholders around a shared vision, minimize risks, and deliver results that matter.

IDENTIFYING STAKEHOLDER NEEDS

Identifying stakeholder needs is a critical step in ensuring the success of IT projects, as it establishes the foundation for defining clear and actionable deliverables. Stakeholders represent a diverse group of individuals and entities, each with unique priorities, concerns, and expectations. These may include business executives, technical teams, end-users, external vendors, and even regulatory bodies. Understanding their needs involves more than just listing requirements; it demands a nuanced approach to uncover the underlying goals and motivations driving their expectations. Failure to accurately identify and address these needs can lead to misaligned objectives, diminished trust, and project delays.

A systematic approach to stakeholder mapping is the first step in this process. Stakeholder mapping involves identifying all individuals and groups who have an interest in the project and categorizing them based on their influence and level of engagement. High-influence stakeholders, such as executive sponsors, typically focus on strategic outcomes like cost efficiency, competitive advantage, or compliance with industry standards. Meanwhile, technical teams and end-users are often concerned with practical implementation and usability. By mapping these relationships, project managers can prioritize communication and resource allocation, ensuring that the most critical stakeholders are engaged appropriately and at the right times.

To truly understand stakeholder needs, direct engagement is indispensable. Methods like one-on-one interviews, group workshops, and surveys allow stakeholders to articulate their expectations and provide valuable context. For example, while a business leader may request "greater system efficiency," probing deeper can reveal specific concerns such as minimizing downtime during peak hours or reducing operational costs. Similarly, involving end-users can highlight practical requirements like interface simplicity or speed, which might otherwise be overlooked in technical discussions. By asking open-ended questions and encouraging dialogue, project managers can gather a more comprehensive view of stakeholder priorities and identify commonalities or conflicts early in the process.

Distinguishing between needs and wants is a crucial aspect of this discovery phase. Stakeholders may express desires that, while appealing, do not align with the project's scope or constraints. It falls to the project manager to evaluate which requests are essential to the project's objectives and which can be deferred or negotiated. This prioritization often involves transparent communication, where stakeholders are guided to understand trade-offs and compromises. For instance, a requested feature might be postponed to ensure timely delivery of core functionalities. By managing expectations collaboratively and thoughtfully, project managers not only clarify deliverables but also strengthen relationships with stakeholders, fostering a cooperative environment that supports long-term success.

ESTABLISHING SMART DELIVERABLES

Defining deliverables using the SMART framework—Specific, Measurable, Achievable, Relevant, and Time-bound—is essential for transforming broad objectives into actionable outcomes. In IT projects, where complexity and ambiguity often challenge progress, SMART deliverables provide clarity and structure. This framework ensures that all stakeholders share a common understanding of what is expected, how success will be measured, and when results will be delivered. Without such precision, projects risk miscommunication, scope creep, and unmet expectations, undermining both efficiency and trust.

Specificity lies at the heart of SMART deliverables. A deliverable must answer key questions: What exactly needs to be achieved? Who is responsible for it? What are the boundaries of its scope? For instance, instead of defining a deliverable as "improving system performance," a specific deliverable would be "reducing average page load time by 30% for users in North America." This level of detail removes ambiguity and aligns stakeholders on the exact outcome being pursued. Specificity also helps teams focus their efforts, avoiding wasted resources on activities that do not directly contribute to the stated goal.

Measurability is equally critical, as it allows progress to be tracked and success to be objectively assessed. A measurable deliverable includes quantifiable metrics or criteria that indicate completion. For example, a deliverable like "implementing a new user authentication system" becomes measurable when paired with criteria such as "system deployment across all regions with less than 1% error rate." Measurability not only keeps teams accountable but also enables stakeholders to evaluate whether the deliverable meets their expectations. It fosters transparency, as everyone involved can see how progress aligns with the predefined metrics at each stage of the project.

The Achievable and Relevant aspects of SMART deliverables ensure that objectives are grounded in reality and aligned with the broader goals of the project. An achievable deliverable considers available resources, technical feasibility, and organizational constraints. Setting unattainable goals leads to frustration and erodes confidence, while realistic ones motivate teams to perform effectively. Similarly, relevance ensures that each deliverable contributes meaningfully to the project's overall success. For instance, an IT infrastructure upgrade deliverable should directly support business objectives like improved customer experience or operational efficiency, rather than addressing unrelated concerns.

Finally, time-bound deliverables establish clear deadlines, creating a sense of urgency and driving accountability. Deadlines should be realistic yet firm, providing teams with a defined timeline for achieving milestones. For example, a deliverable could specify "migrating 100% of customer data to the new platform by June 30, 2025." Time-bound deliverables help prioritize tasks, manage resources effectively, and maintain momentum throughout the project lifecycle. When all aspects of the SMART framework are applied, deliverables become powerful tools for guiding team efforts, managing stakeholder expectations, and delivering results that meet or exceed project objectives.

SETTING COMMUNICATION CHANNELS AND PROTOCOLS

Establishing effective communication channels and protocols is fundamental to ensuring deliverables are clearly understood and consistently tracked by all stakeholders. In IT projects, where teams often span multiple departments, locations, and even time zones, the absence of well-defined communication structures can lead to misunderstandings, delays, and conflicts. By deliberately setting up appropriate channels and protocols, project managers create a framework for seamless information flow, enhancing collaboration and accountability across all participants involved in achieving deliverables.

The first step in this process is selecting the right communication channels based on the project's needs and stakeholder preferences. Email, while reliable for formal documentation, may not be suitable for real-time discussions or collaborative problem-solving. Tools like Slack or Microsoft Teams provide platforms for instant messaging and file sharing, fostering quicker decision-making. Similarly, project management tools like Jira or Trello can centralize updates on deliverables, offering transparency and a single source of truth. It is crucial, however, to avoid over-reliance on any single medium. For instance, while instant messaging is convenient, critical updates should also be documented in formal reports to ensure traceability and avoid miscommunication.

Defining communication protocols is the next step, as these establish the "rules of engagement" for interactions among team members and stakeholders. Protocols should address frequency, format, and audience for each type of communication. For example, weekly progress meetings might be scheduled to provide high-level updates to executives, while daily stand-ups focus on granular task coordination within technical teams. Additionally, protocols should clarify expectations for response times, such as requiring replies to emails within 24 hours or immediate acknowledgment of urgent messages. By setting these standards upfront, project managers reduce ambiguity and foster a culture of accountability.

Another essential aspect is tailoring communication to suit the needs of diverse audiences. Not all stakeholders require the same level of detail or technical depth. For instance, a progress report for business leaders might focus on key milestones and budget adherence, while a report for developers would delve into specific tasks and dependencies. Ensuring that the right information reaches the right audience not only saves time but also prevents misinterpretation. Visual aids, such as Gantt charts, dashboards, or annotated diagrams, can further enhance clarity, particularly when communicating complex deliverables to non-technical stakeholders.

The communication framework must be flexible and adaptable to address evolving project needs. As projects progress, unforeseen challenges may arise, requiring adjustments to the established protocols. For example, if a critical deliverable encounters delays, the frequency of status updates may need to increase to keep all parties informed. Regularly reviewing and refining communication practices ensures they remain effective, promoting alignment and collaboration throughout the project. By investing time and effort into establishing robust communication channels and protocols, project managers lay the groundwork for successful deliverable management and stakeholder satisfaction.

ESTABLISHING SUCCESS CRITERIA AND METRICS

Establishing clear success criteria and metrics is pivotal to defining what constitutes the satisfactory completion of a deliverable in IT projects. These criteria serve as benchmarks for evaluating performance, ensuring all stakeholders agree on the standards of success. Without explicit metrics, the risk of misaligned expectations grows, leading to disputes over quality, delays in approval, and project inefficiencies. Success criteria and metrics not only provide clarity but also foster accountability, enabling teams to focus on tangible outcomes that align with project goals.

The foundation of success criteria lies in aligning them with the project's overarching objectives. For each deliverable, the project manager must consider the specific goals it is intended to achieve. For example, if a deliverable involves the deployment of a new application, success criteria might include technical functionality, user adoption rates, and system stability. Engaging stakeholders in defining these criteria ensures that their expectations are accurately captured and that the deliverable's outcomes contribute meaningfully to broader business or operational objectives. This alignment reduces ambiguities, as every party understands how the deliverable fits within the project's scope.

Quantifiable metrics are at the heart of evaluating success. These metrics should be measurable and relevant to the nature of the deliverable. For instance, success for a software migration deliverable might be measured by a 95% accuracy rate in data transfer or a 20% reduction in system downtime post-deployment. Similarly, user-facing deliverables, such as website updates, might use metrics like a 15% increase in traffic or a 30% improvement in page load times. Quantifiable metrics provide an objective basis for assessment, helping stakeholders to evaluate whether the deliverable meets predefined expectations and supports the intended outcomes.

The process of establishing success criteria must also account for the perspectives of different stakeholder groups. Business stakeholders may prioritize cost efficiency or regulatory compliance, while technical teams may focus on system performance and scalability. Balancing these priorities requires thoughtful dialogue and compromise. For example, while business leaders might push for expedited timelines, technical teams may highlight the need for adequate testing to ensure quality. By reconciling these viewpoints, project managers can define balanced success criteria that satisfy both strategic and operational needs, fostering a sense of shared ownership among stakeholders.

Success criteria and metrics should include mechanisms for continuous evaluation and refinement. Throughout the project lifecycle, interim assessments against these benchmarks can reveal whether deliverables are on track to meet expectations. If gaps are identified, corrective actions can be taken early, minimizing the risk of costly rework or failure at later stages. Furthermore, reviewing success metrics post-completion offers valuable insights for future projects, highlighting what worked well and where improvements are needed. By embedding success criteria and metrics into the project's communication and evaluation processes, teams ensure that deliverables are not only completed but also contribute measurably to the project's overall success.

Documenting Agreements

Documenting agreements is a critical step in ensuring alignment and accountability for deliverables in IT projects. Verbal discussions, while often the starting point for decision-making, can lead to misunderstandings or misinterpretations if not formally recorded. A well-documented agreement serves as a reference point for all stakeholders, detailing the scope, responsibilities, timelines, and success criteria for each deliverable. This process fosters clarity and prevents disputes, enabling teams to focus on execution rather than debating expectations later in the project lifecycle.

The documentation process begins with a comprehensive summary of the deliverable's key elements. This includes its objectives, detailed specifications, and the roles of each stakeholder. For instance, in a project involving the implementation of a new customer relationship management (CRM) system, the documentation should outline not only the technical requirements—such as data migration protocols and system integrations—but also the responsibilities of business teams in providing user requirements and feedback. By capturing these details, project managers create a unified understanding of the deliverable's scope and the contributions required from all parties.

Timelines and milestones are another essential component of documented agreements. A clear timeline specifies not only the final deadline for the deliverable but also the intermediary steps needed to achieve it. For example, a software development deliverable might include milestones for completing initial designs, conducting user acceptance testing, and deploying the final version. Each milestone should be paired with specific dates and responsible parties, ensuring accountability at every stage. When these timelines are documented and shared, they provide a roadmap that helps keep the project on track and prevents delays caused by miscommunication or overlooked dependencies.

Documenting agreements also involves formalizing the success criteria and metrics established during earlier planning stages. These benchmarks must be explicitly stated, leaving no room for ambiguity about what constitutes a "complete" or "successful" deliverable. For example, if a deliverable involves optimizing an e-commerce platform, the documented agreement might specify metrics like a 10% increase in transaction speed and a 15% reduction in cart abandonment rates. Including such measurable criteria in the documentation allows stakeholders to objectively assess progress and verify whether the deliverable meets the agreed-upon standards.

The documentation process must emphasize accessibility and version control. Agreements should be stored in a centralized location, such as a project management platform or shared document repository, ensuring that all stakeholders can easily access the latest version. Changes to the agreement—whether due to evolving project needs or unforeseen challenges—must be meticulously tracked and communicated to all relevant parties. Tools like version-controlled documents or meeting minutes can capture these updates, providing transparency and minimizing the risk of confusion. By meticulously documenting agreements, project managers build a foundation of trust and clarity, enabling seamless collaboration and successful delivery of project outcomes.

REINFORCING EXPECTATIONS THROUGH CHECKPOINTS

In complex IT projects, initial agreements and plans often face challenges as the project progresses. Changing requirements, unforeseen obstacles, and evolving stakeholder priorities can all threaten the alignment of expectations. To mitigate these risks, reinforcing expectations through regular checkpoints is essential. Checkpoints serve as scheduled reviews where teams revisit deliverables, assess progress, address potential misalignments, and reestablish shared goals. This process ensures that all stakeholders remain aligned and engaged, providing an opportunity to course-correct before issues escalate.

Checkpoints are most effective when strategically integrated into the project timeline. They should coincide with critical milestones, such as the completion of a development phase, the initiation of testing, or the rollout of a prototype. For instance, in an Agile environment, sprint reviews naturally function as checkpoints, allowing teams to evaluate deliverables and gather feedback iteratively. In traditional methodologies like PMP or ITIL, checkpoints might align with phase gates, ensuring that each stage meets predefined criteria before advancing. By embedding these reviews into the project workflow, teams maintain a structured rhythm for assessing and refining deliverables.

A key function of checkpoints is to validate progress against established success criteria and metrics. During each review, stakeholders should evaluate whether the deliverable is meeting the agreed-upon standards. For example, if a deliverable involves enhancing system performance, the team might use the checkpoint to compare current results against benchmarks such as response times or error rates. These evaluations not only provide transparency but also empower teams to identify and address discrepancies early. The ability to flag minor issues before they grow into significant problems is one of the most valuable outcomes of consistent checkpoints.

Effective communication is critical to making checkpoints productive. Prior to each review, project managers should circulate an agenda outlining the deliverables being assessed, the metrics under consideration, and any specific topics requiring input. This preparation ensures that all participants come to the checkpoint with a clear understanding of its objectives, fostering focused and efficient discussions. Additionally, the outcomes of the checkpoint—whether updates to timelines, changes to scope, or feedback on deliverables—must be documented and communicated to all relevant parties. This practice ensures that every stakeholder remains informed, even if they were not directly involved in the checkpoint itself.

Finally, checkpoints play an essential role in maintaining stakeholder confidence and engagement. Regular reviews demonstrate the team's commitment to transparency and accountability, reinforcing trust between internal teams, clients, and other stakeholders. Moreover, by inviting feedback and collaboration, checkpoints provide stakeholders with a sense of ownership over the deliverables, increasing their investment in the project's success. This proactive approach not only keeps the project on track but also fosters a culture of continuous improvement and shared responsibility, enabling smoother execution and more successful outcomes.

COMMON CHALLENGES IN SETTING DELIVERABLE EXPECTATIONS

Even the most meticulously planned IT projects face real-world challenges when establishing and managing deliverable expectations. These scenarios often arise from miscommunication, shifting priorities, or unforeseen technical complexities. Addressing these challenges requires a blend of proactive planning, adaptive problem-solving, and effective communication to ensure deliverables remain aligned with stakeholder needs. By examining common scenarios, teams can anticipate potential pitfalls and apply strategies to mitigate them effectively.

One frequent challenge occurs when stakeholders have conflicting expectations about deliverables. For instance, a technical team may prioritize scalability and future-proofing, while business stakeholders focus on rapid deployment and cost efficiency. Such misalignment can lead to frustration, delays, or deliverables that satisfy neither party. Addressing this requires clear communication during the planning phase, where priorities are explicitly discussed and reconciled. Facilitated workshops or stakeholder meetings can help surface differing expectations, allowing the team to define a compromise that aligns with the project's broader goals. Documenting these agreements ensures clarity and reduces the risk of future disputes.

Another common issue arises from evolving project requirements. IT projects often face scope changes due to new business needs, regulatory updates, or emerging technologies. For example, a deliverable initially scoped as a basic analytics dashboard may evolve into a more complex, real-time reporting tool as stakeholder demands shift. Such changes can strain timelines and budgets if not managed carefully. To mitigate this, teams should establish a formal change management process. This includes defining how new requirements are evaluated, approved, and incorporated into the project plan. Regular checkpoints and transparent communication about the implications of changes—such as cost, timeline, or resource adjustments—help manage stakeholder expectations while maintaining control over the project scope.

Unclear or ambiguous success criteria present another significant hurdle. When stakeholders and teams lack a shared understanding of what constitutes a "complete" or "successful" deliverable, approval processes can become drawn out, leading to frustration and inefficiency. For example, a software integration deliverable might be considered "complete" by the development team once functional tests pass, but stakeholders might expect additional documentation or training materials. To address this, teams must invest time early in the project to define specific, measurable success criteria. Incorporating these criteria into contracts, project charters, or requirement documents ensures that everyone shares the same expectations.

Lastly, breakdowns in communication channels can derail the process of setting and managing deliverable expectations. In distributed or multi-vendor projects, miscommunication often results from siloed teams, lack of centralized updates, or inconsistent reporting. For instance, a vendor might misinterpret a requirement due to incomplete or outdated documentation, leading to deliverables that deviate from the agreed-upon specifications. Establishing robust communication protocols—such as regular status meetings, shared dashboards, and collaborative platforms like Jira or Confluence—can significantly reduce these risks. These tools ensure that information flows seamlessly across teams and stakeholders, keeping everyone aligned and informed.

By recognizing and addressing these practical challenges, IT teams can create a more resilient framework for setting and managing deliverable expectations. Anticipating conflicts, preparing for evolving requirements, and maintaining robust communication practices help ensure that deliverables are not only completed but also meet the needs of all stakeholders, contributing to the project's overall success.

KEY TAKEAWAYS AND SUMMARY

Setting clear expectations for deliverables is a cornerstone of successful IT project management, bridging the gap between diverse teams and stakeholders while ensuring alignment on goals, timelines, and outcomes. As the chapter has illustrated, clarity in deliverables does not emerge spontaneously; it is the product of deliberate, structured efforts to establish shared understanding, foster transparent communication, and create robust documentation. By reflecting on the core principles and strategies discussed, teams can build a strong foundation for managing deliverables effectively.

The journey begins with a commitment to understanding stakeholder needs. Projects thrive when teams take the time to listen and gather input from all relevant parties, identifying priorities and potential concerns. This empathetic approach not only lays the groundwork for alignment but also establishes trust, which is critical for navigating the complexities of modern IT projects. By tailoring deliverables to address these needs and balancing technical feasibility with business value, teams position themselves for long-term success.

Equally important is the practice of formalizing deliverables through SMART criteria—specific, measurable, achievable, relevant, and time-bound. This structured framework transforms abstract goals into actionable objectives, enabling stakeholders to visualize progress and success with precision. Establishing success criteria and metrics further strengthens this clarity, ensuring that all parties share a consistent understanding of what defines a completed deliverable. These benchmarks act as a guiding star, allowing teams to stay focused amidst the dynamic nature of IT environments.

Throughout the process, communication emerges as a central theme. Setting clear communication channels and protocols ensures that information flows seamlessly across internal teams, external partners, and stakeholders. Regular checkpoints reinforce these expectations, providing opportunities to assess progress, address emerging challenges, and realign efforts. Documentation serves as the backbone of this communication ecosystem, preserving agreements and providing a reference point for all parties. Together, these practices create a culture of transparency and accountability that minimizes misunderstandings and fosters collaboration.

Ultimately, the key takeaway is that successful management of deliverables hinges on consistency, adaptability, and foresight. IT projects are inherently dynamic, with shifting priorities, evolving technologies, and diverse stakeholder demands. Teams that proactively address these challenges by setting clear expectations, maintaining robust communication practices, and adapting to changes with agility are better equipped to deliver high-quality outcomes. These principles are not merely tools for project success—they are habits that, when cultivated, transform how teams collaborate and build trust with stakeholders.

By implementing the strategies outlined in this chapter, project managers and teams can turn the often-daunting process of managing deliverables into a structured, repeatable practice. This approach ensures not only the successful delivery of individual projects but also the development of long-lasting, collaborative relationships that pave the way for future achievements in IT consultancy and beyond.

Handling revisions, delays, and scope changes through proactive communication.

In the realm of IT projects, change is not an exception but a norm. Whether it is revisions to deliverables, unexpected delays, or shifts in project scope, these challenges are almost inevitable in environments shaped by dynamic business needs, evolving technologies, and the inherent complexities of innovation. This section aims to contextualize the nature of change in IT projects, underscoring why proactive communication is the key to managing these uncertainties while preserving project integrity and stakeholder trust.

At its heart, IT project management involves orchestrating a multitude of variables—technical requirements, resource availability, team dynamics, and stakeholder expectations. Despite meticulous planning, factors such as shifting business priorities, technological constraints, and unforeseen risks often necessitate adjustments. For example, a mid-project regulatory update might require immediate revisions to ensure compliance, while a critical dependency on a third-party vendor could introduce delays beyond the team's control. These situations highlight that the challenge is not avoiding change but navigating it effectively.

The impact of unmanaged changes can be profound. Revisions or delays that are poorly communicated can erode stakeholder confidence, strain team morale, and jeopardize project outcomes. A sudden scope expansion without proper discussion can lead to resource exhaustion and missed deadlines, while a lack of clarity around revisions can create confusion, resulting in errors or duplication of work. Proactive communication emerges as a crucial strategy to mitigate these risks, transforming potential disruptions into opportunities for collaboration and growth.

Recognizing the inevitability of change is the first step. IT projects are inherently iterative, often requiring ongoing adjustments as teams refine solutions, respond to feedback, and adapt to external conditions. This iterative nature is not a weakness but a strength, allowing for continuous improvement. By embracing a proactive communication mindset, teams can address changes with agility, ensuring that stakeholders remain informed, aligned, and confident throughout the project lifecycle.

This chapter explores how effective communication can be a stabilizing force amidst the flux of IT projects. It lays the groundwork for handling revisions, delays, and scope changes with transparency, foresight, and empathy. With the right strategies, change becomes not a roadblock but a pathway to better solutions, stronger stakeholder relationships, and successful project delivery.

PREPARING FOR CHANGE: BUILDING FLEXIBILITY INTO PLANS

In IT project management, change is inevitable, but its impact can be mitigated through careful preparation and flexible planning. Building adaptability into project structures ensures that teams can respond to revisions, delays, or shifts in scope without losing momentum or sacrificing stakeholder trust. Proactive planning creates a framework that accommodates uncertainty while maintaining clarity and direction, positioning the team to handle change as an integrated part of the project lifecycle rather than an unforeseen disruption.

Flexibility begins with recognizing the potential sources of change. These might include shifting client requirements, emerging technological constraints, regulatory updates, or resource availability issues. Identifying these variables during the initial planning phase allows teams to establish contingencies, such as buffer times in schedules or resource reallocation strategies. For instance, projects with interdependent milestones may include slack periods to absorb minor delays without cascading effects on the overall timeline. Similarly, maintaining a prioritized backlog of deliverables can help the team shift focus when circumstances necessitate reorganization.

Another cornerstone of flexible planning is creating a structured change management framework. This involves clearly defining how changes will be evaluated, approved, and implemented throughout the project. A well-designed framework includes standardized procedures for submitting change requests, conducting impact assessments, and aligning stakeholders on necessary adjustments. By institutionalizing this process, teams can manage changes systematically, reducing the risk of ad hoc decisions that might derail the project. For example, an impact assessment matrix can be employed to evaluate how proposed changes affect timelines, budgets, and resources, enabling data-driven decision-making.

Flexibility also depends on open and transparent communication channels. Establishing protocols for regular check-ins and updates ensures that potential challenges are identified and addressed early. Teams should maintain a shared understanding of project priorities, risks, and contingencies to foster collaboration and readiness for adaptation. A team that is informed and aligned is better equipped to navigate the complexities of IT projects. Moreover, stakeholders who are kept in the loop about potential uncertainties are more likely to remain engaged and supportive when adjustments are required.

Preparing for change involves a delicate balance of structure and adaptability. While the project must follow a defined plan, it should also have the elasticity to evolve with changing circumstances. By incorporating contingencies, implementing a robust change management framework, and fostering transparent communication, IT teams can transform uncertainty into an opportunity to refine processes and deliver improved outcomes. Flexibility, built into the foundation of the project, empowers teams to navigate change with confidence and resilience.

COMMUNICATING REVISIONS EFFECTIVELY

Revisions are an intrinsic part of IT projects, driven by the need to adapt to evolving requirements, stakeholder feedback, or unforeseen technical challenges. While revisions are often necessary to ensure project success, their implementation can create friction if not communicated effectively. Clear, timely, and well-structured communication about revisions minimizes misunderstandings, fosters collaboration, and maintains trust among all stakeholders.

The first step in effective communication is transparency about the need for revisions. This requires articulating the *why* behind the change—whether it is a response to new client feedback, a technical limitation, or external factors such as compliance requirements. Framing the revision in terms of its benefits and alignment with project goals helps stakeholders understand its value rather than perceiving it as a disruption. For example, informing stakeholders that a proposed revision will improve product performance or address critical user feedback can turn potential resistance into support.

Timing is equally crucial. Revising a deliverable without prompt communication can lead to wasted efforts, duplicated work, and confusion within the team or among stakeholders. Teams should notify all relevant parties as soon as the need for revision is identified, even if the full scope of the change is still under discussion. Early communication allows stakeholders to adjust their expectations and provides an opportunity for input, fostering a sense of shared ownership over the process. A proactive update, such as "We've identified a potential revision needed due to X, and we're assessing the impact," reassures stakeholders that the team is in control.

Equally important is clarity in outlining the details of the revision. Teams should specify what is changing, how it will affect the project scope, timeline, or budget, and what actions are required from each stakeholder. Utilizing visual aids such as comparison tables, updated project timelines, or change impact summaries can enhance understanding, especially when communicating with non-technical stakeholders. A structured format, such as a change notification document, ensures consistency and reduces the likelihood of critical details being overlooked.

Feedback loops are a critical part of the communication process. Effective revision management includes creating opportunities for stakeholders to ask questions, raise concerns, or suggest alternatives. Regular check-ins or workshops focused on the revisions can foster alignment and provide clarity. For instance, hosting a virtual meeting to walk stakeholders through the proposed changes and their rationale can preempt misunderstandings while demonstrating a commitment to collaboration.

The success of a revision hinges on the way it is communicated. By focusing on transparency, timeliness, and clarity, IT teams can ensure that revisions are not seen as setbacks but as thoughtful improvements aligned with project objectives. Through effective communication, revisions become opportunities to strengthen trust, refine deliverables, and reinforce the team's ability to adapt to evolving needs.

Addressing Delays with Transparency

Delays are an almost unavoidable aspect of IT projects, arising from factors such as resource shortages, unforeseen technical challenges, or shifts in priorities. While delays can frustrate stakeholders and derail project momentum, addressing them with transparency can mitigate their negative impact. Honest, proactive communication not only preserves trust but also fosters collaboration in overcoming setbacks, turning potential obstacles into opportunities for teamwork and problem-solving.

The foundation of addressing delays lies in early recognition and disclosure. Teams should communicate potential or actual delays as soon as they become evident, even if all details are not yet available. Waiting to report a delay until its full impact is clear can cause stakeholders to feel blindsided, escalating frustration and eroding confidence in the project team. By acknowledging the situation early—e.g., "We're encountering challenges with X that might affect our timeline, and we're assessing the scope of the impact"—teams can reassure stakeholders of their vigilance and proactive approach.

Clarity and context are essential when communicating delays. Stakeholders need to understand not just that a delay has occurred, but also *why* it happened and *how* it will be addressed. For example, a delay caused by dependency on a third-party vendor should be explained with specifics: "The vendor's delivery schedule has shifted by two weeks due to unforeseen circumstances, affecting our ability to complete Task Y on time." Providing context frames the delay as a manageable issue rather than an unaccountable failure, helping stakeholders remain solution-focused.

Proposing a clear path forward is equally important. Once a delay has been communicated, teams should present a revised timeline along with actionable steps to minimize its impact. This might include reallocating resources, adjusting priorities, or implementing mitigation strategies such as parallel task execution. For instance, the team could propose advancing unaffected components of the project to maintain progress while waiting for a delayed deliverable. Concrete solutions demonstrate accountability and a commitment to resolving the issue efficiently.

Maintaining open channels for dialogue strengthens stakeholder relationships during delays. Encouraging feedback and questions allows stakeholders to voice concerns and ensures they feel heard. For instance, hosting a status update meeting or sharing a detailed progress report with a focus on the delay's implications invites constructive input. Such engagement not only builds trust but also often leads to collaborative problem-solving, with stakeholders contributing insights or resources to address the issue.

Transparency is the cornerstone of managing delays. It transforms potential tension into an opportunity to reaffirm accountability and reinforce stakeholder relationships. By communicating openly, providing context, proposing solutions, and fostering dialogue, teams can navigate delays with professionalism and resilience. In doing so, they demonstrate their capability to adapt and uphold the project's integrity, even in the face of setbacks.

Managing Scope Changes Responsibly

Scope changes are a frequent occurrence in IT projects, driven by evolving stakeholder requirements, technological advancements, or unforeseen constraints. While adapting to these changes is essential for project success, unmanaged scope adjustments—often referred to as "scope creep"—can derail timelines, inflate budgets, and strain resources. Managing scope changes responsibly requires a structured approach to evaluate, communicate, and integrate adjustments while maintaining alignment with the project's objectives and stakeholder expectations.

The first step in managing scope changes is establishing a robust change control process. A structured process provides a clear framework for assessing the implications of proposed changes, ensuring they are deliberate rather than reactive. This typically involves requiring formal change requests, which detail the nature of the change, its rationale, and its expected impact on deliverables, timelines, and budgets. By channeling all scope adjustments through this process, teams can avoid ad hoc decisions that disrupt workflows and overwhelm resources. For instance, an impact assessment matrix can help identify how a proposed change affects interdependencies within the project.

Once a change request is received, transparent communication is crucial. Teams must present a balanced analysis of the proposed change, including its benefits, potential drawbacks, and trade-offs. For example, if adding a new feature enhances product functionality but extends the delivery timeline, this must be clearly outlined to all stakeholders. Providing options—such as deprioritizing other tasks to accommodate the change within the original timeline—empowers stakeholders to make informed decisions. Ensuring that all voices are heard during this process, especially those of technical experts and end-users, fosters collaboration and consensus.

An integral aspect of responsible scope management is documenting all agreed-upon changes. Once a scope adjustment is approved, it should be formally recorded in project documentation, including updated requirements, timelines, and budgets. This ensures that everyone involved has a shared understanding of the revised project goals and prevents future disputes. Tools such as project management software can streamline this process by centralizing documentation and making it accessible to all stakeholders. A clearly defined scope baseline and a corresponding change log enable teams to track and reference scope changes throughout the project lifecycle.

Ongoing monitoring and communication ensure that the integration of scope changes does not compromise project stability. Regular progress updates should address the implementation of the change, its impact on the overall project, and any new risks that have emerged. For example, if a change introduces dependencies on additional resources, these should be highlighted during status meetings to maintain stakeholder awareness. This iterative communication reinforces accountability and keeps all parties aligned as the project evolves.

Managing scope changes responsibly is a balancing act that requires foresight, collaboration, and discipline. By implementing a formal change control process, communicating transparently, documenting agreements, and continuously monitoring progress, teams can adapt to changes without sacrificing project integrity. This approach not only mitigates the risks associated with scope adjustments but also demonstrates a commitment to delivering value, even in a dynamic project environment.

CREATING FEEDBACK LOOPS FOR CONTINUOUS ADAPTATION

In dynamic IT projects, change is inevitable, whether driven by technological advancements, shifting stakeholder priorities, or unforeseen challenges. To navigate these fluctuations effectively, feedback loops serve as a vital mechanism for fostering continuous adaptation. These loops enable teams to identify issues early, respond to evolving needs promptly, and maintain alignment with stakeholder expectations. By embedding regular opportunities for feedback into the project lifecycle, teams can enhance flexibility, reinforce collaboration, and ensure project outcomes remain relevant and valuable.

The first element of a successful feedback loop is establishing regular intervals for reflection and discussion. These intervals can take various forms, such as sprint reviews in Agile frameworks, milestone meetings, or periodic stakeholder workshops. The goal is to create structured opportunities for all participants—developers, project managers, stakeholders, and end-users—to share insights and assess progress against objectives. For instance, an Agile sprint review offers a space for stakeholders to evaluate delivered work and propose adjustments for upcoming iterations. Such structured touchpoints ensure feedback is not only gathered but also actioned systematically.

Clarity in the feedback process is equally crucial. Stakeholders need clear guidelines on what kind of input is most valuable at each stage of the project. For example, during the early phases, feedback might focus on refining requirements or confirming alignment with business objectives. As the project progresses, input may shift toward usability, functionality, or adherence to timelines. Using targeted questionnaires or focused discussion agendas can help streamline feedback sessions, ensuring conversations remain productive and relevant. Clarity reduces the risk of receiving vague or conflicting feedback, which can derail progress.

To maximize the effectiveness of feedback loops, teams must create an environment where stakeholders feel encouraged to share both positive and critical insights. This involves fostering a culture of trust and collaboration, where all input is viewed as an opportunity for growth rather than criticism. For example, when stakeholders highlight a potential flaw or concern, teams should respond with openness, focusing on solutions rather than defensiveness. By modeling receptivity, project leaders can set the tone for constructive dialogue, ensuring feedback becomes a cornerstone of project success rather than a source of friction.

Technology plays a pivotal role in streamlining feedback collection and integration. Tools such as project management software, collaborative platforms, and real-time communication channels simplify the process of gathering input from diverse stakeholders. For instance, tools like Jira or Trello can include fields for feedback on specific tasks, while shared dashboards can display progress and invite commentary. Automated reminders and feedback forms integrated into these systems ensure that input is not overlooked or delayed, fostering a continuous cycle of adaptation.

Feedback loops also serve as a foundation for iterative improvement beyond individual projects. By documenting feedback and analyzing recurring themes, teams can identify patterns that inform future practices. For instance, if feedback frequently highlights communication gaps during certain project phases, teams can address these proactively in subsequent projects. This meta-level learning transforms feedback loops into a long-term strategy for organizational growth, making adaptation a core strength rather than a reactive necessity.

By implementing structured, clear, and inclusive feedback loops, IT teams can ensure their projects remain agile and responsive in an ever-changing environment. These loops not only facilitate continuous adaptation but also strengthen relationships with stakeholders, empowering everyone involved to contribute meaningfully to project success.

Practical tools for tracking progress and maintaining alignment across teams.

In IT projects, where complexity often arises from diverse roles, distributed teams, and overlapping workflows, tracking progress and maintaining alignment are not just desirable—they are essential. Without a clear and consistent mechanism for monitoring tasks and milestones, projects risk delays, miscommunication, and escalating costs. The role of tools in this context is pivotal. They act as the connective tissue that binds various project elements together, providing transparency, fostering accountability, and enabling informed decision-making. However, tools are only as effective as the strategies employed to implement them, making their selection and integration a critical task for project leaders.

At their core, tracking tools provide a central repository for project data, offering team members and stakeholders a unified view of progress. This "single source of truth" reduces the likelihood of misaligned priorities or conflicting information, a common pitfall in large-scale IT projects. For example, a tool like Jira can ensure that everyone, from developers to project managers, has access to real-time updates on task statuses, dependencies, and deadlines. Such transparency is particularly valuable in Agile environments, where iterative progress demands frequent updates and shared visibility to stay on track. The ability to access this information at a glance simplifies complex coordination efforts and keeps all parties aligned toward common goals.

Beyond visibility, tools are instrumental in fostering accountability within teams. When responsibilities are explicitly assigned within a project management platform, such as Asana or Trello, team members can easily identify their tasks and understand how their contributions impact the broader project objectives. For instance, a well-maintained task board can indicate not only who is responsible for a deliverable but also its current status, any blockers, and the expected timeline for completion. This clarity reduces ambiguity, empowering team members to prioritize their efforts effectively. Moreover, such systems provide a trail of activity that allows project managers to track progress objectively and address issues proactively before they escalate.

Alignment, however, extends beyond technical transparency and accountability—it requires a shared understanding of goals and processes. Tools play a critical role in bridging communication gaps that naturally arise in diverse and distributed teams. For example, collaboration tools like Microsoft Teams or Slack, when integrated with progress tracking systems, can facilitate seamless communication by allowing instant updates and clarifications. Instead of waiting for formal meetings, team members can resolve queries or update statuses in real-time, preventing bottlenecks. Additionally, tools that integrate visual dashboards, such as those provided by Power BI or Tableau, translate raw data into intuitive graphics, enabling non-technical stakeholders to grasp project progress quickly.

However, the reliance on tools must be balanced with an understanding of their limitations. No tool, regardless of its sophistication, can fully replace the human judgment required to interpret project nuances or resolve complex interpersonal dynamics. For example, while a tool may flag a delay in a task, it cannot diagnose the root cause—whether it stems from a miscommunication, a lack of resources, or unforeseen technical hurdles. Similarly, while dashboards can highlight deviations from planned timelines, they cannot resolve differing stakeholder priorities without human intervention. Thus, while tools are indispensable for tracking progress and maintaining alignment, they must be viewed as enablers rather than replacements for effective project management practices.

The role of tools in progress tracking and alignment is multifaceted. They provide a structure that reduces ambiguity, enhance accountability, and foster collaboration across teams and stakeholders. By integrating these tools thoughtfully into workflows, project leaders can address many of the challenges inherent in IT projects. However, their success ultimately depends on the practices and discipline of the teams that use them. As such, the selection of tools must always align with the project's specific needs, ensuring that technology serves as a complement to human expertise, not a substitute.

CENTRALIZED PROJECT MANAGEMENT PLATFORMS

Centralized project management platforms serve as the operational backbone for tracking progress and maintaining alignment in IT projects. These platforms, such as Jira, Asana, Trello, and Microsoft Project, consolidate project data, tasks, and communications into a single, accessible environment. By providing a unified space where teams can plan, execute, and monitor projects, they enable greater transparency, accountability, and collaboration across all levels of an organization. Their significance lies not just in the tools themselves, but in how they support complex, multi-layered IT projects by creating order out of potential chaos.

A core feature of centralized platforms is their ability to function as a "single source of truth." In IT projects, where different teams may operate on varying schedules or methodologies, this singular repository ensures that everyone is working from the same set of data. For instance, development teams using Agile practices can track sprint progress in Jira, while project managers monitor high-level timelines using Gantt charts. This real-time accessibility reduces the risk of outdated information and eliminates the need for endless email chains or meetings to clarify statuses. It also provides an instant snapshot of project health, enabling quick interventions when milestones are at risk.

Equally important is the role these platforms play in clarifying roles and responsibilities. By breaking down projects into tasks, subtasks, and dependencies, they provide a detailed roadmap for what needs to be done, who is responsible, and by when. Tools like Asana or Trello often allow users to assign tasks, set deadlines, and add detailed descriptions, ensuring that every team member understands their contribution to the overall project. This clarity not only minimizes confusion but also fosters accountability. When individuals see how their tasks align with broader project goals, they are more likely to stay motivated and focused. Additionally, automated reminders and notifications ensure that nothing falls through the cracks, even in high-pressure, fast-paced environments.

Another vital aspect of centralized platforms is their ability to support cross-functional collaboration. IT projects often require input from diverse teams—developers, designers, quality assurance specialists, and external vendors—all of whom may have differing workflows or terminologies. A well-implemented project management platform bridges these divides by creating a common framework for communication and coordination. For example, Trello's card-based system allows teams to track tasks visually, while Jira's issue-tracking features help prioritize bugs and feature requests in software development. Integrated comment sections and file-sharing capabilities further streamline collaboration by keeping discussions and resources tied directly to relevant tasks.

Despite their advantages, the effectiveness of centralized platforms depends heavily on how they are adopted and used by teams. Over-complicating workflows or failing to maintain up-to-date information can render even the most sophisticated tools ineffective. Teams must strike a balance between structure and flexibility, tailoring the platform's features to fit their specific needs. For instance, while a complex project with multiple dependencies may benefit from Jira's robust features, a smaller team might find a simpler tool like Trello more effective. Training and buy-in are also crucial. Team members need to understand not only how to use the platform but also why it is essential to the project's success. Without this shared commitment, the platform risks becoming a repository for incomplete or inaccurate data, undermining its purpose.

Centralized project management platforms are indispensable for modern IT projects. By consolidating information, clarifying responsibilities, and fostering collaboration, they enable teams to stay aligned and productive even in the face of complexity. When implemented thoughtfully, these tools not only enhance project efficiency but also build a foundation of trust and reliability that supports long-term success.

Collaborative Communication Tools

In IT projects, seamless communication is critical to ensuring alignment, resolving challenges, and driving progress. Collaborative communication tools such as Slack, Microsoft Teams, Zoom, and Google Workspace have emerged as indispensable components of modern workflows. These tools enable real-time discussions, facilitate the sharing of information, and bridge the geographical and functional gaps that are increasingly common in IT teams. However, their true value lies in how they integrate communication into the broader project ecosystem, enabling teams to stay connected and aligned while balancing the demands of distributed and dynamic environments.

The primary advantage of collaborative communication tools is their ability to provide real-time connectivity. IT projects often require quick resolutions to technical issues, immediate feedback on deliverables, or prompt decision-making to avoid delays. Tools like Slack and Microsoft Teams allow team members to create dedicated channels for specific projects, tasks, or departments, ensuring that conversations remain organized and relevant. For example, a "DevOps Updates" channel can keep developers and operations teams synchronized on infrastructure changes, while a "Client Feedback" thread can centralize discussions about customer input. The immediacy of these tools reduces dependency on lengthy email threads or scheduled meetings, enabling faster collaboration and problem-solving.

Another strength of these tools is their ability to support asynchronous communication. Not all team members work in the same time zones or have overlapping schedules, particularly in global IT projects. Platforms like Slack and Google Workspace allow users to leave messages, share files, and update project statuses that others can respond to at their convenience. This flexibility ensures that progress continues uninterrupted, even when team members are not available in real-time. For example, a project manager in Europe can post a detailed status update in Slack before ending their workday, and developers in Asia can review and respond to it during their own working hours. This continuous flow of information minimizes downtime and keeps the project moving forward.

Equally important is the role these tools play in fostering transparency and inclusivity. By creating centralized spaces for discussions and updates, collaborative communication tools ensure that all team members have equal access to critical information. This is particularly valuable in IT projects, where cross-functional teams often work on interdependent tasks. For instance, a shared document in Google Workspace can provide a live, collaborative environment where developers, designers, and stakeholders simultaneously contribute and review content. Similarly, recorded video meetings or transcripts shared on Microsoft Teams ensure that no one misses out on key decisions, even if they could not attend the session live. Such practices promote a culture of inclusivity and reduce the risks of miscommunication or siloed information.

However, the overuse or misuse of collaborative tools can lead to inefficiencies and even frustration. Constant notifications, redundant channels, or overly casual communication styles can distract team members and dilute the focus on critical tasks. To mitigate these risks, it is essential to establish clear protocols for using these tools effectively. For example, teams can set guidelines for naming channels, structuring messages, and determining when to escalate issues to video calls or in-person meetings. Integrating communication tools with project management platforms like Jira or Asana can further streamline workflows by linking conversations directly to tasks, milestones, and deliverables.

Collaborative communication tools are not just facilitators of dialogue—they are enablers of connection and alignment in complex IT projects. When used effectively, they help teams overcome physical and organizational boundaries, promote transparency, and drive efficiency. However, their success depends on thoughtful implementation, disciplined use, and integration into the broader project framework. By leveraging these tools strategically, IT leaders can create an environment where collaboration thrives, ensuring that communication enhances rather than hinders project success.

VERSION CONTROL AND DOCUMENTATION TOOLS

Version control and documentation tools are pivotal in ensuring consistency, transparency, and traceability in IT projects. These tools, such as Git, Bitbucket, Confluence, and SharePoint, serve as repositories for managing evolving project assets and providing a clear historical record of changes. In complex IT environments, where deliverables often undergo multiple iterations and collaboration spans across teams, version control and documentation tools offer an organized framework to prevent missteps, manage updates, and maintain alignment. Their integration into project workflows is essential for ensuring that all team members are working with accurate and up-to-date information.

The primary function of version control tools like Git or Bitbucket is to manage changes to code, documents, and other digital assets. In software development, these tools allow developers to work on different features or bug fixes simultaneously by creating separate branches. This capability eliminates the risk of overwriting work and ensures that parallel efforts can converge seamlessly. When changes are merged, version control systems automatically highlight conflicts, prompting teams to resolve discrepancies before integration. This systematic approach to managing updates fosters collaboration without sacrificing the integrity of the codebase or other deliverables.

Equally important is the historical tracking capability of version control systems. By maintaining a comprehensive log of changes, including timestamps and author details, these tools provide a robust audit trail. This traceability is particularly valuable in IT projects with regulatory or compliance requirements, where teams must demonstrate accountability for their work. Beyond compliance, the ability to roll back to previous versions is invaluable in situations where updates introduce bugs or regressions. For instance, if a newly implemented feature causes unexpected behavior in a software application, version control allows teams to revert to a stable version while investigating the issue, minimizing downtime and disruption.

Documentation tools like Confluence or SharePoint complement version control by capturing the broader context of project deliverables. These platforms act as centralized knowledge hubs, housing requirements, design specifications, meeting notes, and other critical information. Unlike version control systems, which focus on iterative updates to specific files, documentation tools provide a narrative structure that connects the dots between tasks, goals, and outcomes. For example, a Confluence page can outline the objectives of a new feature, link to the associated Jira tasks, and embed diagrams or screenshots, creating a comprehensive resource for all stakeholders. This centralized access to information ensures that team members, whether new or seasoned, can quickly get up to speed on the project's status and direction.

Integration between version control and documentation tools further enhances their utility. Platforms like GitHub and GitLab offer features to automatically update documentation repositories when code changes are committed, ensuring that technical and project documentation remain aligned. Similarly, linking documentation tools with project management platforms streamlines workflows by associating tasks with relevant resources. For instance, a developer addressing a Jira ticket can access linked documentation in Confluence for detailed guidance, reducing redundancy and ensuring consistency. These integrations eliminate silos and foster a cohesive environment where information flows seamlessly between teams and tools.

Despite their strengths, effective use of version control and documentation tools requires disciplined practices and a culture of collaboration. Teams must establish naming conventions, commit message guidelines, and branch strategies to maximize the clarity and usability of version control systems. Similarly, documentation tools are only as effective as the information they contain. Teams must prioritize regular updates, assign ownership for maintaining accuracy, and avoid creating unnecessary clutter. For example, outdated or redundant documents can lead to confusion and diminish trust in the system. Implementing periodic reviews and clean-ups helps maintain the relevance and reliability of these resources.

Version control and documentation tools are indispensable for managing complexity in IT projects. They provide structure and transparency, facilitate collaboration, and ensure that teams can adapt to changes without losing sight of the project's goals. When used strategically and integrated with other project management tools, they form the backbone of a reliable, efficient, and scalable workflow. Their proper implementation empowers teams to focus on innovation and delivery, confident in the knowledge that their work is secure, traceable, and aligned with project objectives.

PROGRESS TRACKING AND REPORTING TOOLS

Progress tracking and reporting tools are essential for maintaining visibility and accountability in IT projects. Tools like Jira, Asana, Trello, and Monday.com enable project managers and team members to monitor ongoing tasks, evaluate performance, and communicate progress to stakeholders effectively. These tools provide a structured framework for breaking down complex projects into manageable components, ensuring that every contributor understands their responsibilities and timelines. When paired with robust reporting capabilities, they empower teams to make data-driven decisions, address bottlenecks proactively, and maintain alignment across all project phases.

The primary function of progress tracking tools is to decompose large deliverables into smaller, actionable tasks. By doing so, they provide clarity on what needs to be done, who is responsible, and when tasks are due. For example, Jira allows teams to create user stories, assign tasks, and track progress using kanban boards or scrum methodologies. This granular level of detail is especially important in IT projects, where dependencies between tasks can impact the overall timeline. Teams can visualize workflows, identify delays, and allocate resources more effectively, minimizing risks of missed deadlines or overlooked deliverables.

A significant advantage of these tools is their ability to facilitate real-time updates and collaboration. In dynamic IT environments, project requirements or priorities often shift, necessitating rapid adjustments to workflows. Tools like Trello or Monday.com enable team members to update task statuses, add comments, and share files directly within the platform. This transparency ensures that everyone stays informed about current priorities, regardless of their physical location. For example, if a developer encounters a critical bug while implementing a feature, they can immediately flag it in the system, allowing the team to reprioritize efforts accordingly. This instantaneous feedback loop fosters agility and responsiveness, essential traits for successful IT project execution.

Reporting capabilities further enhance the utility of these tools by providing stakeholders with clear insights into project progress. Tools like Asana and Jira generate dashboards and visual reports that summarize task completion rates, milestone achievements, and resource utilization. These reports can be customized to suit different audiences, from high-level overviews for executives to detailed breakdowns for team leads. For instance, a project manager preparing for a weekly stakeholder meeting can generate a status report from Jira that highlights completed tasks, ongoing activities, and any blockers. By presenting this information visually—using charts, graphs, or timelines—the manager can convey progress succinctly and foster confidence in the team's ability to deliver.

Integration with other systems enhances the effectiveness of tracking and reporting tools. Many platforms allow integration with time-tracking apps, version control systems, and communication tools to provide a holistic view of project performance. For example, integrating Jira with Slack can notify team members of task updates, while linking it to GitHub can track the status of related code commits. Similarly, connecting Asana to Google Workspace allows teams to sync project plans with their calendars, ensuring that deadlines are visible and prioritized. These integrations streamline workflows, reduce redundancy, and enable teams to focus on delivering results rather than managing administrative tasks.

However, the success of progress tracking and reporting tools depends on disciplined use and consistent input. Tools are only as effective as the data they contain; incomplete or outdated information can lead to misaligned priorities and misinformed decisions. To address this, teams should establish best practices for updating task statuses, assigning responsibilities, and maintaining regular check-ins. For instance, daily stand-ups or end-of-day updates can ensure that everyone is on the same page and that the tracking system reflects the current state of the project. Additionally, project managers should periodically audit dashboards and reports to verify data accuracy and relevance, ensuring they provide actionable insights rather than overwhelming users with unnecessary details.

Progress tracking and reporting tools are indispensable for driving alignment and efficiency in IT projects. They provide the structure needed to manage complexity, the transparency required for collaboration, and the insights necessary for informed decision-making. By integrating these tools effectively into their workflows, IT teams can navigate challenges confidently, keep stakeholders engaged, and ensure that their projects remain on track for success. When paired with a culture of accountability and a commitment to accurate reporting, these tools become powerful enablers of productivity and achievement.

ALIGNING ACROSS METHODOLOGIES AND TEAMS

In IT projects, the diversity of methodologies and team structures often poses challenges to alignment. Agile teams, operating with iterative workflows, may need to collaborate with teams using structured methodologies like PMP or ITIL. This dynamic becomes even more complex when integrating third-party vendors or geographically dispersed groups with distinct work cultures. Effective progress tracking and alignment tools bridge these gaps by providing a shared framework that accommodates diverse approaches while promoting unified goals.

Alignment begins with establishing a common language for progress tracking. Each methodology—be it Agile, PMP, or Kanban—has its unique terminologies, such as "sprints" in Agile or "milestones" in PMP. Miscommunication can occur when teams interpret terms differently or operate under conflicting assumptions about timelines and deliverables. To address this, project managers can define a shared vocabulary or a "methodology-neutral" framework within the chosen tools. For example, creating a single, overarching project plan in a platform like Jira or Trello allows teams to visualize dependencies and align their individual workflows. Tags or labels can indicate specific methodologies, ensuring clarity while preserving each team's autonomy.

Flexibility in tools is crucial for aligning diverse teams. Tools like Monday.com and Asana allow teams to customize dashboards and workflows, enabling each group to operate in their preferred style while maintaining visibility into the project's overall progress. An Agile team, for instance, might use a kanban board to track user stories, while a PMP-aligned team follows Gantt charts for milestone planning. By integrating these distinct views into a centralized system, all participants can track progress in ways that resonate with their methods. This balance of customization and centralization is vital for fostering collaboration across methodological boundaries.

Regular cross-team checkpoints further enhance alignment. Progress tracking tools often feature automated reminders and integrated communication features that facilitate these interactions. Weekly synchronization meetings, supported by shared dashboards, can ensure that each team is aware of how their progress impacts others. For example, if a development team finishes coding ahead of schedule, this could signal an earlier-than-expected need for quality assurance (QA) resources. Having this visibility helps project managers adjust timelines and resource allocation dynamically, avoiding bottlenecks or idle time. Tools that generate real-time reports or updates can streamline these discussions, allowing teams to focus on actionable insights rather than reconciling disparate updates.

Integration capabilities play a pivotal role in aligning teams using different methodologies. Many platforms, like Jira and Smartsheet, support integrations with tools tailored to specific workflows. An Agile team using Jira can link their work to a QA team's test management system, ensuring seamless handoffs. Similarly, PMP-aligned teams relying on Microsoft Project can integrate their plans with a broader resource management tool to maintain consistency across projects. These integrations reduce redundancy and ensure that data flows between systems, creating a single source of truth for project progress.

Cultural alignment is another dimension of cross-team collaboration. Distributed teams often bring diverse work habits, time zones, and communication preferences to the table. Tools like Slack or Microsoft Teams facilitate asynchronous communication, allowing teams to stay informed without scheduling conflicts. Additionally, progress tracking systems with multilingual support or customizable notification settings can accommodate global teams, ensuring that updates are accessible and relevant to all stakeholders.

A key challenge in aligning methodologies and teams is avoiding over-standardization, which can stifle creativity and efficiency. While centralization is necessary, teams should retain the flexibility to adapt their workflows to project-specific needs. For instance, a creative design team may require looser deadlines and iterative review cycles compared to a development team working on tight deliverables. Progress tracking tools can accommodate this by allowing different levels of granularity within a shared project framework, ensuring that all contributions are valued without imposing unnecessary rigidity.

Aligning across methodologies and teams is about balancing individuality with collaboration. Progress tracking and alignment tools serve as the connective tissue, linking disparate workflows into a cohesive whole. When combined with intentional communication, integration, and respect for diverse approaches, these tools enable IT projects to transcend methodological divides, fostering a unified path toward successful outcomes.

BALANCING TECHNOLOGY AND HUMAN INTERACTION

In the era of digital transformation, technology has revolutionized how IT teams track progress and align efforts. Tools like Jira, Trello, and Microsoft Teams provide unparalleled efficiency, automation, and scalability. However, an overreliance on these tools can diminish the human aspects of collaboration, such as trust, creativity, and mutual understanding. Balancing technology with human interaction ensures that progress tracking doesn't become a mechanical exercise but remains a dynamic and adaptive process grounded in interpersonal connection.

Technology offers incredible precision, but its effectiveness depends on how it complements human relationships. Automated updates, for instance, can reduce the administrative burden of manual reporting, but they cannot convey the nuances of team morale or contextual challenges. A progress dashboard might show that a development milestone is delayed, but it won't reveal whether the delay is due to technical complexity or team burnout. Regular check-ins, one-on-one conversations, and team retrospectives allow managers to understand the story behind the data, ensuring that decisions are informed by both quantitative metrics and qualitative insights.

The human element is particularly vital for fostering accountability and trust. When teams rely solely on technology for updates, there's a risk of disengagement or "checkbox behavior," where individuals fulfill tasks without genuine collaboration or ownership. Face-to-face interactions, whether in-person or via video calls, create opportunities for meaningful dialogue, where individuals feel seen and heard. These moments build stronger interpersonal bonds, encouraging teams to go beyond the bare minimum and work cohesively toward shared goals. Incorporating structured discussions into the use of tracking tools, such as collaborative review sessions, can integrate technology with the relational dynamics that drive success.

Another critical aspect of balancing technology and human interaction is adaptability in communication. While progress tracking tools are excellent for structured updates, they may fall short in situations requiring empathy, negotiation, or consensus-building. For example, when scope changes introduce new priorities, a direct conversation often proves more effective than updating a project management system alone. Tools can record the outcome, but the conversation ensures alignment, mitigates resistance, and fosters a shared understanding of the path forward. Thus, technology should support human communication rather than replace it, enabling teams to adapt dynamically to evolving project landscapes.

One of the risks of over-reliance on technology is the potential for misinterpretation. Text-based updates, devoid of tone or context, can lead to misunderstandings, particularly in high-stress scenarios like delays or critical revisions. Integrating human interaction into the progress-tracking process mitigates this risk. For instance, scheduling a team-wide briefing to discuss major project changes ensures that updates are conveyed clearly, with room for questions and clarifications. These sessions can reduce ambiguity and anxiety, fostering a culture of openness and collaboration that purely technological interactions cannot achieve.

Striking the right balance also requires addressing the limitations of technology in capturing informal collaboration. Many breakthroughs in IT projects occur during impromptu conversations, brainstorming sessions, or hallway chats—moments that are rarely captured by tracking tools. To preserve this creative spontaneity, teams can adopt hybrid approaches that combine structured tools with unstructured spaces for interaction. For example, an Agile team might use digital boards for sprint planning while holding in-person stand-ups to discuss ideas informally. This combination ensures that the benefits of technology are harnessed without stifling organic collaboration.

Lastly, balancing technology and human interaction involves fostering a culture of continuous feedback. While tools like dashboards and reports provide static snapshots, real-time human feedback drives continuous improvement. Regular feedback loops, such as team debriefs or individual check-ins, encourage candid discussions about what is working and what isn't. Technology can facilitate these sessions—by providing data or visualizing progress—but the insights gained from human dialogue often uncover deeper issues or opportunities for innovation.

Technology and human interaction are not opposing forces but complementary dimensions of effective progress tracking and alignment. Technology enhances efficiency and scalability, but human interaction adds depth, creativity, and emotional intelligence. By intentionally integrating both, IT teams can achieve not only operational success but also a workplace culture that values collaboration, adaptability, and mutual respect. This balance ensures that even in a digital age, the human touch remains at the heart of project management.

Common Pitfalls and How to Avoid Them

While tools and strategies for progress tracking and team alignment can significantly enhance project outcomes, improper use or neglect of critical aspects can lead to inefficiencies, miscommunication, and even project failure. Recognizing common pitfalls and adopting measures to avoid them ensures that these tools and strategies are implemented effectively, supporting rather than hindering the project.

One frequent pitfall is **over-reliance on technology at the expense of communication and context**. Project management platforms and tracking tools are invaluable for maintaining visibility, but they can inadvertently create a sense of detachment among team members. Automated progress updates, while efficient, often lack the nuance of direct human interaction. This can lead to a false sense of progress, where metrics appear satisfactory but underlying issues remain unaddressed. To mitigate this, teams should pair technological updates with regular discussions—such as check-ins or stand-up meetings—to contextualize progress and address any challenges that data alone might obscure.

Another common issue is **unclear ownership of responsibilities within tracking systems**. When multiple stakeholders interact with a shared platform, ambiguity can arise over who is responsible for specific tasks, updates, or approvals. This often results in delays, duplicate efforts, or missed deadlines. Avoiding this requires clear assignment of roles within the tool and explicit guidelines for updating statuses and dependencies. Regularly revisiting these assignments in team meetings ensures everyone understands their responsibilities and remains accountable.

Tool fatigue and information overload also pose significant challenges. IT teams frequently juggle multiple platforms—one for project management, another for communication, and yet another for documentation. While these tools are meant to streamline workflows, overuse or poor integration can create silos and overwhelm team members. To avoid this, organizations should standardize their toolkit, ensuring that tools are interoperable and serve distinct purposes without overlapping functionalities. Simplifying processes and conducting regular audits of tool usage can help eliminate redundancies and focus efforts on the most effective platforms.

A related pitfall is the **misalignment of tool configurations with team needs or project methodologies**. For example, a Kanban board designed for Agile teams might fail to accommodate a waterfall-based project's linear milestones. This disconnect can lead to confusion and frustration among team members, reducing engagement and productivity. The solution lies in customizing tools to align with the team's workflow and ensuring adequate training. By tailoring platforms to fit the specific demands of the project, teams can maximize usability and effectiveness.

Delays and misalignment can also result from **ineffective reporting practices**. For instance, generating overly detailed reports might burden stakeholders with unnecessary information, while overly concise reports may leave critical updates unaddressed. Striking the right balance requires understanding the audience for each report—what level of detail stakeholders need and how frequently updates should be shared. Teams should also standardize report formats to maintain consistency and clarity, reducing the time spent interpreting data.

Resistance to adopting tools and processes is another common barrier. Even the most robust systems will fail if team members are reluctant to engage with them. This resistance often stems from a lack of understanding about the tool's benefits or from poorly implemented change management. To overcome this, leaders should involve teams in the selection process, provide comprehensive training, and create opportunities for feedback. Highlighting how tools reduce workloads or improve outcomes can also help foster buy-in.

Lastly, one of the most significant pitfalls is **focusing exclusively on short-term tracking without long-term alignment**. It's easy to get caught up in daily or weekly metrics, losing sight of broader project goals. This narrow focus can lead to misaligned efforts, where team members optimize for immediate tasks while neglecting overarching priorities. To prevent this, teams should integrate milestone reviews into their workflows, regularly revisiting project goals and ensuring that short-term activities contribute meaningfully to long-term objectives.

While tools and strategies for progress tracking and alignment offer immense potential, their misuse or mismanagement can introduce new challenges. By addressing these common pitfalls—such as over-reliance on technology, unclear responsibilities, tool fatigue, and resistance—teams can ensure that their efforts are directed toward sustained success. Proactive planning, open communication, and continuous evaluation are key to maximizing the benefits of these systems while minimizing their drawbacks.

KEY TAKEAWAYS AND RECOMMENDATIONS

Effective progress tracking and maintaining alignment across teams are essential for the success of any IT project, especially in environments characterized by complexity and constant change. While tools and strategies facilitate transparency and collaboration, their true value lies in their thoughtful implementation, integration with human processes, and adaptability to project needs. By distilling the insights discussed, several actionable recommendations emerge for ensuring optimal outcomes.

A primary takeaway is the importance of **choosing the right tools for the project's scope and methodology**. Not all tools are created equal, and selecting platforms that align with team workflows, technical requirements, and organizational objectives is critical. Leaders should prioritize platforms that balance functionality with usability, ensuring they cater to both novice and advanced users within the team. Regular training and customization of these tools can enhance their relevance and engagement, making them an integral part of the project lifecycle.

Another crucial insight is that **progress tracking is not solely about metrics but also about fostering collaboration and trust**. Numbers, timelines, and visual boards provide essential data but must be accompanied by open communication channels that allow team members to raise concerns, ask questions, and provide input. Building a culture of transparency, where updates are not just shared but also discussed, helps teams stay aligned and motivated. Leaders should encourage frequent touchpoints—stand-ups, milestone reviews, and retrospectives—to complement data-driven updates with qualitative feedback.

The balance between **automation and human oversight** emerges as a recurring theme. While automated updates and reporting can save time and reduce errors, they must not replace the nuanced understanding that comes from personal interaction. Teams should integrate automated tools into their processes but ensure that critical updates, especially those involving risks or significant changes, are accompanied by personal communication. This dual approach ensures efficiency without sacrificing context or connection.

Avoiding common pitfalls, such as **tool fatigue, lack of ownership, and misaligned reporting practices**, is another vital consideration. Projects often falter not because of inadequate tools but due to poor implementation or overuse. Leaders should regularly audit tool usage, clarify responsibilities, and standardize reporting formats to prevent inefficiencies. Limiting the number of platforms in use and ensuring they serve distinct, complementary purposes can significantly enhance team focus and cohesion.

To sustain long-term alignment, it is imperative to **connect short-term tracking with overarching goals**. Teams must regularly revisit the "why" behind their work, ensuring that daily efforts contribute to broader project milestones. This alignment fosters a sense of purpose, helping team members understand how their individual contributions drive collective success. Regular milestone reviews and goal-setting sessions can anchor short-term activities to the larger vision, maintaining momentum and direction.

In terms of recommendations, leaders should:

1. **Invest in training and support for tools** to ensure all team members are comfortable using them effectively.

2. **Establish clear protocols for updates and responsibilities**, reducing ambiguity in progress tracking and reporting.

3. **Encourage a feedback culture** where tools and processes are continuously refined based on team input.

4. **Integrate regular alignment sessions** to connect progress metrics with long-term objectives, fostering a shared understanding of success.

5. **Balance tool reliance with human connection**, using platforms to enhance rather than replace interpersonal communication.

Progress tracking and alignment tools are indispensable, but their success depends on thoughtful implementation, human-centric integration, and a commitment to continuous improvement. By embracing the strategies and avoiding the pitfalls outlined, teams can harness these systems to drive clarity, collaboration, and consistent progress. The ultimate goal is not just to track work but to empower teams to deliver their best, united by shared purpose and clear direction.

Discover more

Author

Other books

www.ingramcontent.com/pod-product-compliance
Lightning Source LLC
Chambersburg PA
CBHW071021240526
45469CB00006BD/2026